TURNING POINTS IN HISTORY

General Editor: SIR DENIS BROGAN

THE DISCOVERY OF AMERICA

BY

G. R. CRONE

Illustrated

HAMISH HAMILTON

LONDON

First published in Great Britain, 1969
by Hamish Hamilton Ltd
90 *Great Russell Street London WC*1
Copyright © 1969 *by G. R. Crone*

SBN 241 01511 1

Printed in Great Britain
by Western Printing Services Ltd
Bristol

TO

JOHN KIRTLAND WRIGHT

CONTENTS

Contents

LIST OF ILLUSTRATIONS

ix

INTRODUCTION

THE FIRST systematic accounts of the Age of Discovery were written by sixteenth-century chroniclers, Portuguese, Spanish and Italian. They made use of the brief narratives published, on the return of the voyagers, to meet eager popular demand. These were meagre and had often been obtained clandestinely by the printers, for the authorities were unwilling to release detailed accounts, and the chroniclers were obliged to supplement them from their own knowledge or the reminiscences of those who had known the explorers. Since they were usually in receipt of royal patronage and approached their task with strong national prejudices, they were extremely partisan in their treatment of international problems. Also, in the countries which entered the overseas adventure later or less energetically, little importance was attached to recording the doings of their early navigators. The story is further complicated by the fact that many of the prominent figures were men of humble or obscure origin, and therefore unknown until they came into public notice, when it was usually too late to collect details of their early careers; a final difficulty was their practice of moving from the service of one country to another, leaving their motives to be guessed at. Thus we know very little of as notable an explorer as Bartholomew Diaz, the first to round the Cape of Good Hope, and not a great deal more of John Cabot's life before he came to England.

These histories must also be used with caution, for their authors composed them in a style which, following classical models, turned them into panegyrics of monarchs or others in high authority. Furthermore, no one at the time, apart from kings and their secretaries, was in a position to form an overall appreciation of the course of events; all the essential material—royal charters, official correspondence, instructions, financial accounts, explorers' log books—were inaccessible in the court archives where, if they escaped destruction, they awaited the historians of the nineteenth century. Given these conditions and the circumstances in which the discoveries took place, it is not surprising that various partisan and imperfect versions of events were in circulation for more than two centuries, until more critical historical standards were applied.

The bio-bibliographical history of Columbus is a good, perhaps the best, example of the evolution of a conventional portrait of an explorer. The discovery of America was an act of divine providence, therefore the Discoverer must be an exceptional personage, endowed with exceptional qualities of wisdom, courage and perseverance, and divinely guided. Since America was discovered by sea he must also be an outstandingly skilful navigator and gifted in the science of sciences—astronomy. In a crisis it is he who takes the correct decision and saves the day. All who oppose or seek to hinder him are villains, and if his career does not end in the full blaze of glory, then it is due to their evil machinations, or, let it be whispered, the ingratitude of monarchs. This attitude persisted into the nineteenth century, until the great national archives were opened to historians, and steps were taken to calendar them and to publish select documents.

The first important step was taken by the Spanish historian, Martin Fernandez de Navarrete, who published three volumes of documents relating to the early voyages under Spanish auspices. These presented a reasonable picture of the organization of Columbus's first voyage and of his subsequent relations with the Crown, the general effect being to fill out the conventional picture of his career. At that time American historians were interesting themselves in the early history of their continent and were understandably anxious to sustain the thesis that a great country must have a great man as its discoverer. Using the documents published by Navarrete, Washington Irving produced the first full biography of the Admiral in English, which has formed the basis of many subsequent, and generally accepted, accounts. The Discoverer as romantic hero made a strong appeal to the sensibilities of the time. In France the poet Alfred de Lamartine wrote an impassioned, if slightly inaccurate, summary with the theme 'Colomb: instrument de la Providence', while in Germany Alexander von Humboldt, called 'the father of modern geography', was equally enthusiastic, but much more learned.

However, the new school of historians in various countries, partly inspired by patriotism, were beginning to probe chinks in the Admiral's armour, and the whole problem of his share in the Discoveries was ventilated during the celebrations of the fourth centenary in 1892. The Italian and Spanish governments published voluminous series of records and critical studies of certain aspects, while the private archives of the Columbus family were printed by the Duchess of Berwick y Alba. Thus there was much for supporters and critics to work upon. The most severe of the critics was Henry Vignaud who set about with great relish and industry to overturn the conventional image of the Admiral. Vignaud maintained that Columbus had no intention of reaching the Indies on his first voyage, and that therefore his project was not founded on learned views about the sphericity of the earth; all he had done was to seek for islands in the Ocean, as many had done before him. On this voyage moreover much of the credit must be given to the Spanish navigators, the Pinzon family, who had been wrongfully abused; in any case America had probably already been sighted by the Portuguese. Vignaud's many contentions have not been generally accepted; if they were correct, it would appear that the biographers of Columbus, his son Ferdinand and Bishop de Las Casas, had not only forged the critical documents, or at least amended them, but had succeeded in planting them in the Spanish archives. Even so his critical works were a great stimulant to the more objective study of the Age, obliging the contenders to examine not only the original sources but also to extend their studies into adjacent fields of research. Since the publication of Vignaud's books, the outlook and procedure of historians has developed in a revolutionary way. Historians today, without completely dethroning the individual, place much more emphasis on economic factors, on 'forces' and 'movements'; without subscribing wholeheartedly to the proposition that all history is economic history, it is necessary to take a wider view than excessive concentration on the doings of one individual, if a rounded view of the Age of Discovery is to be obtained. As early as 1848 Karl Marx and Friedrich Engels were writing, in the Communist Manifesto: 'The discovery of America, the rounding of the Cape, opened up fresh ground for the rising bourgeoisie. The East-Indian and Chinese markets, the colonization of America, trade with the colonies, the increase in the means of exchange and in commodities generally, gave to commerce, to navigation, to industry, an impulse never before known, and thereby, to the revolutionary element in the tottering feudal society, a rapid development.'

Looking back, we see the early navigators as the forerunners of a great movement of population from Europe across the Atlantic which has helped to shape the world as it is today. We must therefore endeavour to understand the political, social, and scientific

forces which drove them forward. We require to know the actions
of their contemporaries in the courts, on the field of battle, and on
the high seas; in the counting house and in the study, at home and
among the wonders and trials of the astonishing new world, so far as
these are relevant to the story. In studying the achievements of
Columbus in particular, I began by establishing as clearly as possible
what actually happened on the first voyage and among the islands,
and worked back from there to the preceding events. This led to the
subject of his relations with the Spanish sovereigns and with the
Italian financial houses in Portugal, and then on to what can be
ascertained—and it is not a great deal—of his early life. Out of this
emerged a coherent picture which could be fitted into the political
history of fifteenth-century Europe and into his subsequent conduct, of which we know much more. No attempt has been made to
provide a personal biography of the Admiral, of which there are
many.

Chapter I

THE MEDIEVAL WORLD

THE ACHIEVEMENT of Christopher Columbus undeniably made a great contribution to the emergence of the modern age and placed him firmly among the great men of the Renaissance. Like them, he had been stimulated by the recovery of ancient learning into looking with a new curiosity at the world around him and in speculating upon its limits. At the same time he was conservative in his basic outlook, so that, paradoxically, the discoverer of the new world continued to the end of his career to draw arguments and ideas from the conventional works of medieval cosmographers. It is necessary from the outset to emphasize this aspect of the Columbus epic if the springs of his motives and aims are to be uncovered, and to examine however briefly the medieval image of the world which sustained his life's work.

This image was itself largely derivative, a compilation from the writings of Greeks and Romans, received in part through Arab intermediaries, often garbled or misunderstood. To the contemporaries of the young Columbus, the known world was much narrower and more commonplace than that of their classical predecessors, although the bolder travellers and seamen had begun to probe its bounds. The powerful limiting factor was the advance of Moslem power through most of the Asian lands to the south-east, and through North Africa to the Atlantic. The principal counter to this threat, the Crusades, had failed to establish a permanent line of defence in Syria and the Holy Land, and, more alarmingly, Constantinople, the very heart of Christian civilization in the eastern Mediterranean, was clearly about to fall to the Ottoman Turks. On the west, the Ocean Sea presented a formidable barrier, of which medieval men knew even less than they did of the Asian lands behind the Moslem front. The northern margins were as unpromising as the Ocean or the steppes of Asia, perhaps even more so, for their legendary darkness, extreme cold, and frozen seas were abhorrent to the peoples of the Mediterranean. They were moreover the home of that ruthless race which, exercising through their ships a mobility comparable to that of the Mongol hordes, had ravaged the coasts from Ireland to the eastern Mediterranean. The Age of the Discoveries, when the frontiers of the known world exploded to encompass the globe, was in fact preceded by a phase of contracting boundaries, as though Europe were recoiling upon itself before the great leap forward.

How then did the world appear to Columbus and his contemporaries? We must first dismiss any suggestion that scholars had doubts as to the earth being a sphere, for this concept never entirely died out during the Middle Ages. It was the essence of the science of astronomy as set out by the Alexandrine sage, Claudius Ptolomaeus, for without it an understanding, or application, of that science was impossible. Throughout the darkest days of medieval scholarship, astronomy maintained its pre-eminence among studies, for clerics and laymen alike regarded it as conferring invincible power upon its practitioners, especially in its extension as astrology. Indeed, God himself was regarded as the Great Astronomer. On the other hand, the study of geography, in so far as it had any independent status, occupied a very lowly place in the scheme of knowledge. Much of what passed for it had little relation to the theory of the earth's rotundity. The popular manuals opined that the earth was round, like a ball, or that the earth occupied a place in the universe similar to that of a yolk in an egg, and thereafter continued with conventional descriptions of countries and peoples. In a very popular treatise, the work of a fourth-century Roman, Macrobius, known as *De somnis Ciceronis*, the idea was usually illustrated by a very simple diagram. This was a circle divided horizontally into latitudinal zones or *klimata*. By itself, without reference to the text, this diagram encouraged the view that the known world was a flat, circular disc, and it is this form which was popularized by the monastic draughtsmen who produced the decorative, circular *mappae mundi*, such as the World Map of *circa* 1300 in Hereford Cathedral. Since these were the main source of instruction for the ordinary layman, being exhibited in churches or drawn in service books or other edifying manuals, they helped to establish the idea of a flat earth in lay minds. This was strengthened by the influence of the Church, which for theological reasons disliked the deductions which followed from the theory of the sphere—the notion of other lands out in the world ocean, and therefore isolated from the bearers of the Gospel, or of antipodal continents, where men must walk head downwards (in relation to the dwellers in Christendom).

This type of medieval map, however, arose from a misconception of Macrobius's doctrine, assisted by the simplicity of the 'single circle' diagram. In fact, the complete Macrobian diagram consisted of two circles, thus portraying the globe as two hemispheres—a western hemisphere containing the inhabited lands as then known, and the corresponding eastern hemisphere. Understandably, since nothing was known directly of the latter, the second circle was left entirely blank. For this reason, or possibly simply for convenience in compiling the manuscripts, it was often omitted, and the concept of the earth as a single disc was perpetuated, an interesting instance of the gap, always considerable at any period, between the experts and the uninitiated populace.

Those who accepted the rotundity of the earth naturally accepted also the scheme of *klimata* which was developed from it. From knowledge of the apparent movement of the sun, the consequent passage of the seasons, their duration and characteristics, the varying length of day and night, and the observable changes in average temperatures from south to north, the Greeks had distinguished these latitudinal zones, each of which had approximately the same climate (in our sense of the word), were inhabited by similar races of men and animals, and had comparable resources in plants and minerals. Five such zones were recognized: the northern, or Arctic zone, uninhabitable on account of the cold; the northern temperate, and therefore habitable, zone which was theoretically bounded by the Tropic of Cancer but was in practice extended some distance to the south; the torrid zone between the tropics, uninhabitable on account of the great heat, and finally, to the south of Capricorn, the southern temperate and Antarctic zones. Since it was generally believed that the *oikoumene* (that is, the lands of which they had knowledge—parts of Eurasia and North Africa) was surrounded on all sides by the Ocean, it was concluded that there were similar land-masses elsewhere on the globe, one in the southern temperate zone of their own hemisphere, and two in the opposite hemisphere similarly isolated in the Ocean. The whole surface of the globe was therefore divided up into four great land-masses by the impassable equatorial ocean which was intersected by another branch which embraced both Poles.

This hypothesis in turn raised a number of problems which were to puzzle those adventurers who in the fifteenth century contemplated sailing out into the Ocean Sea. What was the truth in the allegation of the uninhabitability of the southern lands? Some argued that these lands could not be reached across the torrid zone, and in any case must be uninhabited, an argument derived from the scriptural injunction to bear the Gospel to all men; if the torrid zone were impassable, this command could not be carried out, and therefore the human race must be confined to the *oikoumene*. Others argued that there were benighted races waiting to receive the Gospel and that it was the duty of Christians to carry the Word to them.

Those who held this view were supported by the fact that the impassable tropical belt was being narrowed by the activities of travellers. The Greeks had never been dogmatic on this point, and hints could be found in their records of lands 'lying under the Equator' or, as we should say, on or near the Equator. Taprobana (Ceylon) was known, for example, to be within five degrees of the Line, and the Greek sailing directions, such as the *Periplus of the Erythrean Sea*, described countries on the East African coast in a similar low latitude. Then there were reports from later travellers' tales which filtered through from Arabs, and from the few Christians who had ventured southwards; from Arab merchants came reports which suggested a considerable extension southwards of the Indian Ocean, while fourteenth-century Franciscan friars had penetrated to the upper Sudan, and still further south on the east coast, perhaps as far as Zanzibar. These stories seemed to discredit the existence of these hypothetically uninhabitable lands, and led men to consider whether there might not well be local circumstances which mitigated the supposedly intolerable heat. Cardinal d'Ailly, for instance, surmised that altitude above the sea would have a modifying effect. It was also argued that, as the length of the day at the Equator was at some seasons shorter than in lands near the Pole, the greater heat had not to be endured so long as to be absolutely prohibitive of human life.

Given the possibility that all seas might be navigable and most lands inhabitable, the next problem concerned their precise situation, dimensions and relations to each other. There was no unanimity even on the longitudinal extent of the *oikoumene*. Its breadth from west to east could only be estimated, although the thirteenth-century *Travels* of Marco Polo hinted that Asia extended much further to the east than Greek geographers had allowed. Claudius Ptolomaeus, the best authority, had concluded that the continent extended halfway round the world along its mean parallel. There were several comparatively accurate estimates for the equatorial circumference, the Greek astronomer, Eratosthenes, having arrived at a figure of approximately 25,000 miles. Allowing for the convergence of the meridians, this would give a rough figure of 6,250 miles for the breadth of Eurasia from west to east, an overestimate of about twenty-five per cent. If the other land-mass in the northern hemisphere was of comparable size, it was only to be concluded that the ocean between them must be relatively narrow. Whether for this or for other reasons, Roman writers had in fact asserted that, with favourable winds, it was a few days' sail only from Spain across the Atlantic to India, in other words some portion of the Asian coast.

The width of this intervening ocean was, however, a matter of dispute, depending on what view was taken of the relative proportions of sea and land on the earth's surface. Some authorities considered that the seas occupied a relatively small area. Evidence for this was drawn from Biblical texts—the prophet Esdras had declared: 'Thou didst command that the waters should be gathered in the seventh part of the earth: six parts hast Thou dried up.' Others, Cardinal d'Ailly for one, came to the conclusion that the seas occupied rather more than a quarter of the whole area. Whichever of these figures were adopted, such estimates encouraged the belief that the Ocean must in places be quite narrow. Thinking along these lines, some writers had discussed the possibility of travelling round the globe and returning to one's starting place, and this was given picturesque expression in popular manuals on 'the image of the world'. As a mid-thirteenth-century compiler phrased it: 'If there were no obstacles, a man could go round the earth as a fly crawls round an apple.' Another writer, known under the name Sidrach, answers the question 'Can a man go round the world dry-shod?' in this way: 'There are too many obstacles: first, mountains, savage beasts and waterless deserts, then one comes to the great crevice of the putrid sea.' This last obstacle was one of the ocean channels depicted on the Macrobian diagram.

If medieval men had somewhat confused ideas about the surface of the globe as a whole, and viewed the outer world 'as through a glass darkly', the world nearer home, depicted on the *mappae mundi*, was strewn with semi-mythical marvels, and peopled by savage men, producers of exotic wares, and monstrous beasts. Since the many 'Books of Marvels' which described this nightmare world consisted largely of snippets from classical writers, distorted and misunderstood, it is not strange that these semi-fictions should have gained wide currency. However, from the thirteenth century onwards, scholars had striven to reduce this chaotic lore to order. Foremost among them was the distinguished scholar Cardinal Pierre d'Ailly (1350–1420).

This remarkable Frenchman won distinction as a university teacher, a prelate of the Church, a cosmographer, and an astrologer. In the last rôle he is remembered for having foretold the French Revolution three hundred and fifty years before its outbreak! After referring to the seven great conjunctions of the planets Saturn and Jupiter and the political upheavals which had accompanied them, he wrote of the eighth, forecast for the year 1789: 'This said, if the world lasts until that year, which only God knows, there will be great, many and astonishing changes in the world, principally in law and religion.' In his *Imago* d'Ailly demonstrated the sphericity of the earth, actually making the calculation that if a man set out walking at a steady rate of twenty miles a day he would complete the circuit in four years, sixteen weeks and two days. He also had sensible things to say about maps: the Macrobian circles must be regarded, not as plane surfaces, but as hemispheres, and the *mappa mundi* would be better portrayed on a globe. He also quoted Aristotle and Seneca on the proximity to Spain of India, a statement which Columbus particularly noted. The second part of d'Ailly's treatise contains a geographical description which also assists in understanding Columbus's conception of the world, a world very similar to that depicted in the circular world maps. On it the layman could see the circle neatly centred on Jerusalem in accordance with Biblical texts, such as that of Isaiah—'It is He that sitteth upon the circle of the earth.' In the extreme east was Paradise, or the Garden of Eden, usually represented as a small circular island with Adam and Eve, the serpent and the tree. The whole was surrounded by a wall of flame, signifying that it was not accessible to mortals; indeed, some authorities considered the whole concept symbolic and that Paradise was not to be found on earth. Others compromised, placing it on the summit of an exceptionally high mountain. Whatever its precise position, the surrounding region was traditionally held to enjoy a delightful, temperate climate. This spot was later referred to by Columbus as the 'beginning of the East'. From Paradise came the four great rivers which, after flowing underground, reappeared as the Ganges, Tigris, Euphrates and Nile. Near Paradise also was the marvellous and mysterious country known to all as India. Its bounds were variable and far-flung: in the south-east it extended across the

Equator to the Tropic of Capricorn and the land of Pathalia, surrounded by the great arm of the sea which stretches from the Ocean
between India and further Spain; in the west it extended to the
African shores. Thus three Indias were recognized: one in north-
east Africa (the 'horn' of Africa), another in India proper, and a
third in the south-east of the Asian continent. Their common characteristic was that they were all washed by the great 'Sea of India'.
What was known of the further parts of this great country was a
medley of facts and fancies drawn from Greek, Roman, Hindu and
Arabic sources. By common consent it was a land of benign climate,
of sweet-smelling trees and forests so tall that they touched the
skies,* a land of strange birds, especially parrots. But it was the
wealth in gold and precious stones which dazzled all commentators.
There were even tales of a great mountain of gold, vaguely located
but probably identifiable with the mount Mweru, the Hindu centre
of the universe. Its varied peoples were equally astonishing and
included the eaters of human flesh and the dog-headed men. However, some more sober and apposite knowledge of India proper
had filtered through: its great size, its ancient cultures and its peace-
fulness. Undisturbed by foreign inroads, its peoples, long settled in
their land, were numerous enough to sustain five thousand cities.

Somewhere to the north of Paradise was to be found the land of
Seres, as the Romans knew it, but popularized by Marco Polo as
Cathay. Its people, having no wish for contact with the outside
world, kept themselves to themselves. It was known, however, that
they obtained silk from the leaves of a tree—a confused reference
to the raising of silkworms on mulberry leaves. But the country
never reached the fame which India enjoyed, until Marco Polo
described its age-old civilization in his *Travels*: Cathay is the wealthi-
est country in the world, with a vast trade in precious stones, spices,
pepper and other fine wares. Two cities are particularly lauded:
Zaitun, one of the best harbours in the world frequented by great
numbers of ships, so that for 'one Shippe that cometh into Alexandria there cometh 100 unto it', and Quinsay, noble capital of Mangi,
one hundred miles in compass, with 1,200 bridges of stone. His
report on the return voyage through the 'Sea of India' also gave wide
currency to the notion that it was filled with an immense number of
islands (7,448!) which provided convenient homes for mythical men
and animals. To such tales the Arab romancers added their quota,

* Dr. J. K. Wright has suggested that this was a reference to the forested
Himalayas.

particularly when in the course of time the more extraordinary fantasies were banished from the mainland.

In the West, the familiar world was similarly bounded by the encircling ocean which through the centuries came to possess its own complement of islands, mythical and otherwise, though they were never credited with such exotic mysteries and treasures as were the oriental islands. The Fortunate Islands, or Hesperides, identified as the Canaries, were known to Greek and Roman geographers, as were the Madeira group. The meridian of the former was chosen by Ptolemy as the zero from which he calculated his longitudes to the east; thus for centuries they were at the 'end of the west'. In the north-west, classical knowledge did not extend beyond the island of 'Thule', variously identified as the Shetlands, a portion of the Norwegian coast, or Iceland. The latter island however did not enter into European consciousness until the Norse voyages of the tenth and eleventh centuries. As to the far north, beyond the parallel of Thule, western skippers were sailing round the North Cape and into the White Sea as early as the time of King Alfred.

All contact with Central Asia and the East did not cease with the decline of Mongol rule and the more troubled times which followed. There was a steady demand among the local chieftains for the luxury goods and technical devices produced by the skilled craftsmen of the Byzantine Empire and the Mediterranean centres. Mechanical devices, such as musical boxes, fountains and other water-works, were popular, also specialized products such as Venetian glass, and highly bred horses. In return, they offered silk, perfumes, precious stones and other oriental specialities. This commerce probably never assumed large proportions—the items were small and of high value, the kind of articles which could be carried by an adventurous merchant on his person—but it kept interest in the East alive, and those who returned would bring some details of the eastern peoples and their high culture: such information, for example, as enabled Fra Mauro, the mid-fifteenth-century Venetian cartographer, to depict the great rivers of China with considerable accuracy. In the later centuries, pepper and spices also were reaching the eastern Mediterranean from south-east Asia; though the traffic was in the hands of Chinese, Arab, Indian, Persian and other traders and its terminus was controlled by the rulers of Baghdad and Cairo, details of its source and cultivation and of the route it followed became vaguely known to the Italian merchants who purchased the cargoes. It is also clear that merchants from the West penetrated along these trade routes in the course of business and brought back general and topographical information which might or might not reach the cosmographers and map-makers. The extent to which it did so depended upon political conditions, and with the advent of the Ottoman Turks these became increasingly difficult. A further limiting factor was that these travellers were uninterested in matters not strictly commercial, and had not the urge, or perhaps even the ability, to put their observations down on paper. However, in spite of the dangers presented by the Ottoman Turks, it is significant that Portuguese agents late in the fifteenth century were still able to send valuable information back to Lisbon. The door between East and West remained ajar.

All these concepts and beliefs dominated the mind of Columbus when he was formulating his grand enterprises, particularly the wealth of Cathay, and the significance of the ports of Zaiton and Quinsay. To that extent he was a man of the Middle Ages. His significance in history is that, in pursuing aims nurtured in that culture and to some extent personal in character, he demolished the whole structure with the yardstick of factual observation and set the course of European history in a new direction. It is surely an irony that he never quite appreciated the true character of his achievements and remained partially under the influence of the old ideas to the close of his life.

Chapter II

IRISH AND NORSE NAVIGATORS
IN THE ATLANTIC

TO THE men of the classical world the contrasts between their own Mediterranean and the great ocean west of the Pillars of Hercules were a constant source of wonder. The familiar sea which held their universe together was virtually land-locked and tideless, its contours so broken by peninsulas and archi-pelagoes that no great distances separated the northern from the southern shores. Their great, populous cities were closely linked, at least through outports, to the life-giving sea, whose traffic in war and peace could be controlled at the many narrow passages and straits. Following on the older maritime empires of Phoenicia and Crete, the traders and colonists of the Greek city states, with Athens in the van, had carried their culture over much of its littoral, and the empire of Rome in its turn was founded on control of the western Mediterranean. Those who dwelt around this Middle Sea were well aware of their unique position, the result of centuries of trial and error in adjusting culture to environment, and in their self-centred pride they regarded with disdain the less fortunate peoples, the *barbaroi* who dwelt on the landward margins of their favoured world.

West of the Pillars, everything appeared to suffer a change. In place of the orderly and harmonious procession of the seasons, the stability of their secular civilizations, and their busy markets and harbours, was a vast, empty world of waters—strange, incomprehen-sible, and therefore terrifying. Without known bounds, stretching away unendingly towards the setting sun or into the northern dark-ness, this mighty and restless mass fascinated, even while it repelled, them. The empty seas and wild coasts, lacking fine harbours, the strange phenomenon of the tides, the constant succession of cyclonic storms swirling in from the west, the mists and fogs, were a fitting background to the tough, uncouth peoples who alone, faced with these dangers, could win a precarious livelihood from the harsh environment.

In the pages of Caesar's *De Bello Gallico* we can read an assessment of these novel conditions by a percipient and hard-headed Roman. In his campaign against the Veneti, his problem was to get to grips with their strongholds, protected by the tidal rise and the surrounding shallows. During most of the summer the Roman ships were weather-bound, and intimidated by the dangers of the open sea and the absence of safe refuges. The coastal waters, however, had no terrors for the enemy ships. Strongly built of oaken timbers and iron bolts, with high bows, flat bottoms and leathern sails, they could negotiate heavy seas and sudden squalls as successfully as the coastal channels and shallows. Against this the one advantage that Caesar could claim was that in certain conditions, when the crews took to the oars, his ships were faster. It was only when, by means of a stratagem, he succeeded in dismasting his opponents, that he could bring the full weight of the Roman fighting men to subdue his foes. The advantages of the sailing ship over the galley were fundamental in Atlantic history: however strongly the advocates of early crossings may argue, the galley was definitely not the instrument for the navigation of the deep waters.

It was above all the vastness of the Ocean which most impressed the ancients. It is indeed a formidable expanse of water, though later voyagers found it to be dwarfed by the immensity of the Pacific Ocean. The northern half is 16·5 million square miles in area, some four times the size of Europe. At its narrowest, apart from its Arctic margin, it is 1,700 miles across, between Africa and Brazil; its greatest width is 4,000 miles. Few islands break this great expanse in the west. The Canaries and the Cape Verde Islands rise on the outer edge of the African continental shelf, while summits of the mid-Atlantic ridge emerge as the archipelago of the Azores. But the exploration of the Atlantic was not simply the conquest of space; it necessitated overcoming a great complex of natural phenomena of global range, and unless its history is to be a mere catalogue of voyages, a general understanding of these features is necessary.

The system of winds and currents which rules in the North Atlantic has well-marked features, regular and, within limits, predictable. Seasonal variations result from the shifting of the principal belts northwards and southwards, 'following the sun', and within them there can be quite considerable local fluctuations, particularly in higher latitudes. The mainspring of the circulation, atmospheric and hydrographic, is the enormous amount of solar energy concentrated in the Tropics and diminishing to north and south. As a result, a general low-pressure system is established within the Tropics, with two high-pressure belts in middle latitudes, the Azorean in the north and the mid-south Atlantic beyond the Line. This movement of air- and water-masses is further modified by the rotation of the earth. The resulting planetary winds are the north-easterlies and the south-easterlies, on each side of the Equator.

Within the northern tropics, therefore, the prevailing winds are from the north-east, and these sweep steadily across to the Caribbean. As the Equator is approached and the air-masses rise along the inter-tropical front, these give place to a belt of light variable winds and calms, known as the Doldrums. To be becalmed in this area under the tropical sun was dreaded by seamen as much as a struggle against a severe storm. North of the north-easterlies, after another zone of calms (the Horse latitudes), the prevailing winds, flowing away from the high-pressure area centred on the Azores, are predominantly south-westerly to westerly, bringing stormy weather in winter to north-western Europe. The south-west corner of the North Atlantic, particularly the Caribbean, along the inter-tropical front, is an area of occasional but very severe tropical hurricanes, which alarmed and hampered the early Spanish voyagers. The ocean currents follow a similar course. In the east the cool Canaries current flows southwards and bifurcates near the island group, one branch continuing south-east as the Guinea current. The main branch, the North Equatorial Current, continues westwards and having swept past the Antilles and been joined by the South Equatorial Current flows up the American coast and north-eastwards as the Gulf Stream. Under the influence of the Westerlies, the surface water continues for a considerable distance as the Gulf Stream Drift, raising appreciably winter temperatures along the western shores of Britain and Scandinavia. In the centre of this vast circular movement, and associated with the calms of the Horse latitudes, extends the Sargasso Sea, an area of floating vegetation, originating in the Caribbean, which, however, is not sufficiently thick actually to impede navigation.

The waters adjacent to the Iberian peninsula and north-west Africa, therefore, are subject to south-easterly winds and a southward-flowing current, modified by local onshore winds in the summer, due to the heating-up of the interior of continental Africa. Further south these winds blow more strongly and steadily across the Ocean. The northern half is under the influence of the Westerlies, particularly strong and turbulent in the winter and blowing away from the great land-mass in the west. In winter these sweep on between Iceland and Scandinavia until deflected by the outward-flowing Arctic air-mass: in summer, as the belt of warmer temperature moves northwards, variable and northerly winds facilitate passage across to north-eastern America. In this area a cold dense current flows southwards between Greenland and Labrador and, meeting with the warmer water of the Gulf Stream, produces the notorious fogs to the south-east of Newfoundland.

The course of Atlantic exploration is related to increasing knowledge of this system of winds and currents in the eastern Atlantic and to the recognition of an outward, southerly route and a more northerly return. Although there are traditions associating Basque and other seafaring communities of the western seaboards with long voyages out into the Atlantic, and in spite of the fact that Genoese and Venetians sighted the archipelagoes of Madeira and the Canaries in the fourteenth century, it was the Portuguese who in the following hundred years through long and painful experience learned to comprehend the system of winds and currents, and who devised courses accordingly to make the most of situations favourable to navigation, and to avoid as far as possible areas in which progress was hampered. The gaining of this knowledge went hand in hand with the evolution of a type of vessel designed to sail close to the wind, to withstand a long voyage in stormy seas, and to be manœuvrable in confined waters.

In the African sector their progress southwards was delayed at first by the character of the coasts. Low shores, shallows, banks and reefs, the lack of sheltered harbours and supplies of fresh water, the sparse and hostile populations, made coastwise sailing slow and dangerous, where it did not discourage it severely. On the other hand, to stand out to sea was a hazardous undertaking to the inexperienced, and meant a long beat back against wind and current. For years therefore Cape Non (modern Cape Nun) stood as the limit of navigation, and the general feeling was expressed in the popular saying noted by the chronicler Azuara: 'Whosoever passes Cape Non, either returns or not.'

As the Portuguese grew bolder and more experienced, their practice on the return voyage from their African settlements was to stand well out to sea, to 'get round' the north-easterly winds. They then picked up the Westerlies in the neighbourhood of the Azores and ran back to Lisbon. As they proceeded further south and entered the

Gulf of Guinea, these return sweeps became wider and may eventually have touched the margins of the Sargasso Sea.

This practical knowledge was for long confined to seafaring men. Scholars, in so far as they thought of the Ocean at all, continued to picture it as dangerous and unnavigable, subject to a terrifying assortment of natural phenomena.

It was customery to relegate to this limbo those imaginary islands where culture heroes, satanic spirits and extraordinary monsters found their last home. But there was also another, pleasanter, aspect to the solitude of the Ocean. From early times men were haunted by the thought that far in the west there was a land in which the souls of the departed would find eternal rest. The symbolism of this does not require to be laboured: the sun rises in the east and passing its zenith sinks in glory behind the western rim, and so the souls of men, after the heat of the day, take flight to an island home beyond the sunset. Throughout the centuries this central concept found individual expression in the cultures of many nations and peoples, and was taken over to some extent by the early Church. Plato's great continent of Atlantis was placed in the Atlantic west of the Straits of Gibraltar, and the story of this Utopia, eventually destroyed by earthquakes and sea floods, continued, and continues, to intrigue the popular imagination. Many have tried to fit it into the geophysical history of the Atlantic and to locate it near the mid-Atlantic ridge, but geological time, if no other factor, is against this solution.

Another element in the legend of the western elysium was derived from the romances of the later Latin writers. J. K. Wright, using Claudian's *Epithalamium* as a basis, has paraphrased their attitude in the following words: 'With the crystallisation of Latin literary forms there appeared a stereotyped conception of the ideal landscape in which the essential elements were always the same: a rich meadow shaded by laurels, myrtles, and elms and watered by a murmuring stream, clear and cool: a placid spot where eternal spring prevails and where rain and storm, frost and heat are alike unknown.' These fancies, combined with elements from the Labours of Hercules, were located by them in the Islands of the Hesperides (the Canary Islands) while the nearby Peak of Tenerife stood for the lofty pillars that 'divide the heavens from the earth', and perhaps also for the giant Atlas who intervened on Hercules' behalf. The Atlantis legend has also been associated with the mysterious city of Tartessus (the Biblical city of great wealth, Tarshish) which the German archaeologist Adolf Schulten located in or near the mouth of the Guadalquivir, north of Cadiz. Others have argued for a site in the Gulf of Sirtes; 'But as earthquakes and floods broke out . . . the island of Atlantis sank into the Ocean and was seen no more. And therefore the Ocean at this place became unnavigable, and has remained unexplored, for the muddy shallows left by the submerged island made it too difficult.'

A lost island in the far west also figures in early Irish tradition, with its tales of Tir-nan-Og, the land of eternal youth, where there is no grief, sickness or death. As in so many other spheres of human activity, the central motif was taken over by the early Church and decorated with incidents of religious significance. Perhaps the oldest of these legends is embodied in the Voyage of Bran. 'This tale as it has come down to us consists in the main of two poems, in one of which a fairy woman lures Bran overseas by picturing the delights of the Elysian island lost in the ocean, while in the other the sea-god Manannan son of Ler prophesies of Mongan who was to be begotten by him in a later age.'* The extent to which the story was originally localized is demonstrated by the fact that Manannan was the divinity of the sea which washes Ulster on the east. In the course of time the number of voyagers multiplied and their ventures took them further afield. The best known of these is related in the Navigation of Saint Brandon. The saint is an historical figure who flourished around the year A.D. 600 and is mentioned for his feats at sea by writers in the eighth and ninth centuries, though his Navigation was not written down until the tenth. The story as it has reached us has obviously been moulded into a mystical framework: it occupied seven years and Brandon is bidden to celebrate the great festivals of the Church at certain points. Directions and distances are, not unexpectedly, vague, the figure forty being often used. The islands visited by Brandon and his companions and their adventures *en route* are largely fantastic in character, for example the landing on the back of a whale, the island of talking birds, the sparkling crystal island, the curious ancient hermits who helped and directed them on their way, and many other tales.

Beneath them all there is, however, an undoubted substratum of truth. The island of Sheep is to be identified with the Faroes, and it is important to note that these constitute the centre of their voyages, while the island of Birds is probably one of the Western Islands of Scotland. Two other features are associated with ice—the island of crystal is without doubt a reminiscence of an iceberg, while the

* See Flower, R.: *The Irish Tradition*, 1947.

'thick curdled mass' of the sea describes an ice-floe, and the marvellously clear water suggests a visit to a Norwegian fjord. Brandon was undoubtedly, on other evidence, a great traveller, who visited Wales, Britain and the Hebrides, and in the Navigation we have either a description of a voyage to the Faroes and perhaps Iceland, or an account of the region which was obtained at the end of a voyage in that direction. Attempts have been made to show that he voyaged far to the south, reaching the Canary Islands and even the West Indian Islands, but what evidence there is points to a northern voyage. This is supported by the statements of the later Irish scholar, Dicuil, who gives a recognizable description of Iceland and states that this island had been reached by the Irish before it was settled by the Vikings. Some have also endeavoured to stretch the evidence to make the Irish the first discoverers of America, but this is more than the story can carry. It is also possible that some of the details were derived from the Vikings who had arrived in Ireland in the mid-ninth century, before they reached Greenland.

The Norsemen reached Iceland via the Faroes, and were settled there by the end of the ninth century. The southern coasts, warmed by the Gulf Stream Drift and enjoying a somewhat milder climate than that of today, offered, in contrast to the desert interior, sufficient resources to sustain a hard way of life, though the economy prospered with the exploitation of the adjacent fishing grounds. One important deficiency was timber, as the woods were gradually cut down. It was thus an environment which provided a stable base for colonization, while stimulating a search for the means to a richer life. Though Greenland is no great distance from Iceland, the East Greenland Current brings much ice right down the eastern coast so that it is difficult to approach for much of the year. Consequently it was the probably accidental discovery of the more congenial area of south-east Greenland which led to its settlement. In Greenland, in the prevailing conditions, it was just possible to raise sufficient fodder on small patches at the head of the fjords to winter cattle and to maintain a small agricultural community, an achievement which would not be possible today. The main deficiency was bread-corn, most of which had to be imported, as well as timber for the dwellings. In return the Greenlanders exported a rough frieze cloth made from locally raised wool, walrus tusks which competed with ivory on the European market, and, to satisfy the demand of feudal sportsmen, numbers of white falcons.

Nevertheless, the balance was a delicate one, for the Greenlanders had passed beyond the bounds of the medieval agricultural area; with the slight deterioration of climate, the balance tipped against them and the community faded away through under-nourishment and probably from attacks by the Eskimos. Nevertheless, incredible though it may appear, within a hundred years of the Norse arrival in Iceland they had extended their culture-area to south-west Greenland and maintained this connection for almost four centuries until the trading voyages to Norway ended in 1367. At the most, the two settlements, the eastern settlement around Brattahlid, to the north-east of Cape Farewell, and the western settlement about two hundred miles further north, had a maximum of three thousand souls, before the effects of isolation and inbreeding began to tell. Not only was the voyage to Iceland and Norway hazardous for much of the year, but even communication between the two settlements was troublesome. Thus the Greenland territory was not a strong base for a further advance into the unknown. That a small European community existed in the Arctic and had some knowledge of the American continent is certain: the intriguing problem is the extent of that knowledge, the use, if any, made of it, and its subsequent effect on the course of exploration.

The detailed story of the Norse voyages to America is found in the Icelandic sagas compiled in the fourteenth and fifteenth centuries, that is, at the end of the medieval colonization of Greenland. The sagas are clearly based upon earlier accounts now lost and on oral tradition of events which had occurred four and five centuries earlier. It is not strange, therefore, that there are differences and confusions between the various accounts. Taking these as they stand and reconciling them as far as possible, the following story can be constructed. In the year 986, a certain Bjarni Herjolfsson while on a voyage to Greenland was driven far off-course by northerly and easterly gales. Finally, after some days of thick fog, the weather cleared and he found himself off a pleasant land, not mountainous but well wooded, with low hills. Although the crew wished to renew their supplies of water and firewood, Bjarni refused to land. Then, sailing northwards, for another two days, to regain course, he sighted another land, this time flat and wooded. Again he did not land, and after three more days, aided by a south-westerly wind, he reached a third land of mountains and glaciers. Again he sailed away without landing, and with the same favourable wind made southern Greenland safely. Nothing was done to follow up these discoveries for fourteen years, until Bjarni sold a ship to Leif Erikson, the son of Eric the Red, who was proposing to organize a voyage to the west.

Leif wished his father to lead the expedition, but on the way to the embarkation Eric stumbled and, disturbed by the omen, refused to proceed. Leif finally set out in command with a crew of thirty-five. There is a vivid description of the effect such Norsemen had upon the peoples they encountered on their ruthless raids, not as they appeared to an American Indian but to a Greek contemporary in Moslem service. Ibn Fudhlan wrote: 'I never saw people more perfectly developed; they were tall as palm trees and ruddy of countenance, with red hair. They wear neither coat nor caftan, but the men have only a coarse cloak, which they hang over their shoulders so that one hand is left free. Every man carries an axe, a knife or a sword with him; they are never seen without their weapons. Their swords are broad and decorated with wavy ornamentation and Frankish work.'*

Leif reversed Bjarni's route and started in the north. He first sighted a grassless land of flat rock backed by great glaciers. After landing and finding it devoid of value, he gave it the name of Helluland, that is, land of flat stones. Putting out to sea they came to Bjarni's second land and again went ashore: 'This land was low-lying and wooded, and wherever they went, there were wide stretches of white sand, and the slope from the sea was not abrupt.' On account of the trees, he called it Markland, land of woods. Sailing for two days on a general south-easterly course he finally sighted a cape with an island lying to the north of it. Continuing west through the channel between island and cape, his vessel was eventually stranded at low tide a considerable distance from the sea. They then landed at the mouth of a river rich in salmon which issued from a lake, into which they subsequently towed the boat. By the lakeside they built a large house and booths for the winter. The new land was indeed pleasant. Immediately on going ashore, they were attracted by some dew on the grass. 'It happened that they touched the dew with their fingers and put it to their mouths, and they thought they had never tasted anything so sweet before . . . The land was thought to be so fertile that it was unnecessary to store cattle fodder for the winter, for there was no frost and the grass did not wither much.' The country lay to the south of Greenland, as day and night were more equally divided.

One evening, a German among the crew returned with strange

* Quoted from Herrmann, P.: *Conquest by Man.*

news: 'I have something fresh to report. I have found vines and grapes.' 'Is that true, foster-father?' said Leif. 'Certainly it is true,' he replied, 'for I was born where there is no lack of them.' Accordingly they named the country Vinland, that is, Wineland, and in the spring, having loaded a cargo of grapes and timber, they sailed away. *En route* for Greenland they rescued fifteen men from a ship wrecked on a reef, and all returned safely to Brattahlid. Leif was later called 'Leif the Lucky', but the rescued party was less fortunate, for most of them died from their privations during the following winter.

A year later Thorvald, Leif's brother, sailed for Vinland and wintered at Leif's settlement. The next year he again returned, examined the country to the north, and sailed east to a cape where he was killed in a brush with the natives. The cape was called Krossanes (Crossness) after Thorvald's grave. In 1008 another brother, Thorstein, attempted to reach Vinland, but was unsuccessful. After another interval of twelve years, an Icelander, Thorfinn Karlsefni, returned to Helluland, Markland and the off-shore island. Two days' sailing to the south brought him to Keelness and he named the white beaches 'Furdustrands'. Beyond, they found an island in a fjord with strong currents, which they called Straumsfjord. After the winter Karlsefni pushed southwards to a river which flowed from a lake. In this area, which he named Hop, they found vines and self-sown wheat. After wintering there he returned to Straumsfjord where he spent the following winter and then sailed back to Greenland.

The last voyage to Vinland of which there are any details took place in the year after Karlsefni returned to Greenland. Freydis, Eric's daughter, persuaded two Icelanders, the brothers Helgi and Finnbogi, to join with her in a voyage to Leif's camp. Two ships with a total complement of ninety-five men and five women formed the expedition. No incidents are recorded for the outward voyage, and the camp was reached safely. During the winter Freydis persuaded her husband to overpower the brothers and their men. As each man was brought bound out of the house, Freydis had him slain. 'Now all the men were killed, but the women were left, and no one would kill them. Then said Freydis, "Hand me an axe", so they did, and she killed the five women who were there, and left them dead.' In the spring they returned to Greenland in the ship which had belonged to the brothers. Though Freydis had threatened with death anyone who reported the murders, gossip was soon in circulation; whereupon Eric the Red tortured three men and so extracted a full account from them. 'Then said Leif: "I cannot bring myself to treat Freydis, my sister, as she deserves, but I predict of them that their stock will never be worth much." And the end of it was that no one from that time thought anything but ill of them.' However much this gruesome tale may have appealed to its Icelandic audience, it adds little to the story of Vinland.

In these accounts similar details are given of different lands, for instance the sandy beaches are located on the second and third islands. Such conflict of detail does not make it easy to locate Vinland precisely. Distances are also often omitted except in Bjarni's voyage, which is therefore the easier to trace. Accepting that a day's sail is approximately equivalent to a hundred miles and using the descriptions of the three lands, it would appear that he made his first landfall in southern Labrador. Two days in a northerly direction would put him two hundred miles further up the Labrador coast. It seems clear that the third landfall was on south-east Baffin Island, though this is more than three hundred miles on. However four hundred miles further in a general north-easterly direction would bring him from Baffin Island to western Greenland.

With the succeeding voyages the distances are vaguer and a number of elements difficult to reconcile among themselves are introduced, so that identification is more speculative. The narratives are given more dramatic form: Leif's stumble and consequent refusal to lead the expedition, and the bloody drama of the last voyage, are literary embellishments, suggesting that the saga writers were principally interested in a good story. The details also bring to mind the old accounts of the mysterious western islands—the mild and pleasant climate, the extraordinarily refreshing water (perhaps a reminiscence of the fountain of youth), the growth of pasture throughout the year, and particularly the grape-vines discovered by the wandering German. Many commentators have accepted these as facts and on this basis have worked out a course for Leif running far to the south. His Helluland is indisputably southern Baffin Island and Markland is Labrador. On the basis of the grapes and meadows (wild grapes are not found north of 47° latitude and frost-free winters do not occur north of Massachusetts), Vinland is generally placed in the Cape Cod area, with the conveniently-named Martha's Vineyard as the camp site. Several of the topographical details can be fitted into this frame, for instance the long white strands with the extensive beaches south of Cape Cod, although other accounts place them further north.

But is it necessary, or correct, to give so much weight to the more picturesque details? Do not the sagas give Leif's Vinland all the attributes of a medieval western island? The present writer inclined to this conclusion before he realized that Fridtjof Nansen, the explorer and authoritative historian of the Arctic, had advanced this hypothesis many years ago. Further support for it can also be drawn from medieval Icelandic geographies. J. K. Wright states, for instance: '. . . An Icelandic geographical description of the world, dating perhaps from our period (i.e. 12th–13th centuries) contains the following remark: "Not far from Markland is 'Wineland the Good' which some affirm extends from Africa, and if this is so, an arm of the sea separates Wineland from Markland." This conception of the world appears to link Wineland, if not with the western traditions, at least with the riches of the tropics. The story of the vines— their finding by the German before his companions had seen them, and the odd statement that the Norsemen brought away a cargo of grapes the following spring—give the tale an air of unreality. Wine has for long had a sacramental connotation, particularly in the early Christian centuries, so that it is not odd that it should be introduced as one of the products of a distant land beyond the horizon. The real significance of the place-name Vinland is also a matter of dispute: some authorities argue that it is more properly to be derived from *Ven*, signifying a grassy plain. If the association with wine be put on one side, a more northerly location may be sought, based on the topography of the area in which Leif wintered.

Allowing that no coherent account can assimilate all the details in the narratives, a fair case can be made out for southern Labrador and the Belle Isle area. The cape projecting northwards which could be Cape Norman or Cape Bauld, Newfoundland; the island to the north, Belle Isle; the fjord, the Strait of Belle Isle; the westward-trending coast with many islands, and the swift current can be accommodated without unduly stretching the evidence. Some support for this location can also be obtained from the geography of the Norse voyages reconstructed in the maps drawn by the Icelanders Sigurdur Stefansson, around 1590, and by Hans Poulson Resen in 1605. Stefansson has 'the Vinland Cape' prominently displayed, and to the west of it, beyond a long narrow inlet, is Vinland with 'the land reached by the English', a reference to the voyages of the Cabots or John Davis. Immediately to the north, with a continuous outline, are Markland and Helluland. The latter with respect to Greenland appears to be in the correct position for south

Baffin Island. A legend states that the southern portion of the whole area is separated by a gulf or strait from America. Resen's map is basically similar to Stefansson's, and clearly places the 'Vinland Cape' north of 'Terra Corte Realis', in other words Newfoundland. This is not, obviously, contemporary evidence for the suggested location: it merely demonstrates where Icelandic scholars, in the great age of discovery, thought the Norse voyagers had been. To this extent it tells against an extreme southerly position for Vinland.

In the past, claims have been made for several sites along the eastern coast of America on the basis of alleged relics of Leif's settlement. With one possible exception, none of these are acceptable to professional archaeologists. The exception is a settlement site at Cape Bauld, the extreme northerly point of Newfoundland. Since 1961 the site has been excavated by the Norwegian scientist, Helge Ingstadt. In preliminary reports, he suggests this to be contemporary with the Norse voyages to America.

The settlement consists of the foundations of seven turf buildings, including a large room with an open hearth. Carbon-14 tests of charcoal samples give dates centring around the early tenth century. Ingstadt's definitive results have yet to be published so that it is too early to attempt to relate this find to the general history of the Norse voyages. Should however the evidence be sufficient to link the site with one of the known voyages, it would be very strong support for a location in northern Newfoundland.

Another recent development which stimulated interest in the Vinland problem was the publication of a manuscript world map claimed to include the earliest cartographic representation of any part of the Americas, with a delineation of Greenland 'so strikingly accurate that it may well have been derived from experience'. The map, by equating its script with that of the accompanying text, is assigned to the year 1448. Since this is half a century before Columbus's discovery, it is not strange that its publication should have caused much excitement. As it stands, it depicts Vinland as a large island to the south-west of, and at least twice the area of, Greenland as shown. The principal features of the elongated island are two large rivers or inlets on the east coast which flow in a north-easterly direction. Assuming that Vinland and Greenland are intended to be on the same scale, the former extends southwards to the neighbourhood of Boston, Massachusetts. If this is accepted, the northern waterway, which is represented as having its source in a large lake, is Hudson Strait and Bay, and the broader, southerly waterway is the

Gulf of St. Lawrence. On these assumptions, the representation on the map supports a southerly location for Vinland. It may be pointed out, however, that since the map has no scale or net of meridians and parallels, and has clearly been compiled from several sources, the extent of Vinland cannot be defined with certainty. It is possible, therefore, that the southern river is Hamilton Inlet and that the whole island lies north of the Gulf of St. Lawrence.

Legends on the map state that Bjarni and Leif discovered Vinland together: 'sailing southwards amidst the ice' they reached 'a new land extremely fertile and even having vines, the which island they named Vinland'. (The reference to ice seems incongruous in relation to vines.) It also records a visit to Greenland and neighbouring regions, 'that truly vast and very rich land', in 1117 by Bishop Eirik Gnupsson, who remained a 'long time in both summer and winter' and returned north-eastwards to Greenland. This either corrects the date of the Bishop's visit, previously assigned to the year 1121, or implies that he made two; it also enlarges the duration of his visit.

If the Vinland Map embodies independent, early Norse information, it has an important place in the history of Vinland. Its true character and importance, however, turn largely on the question of its date. Without going into the palaeographical arguments, it is fair to say that the date of 1448 is subject to some doubt. Another difficulty is the apparent accuracy of the outline of Greenland, which was not circumnavigated until the nineteenth century. It is generally accepted that firstly this great island could not have been circumnavigated at an early period, despite a somewhat milder climate; secondly that there seems no motive for the Norsemen to have undertaken such a voyage; and thirdly that the Norsemen did not use or make charts. It is possible that the map was reconstructed in or before 1448 from oral tradition and a study of the sagas, though even this hypothesis would not explain the Greenland outline. On the cartographic side, a solution to the puzzle may result from a further study of contemporary maps and charts of the northern Atlantic. For the present it remains an enigma.

Some commentators, on the basis of the statements relating to Bishop Gnupsson's visit, approximately a century and a quarter after its discovery, have argued for a continuous occupation of Vinland over a considerable period of time. It is true that there is a statement that a ship brought timber from Markland in 1347, but this is not in itself evidence for the existence of a settled community.

If it was known that the country was rich in resources, pleasant and accessible, it is difficult to understand why the vigorous, thrusting Norsemen did not exploit their discovery, or why when the Greenland settlements were in difficulties they did not attempt to remove to this paradise. One factor militating against the maintenance of a connection with Vinland may have been the physical conditions in the seas south-west of Greenland, in relation to medieval navigation. For the greater part of the year, this area is under the influence of the strong westerlies blowing away from the American coast and bringing severe storms; at times, also, heavy fogs persist. These conditions were often too much even for the improved vessels of the early Portuguese and English adventurers. Cabot was lost on his second voyage and it is not known how many of his fleet returned; similarly Gaspar Corte Real, after a successful first voyage, disappeared without trace on his second venture. Then Miguel Corte Real, searching for his brother, was himself lost. Thus, over a period of five years, the commanders of three out of five expeditions failed to return. That two were lost on second voyages suggests that the dangers increased as adventurers pushed into the unknown. And the hazards of this area also took their toll of Elizabethan seamen.

It may be tentatively concluded therefore that Vinland did not lie a considerable distance to the south; that it was not occupied for any length of time, and that, if a connection with any part of America was maintained from Greenland, it was through spasmodic voyages to Labrador for timber and other easily obtainable products.

The later history of the Greenland settlements may be briefly sketched. They stood on the margin of the known world, precariously balanced on the edge of disaster. Periodically they received a visit from a royal trading vessel which brought much-needed supplies and carried back the scanty products of the inhospitable land. The settlements were also included in the organization of the Church, a bishopric of Greenland and the neighbouring regions being instituted in the early twelfth century. Their story is thus one of gradual decline. The Western Settlement was abandoned or destroyed about 1340, and thirteen years later, on receipt of news of the parlous condition of the Eastern Settlement, a Norwegian party sailed under one Paul Knutson to its relief. This voyage was undertaken at the direction of the Norwegian King 'for the sake of our predecessor who in Greenland established Christianity . . . and we will not now let it perish in our day'. Political events in Norway, however, diverted attention from this distant outpost, and the last recorded sailing of a trading ship was in the year 1369. It would seem that the settlers either perished from starvation and scurvy or were overwhelmed by Eskimo attacks from the north.

Throughout most of the fourteenth century, therefore, even if spasmodically, Norway and Iceland were in contact with Greenland, and the question then arises as to what extent the sailors and scholars of southern Europe were conscious of this land in the distant west. In the mid-fourteenth century Italian chart-makers extended their work to include representations of the Scandinavian countries and Iceland, and an increasingly accurate delineation of that island appears on their charts. They stop short, however, of including any representation of Greenland, until the following century, when on a chart in the Ambrosiana Library, Milan, there appears to the west of Ireland a large rectangular island labelled *Isola Verde* (Green Island); immediately to the south of it is a smaller, circular island named *Illa de Brasil*. But this chart is generally ascribed to the late fifteenth century; this date together with the position of the islands makes it difficult to accept it as an early cartographic representation of Greenland.

There is, however, one document which throws light on the knowledge of Greenland but which, tantalizingly, stops short of answering all the problems. This is a summary of information recorded by an English Minorite friar who visited Greenland in 1360. He is described as a mathematician of Oxford who took with him an astrolabe and made a number of observations for latitude, none of which, regrettably, have survived. He is generally identified as one Nicholas of Lynn, though Professor Eva Taylor suggested that he was another contemporary, Hugh of Ireland. On his return to Norway the friar gave a detailed account of the Arctic lands based on his experiences. He was impressed by the steep-sided fjords with their rock slopes bare of vegetation and their summits capped by clouds, the long ice-bound winters, and the contrast between the frozen sea on the east coast and the open water on the west. He recorded also the quantities of drift-wood washed up on the shore—a characteristic feature which centuries later assisted Nansen in planning the voyage of the *Fram*. He may even have visited Markland for he spoke of having seen, a short distance inland, clearings in the woods where trees had been felled. This cannot have been Greenland, but the description would accommodate Labrador. Except for a statement that he exchanged his astrolabe for a book with a priest, there is no mention of the Greenland settlers, but there is one intriguing reference to people 'not four foot tall', probably the Eskimo. Other details concern channels through which the sea flows swiftly, whirlpools and a somewhat complicated distribution of Arctic lands and seas. Where Greenland fitted into all this is often difficult to determine, but there is little doubt that embodied in the narrative is a visit to Greenland.

Nicholas wrote an account of his experiences for King Edward III in whose service he travelled. This has since disappeared, but an otherwise unknown scholar, Jacobus Cnoyen of 's Hertogenbosch, incorporated it in a work entitled *Inventio Fortunatae*. This was apparently a description of the world which included much about the Arctic lands derived not only from Nicholas but from older Norse geographies, and details about King Arthur's legendary activities in the Arctic, not recorded elsewhere. This work is also lost, but was well known to scholars of the period 1490–1580. One of these, the celebrated Gerardus Mercator, made a summary of the *Inventio* at the request of his friend Dr. John Dee, the Tudor cosmographer, and it is from this that our knowledge of Nicholas of Lynn stems. There are several interesting references to the *Inventio* by later geographers. Johannes Ruysch, who claimed to have made a voyage to the newly-discovered lands about 1500, used it in compiling his map of the world published in Rome in 1507. Also, if the Admiral to whom a certain John Day wrote in 1496 about the activities of the Bristol men in the Atlantic was Columbus, then the latter seems to have been anxious to obtain a copy of the work. We do not know whether he was eventually successful, but since this was several years after his first voyage of discovery, it is no evidence that Columbus was influenced in planning his enterprise by news of Greenland.

A summary of a lost compilation which has itself disappeared might not be thought to be a reliable authority for a fourteenth-century voyage to Greenland: many of the details however are acceptable. Contemporary Franciscan friars were noted for their zealous, wide-flung journeyings; the town of Lynn, with other east-coast ports, was then trading with the North, and Oxford mathematicians were well versed in the use of the astrolabe. One further point is worth making. The sole place-name mentioned in this connection is *Grocland* (accepted as identical with Greenland); the names Vinland and Markland do not occur. If these were prominent in the minds of contemporaries, it is surely noteworthy that Cnoyen, a man clearly aiming at collecting all available information on the Arctic regions, made no mention of them.

In the following century the number of merchants and travellers from southern Europe who visited the North began to increase. An itinerary compiled at Bruges for the use of merchants mentioned the stages Bergen–Iceland and Iceland–Greenland. One traveller, the Venetian Pietro Querini, was shipwrecked on the north Norwegian coast, journeyed through Sweden and returned to Venice. The recital of his experiences greatly interested the cartographer Fra Mauro, who included details in his great world map, completed in 1459. His assistant, Andrea Bianco, who incidentally had worked in London for some time, may also have known of them, since the North is figured on charts contained in his atlas of 1436. On one of these he drew, on the western edge of the sheet and at no great distance from Norway, a relatively long piece of coastline, with the names *Ya Rouercha* and *stocfis* on it. The latter is generally taken to stand for 'stockfish', an English word associated with English voyages to Iceland. If the identification with Iceland is correct, then what he knew of that island was that it was very large, in relation to Scandinavia, and lay to the west of Norway. Of what lay beyond, he was apparently ignorant.

Shortly before Bianco was working on his charts, a Danish scholar, Claudius Clavus (or Swart), visited Rome, bringing with him a geographical description of the northern lands. This aroused much interest and a cartographer was set to work constructing a map under Clavus's direction. On this map Greenland is depicted as a long, narrow peninsula, springing from northern Norway and extending to the south-west; Iceland appears as a crescent-shaped island with its longer axis from north to south, and the south-west peninsula of Norway runs out westerly into the Atlantic. Among these distortions, there are some accurate data: especially noteworthy is the correct placing of the southern tip of Greenland, on the same parallel of latitude as Bergen. These may be due to use of the table compiled by Nicholas of Lynn, but it is difficult to explain the other fantasies. That this map with its misconceptions should have been accepted and later incorporated into the world map of Claudius Ptolemy testifies to the lack of reliable knowledge of the North among scholarly circles in Rome, for Fridtjof Nansen showed that its outline of Greenland was derived from that of Norway on a Catalan chart, and also that the nomenclature on the peninsula is fictitious. Whether this was due to Clavus or to the cartographers' misunderstanding of his instructions cannot now be determined; the point to be noted is that far from advancing knowledge, the Clavus map put into circulation a false image which deluded cartographers for a century or more.

What then did the southerners in the opening years of the fifteenth century know of the North? Very little information on Vinland is to be found in contemporary Icelandic literature, and still less in southern European geographies. The earliest literary reference is in Adam of Bremen's history of the northern lands, *circa* 1050, where the vines are mentioned, but this attracted little notice. The references in Norse literature are scanty and confused: it is sometimes referred to as lying in the dark and wild ocean beyond Greenland. As for Greenland itself, southern scholars could not obtain a clear picture of its position from the *Inventio Fortunatae*, nor did Clavus show its correct relation to Scandinavia. On the other hand, sailors and merchants frequenting Icelandic ports may have picked up more accurate details. That this information reached the notice of Columbus and other explorers is not impossible, but if it did it seems unlikely that tales of an inhospitable land in the far north would have given them much encouragement to launch out into the central Atlantic.

The conclusions which can be drawn are that some persons in southern Europe in the earlier decades of the fifteenth century were aware of the approximate position of Iceland and of the importance of its fisheries, and rather fewer had a vague idea of Greenland lying beyond, in a northerly direction. But it is highly improbable that they associated this distant country with southern lands, on the western side of the Atlantic.

Chapter III

ATLANTIC VOYAGES OF THE PORTUGUESE

WHILE SEAMEN and merchants of southern Europe were establishing contact with Scandinavia and Iceland, some of their contemporaries were already set upon a course which was to lead them to dominance of the oceans of the world, expectation of the riches of the tropics providing a stronger impetus to advance than the unexciting produce of the northern fishing grounds. In the van of this expansion into the Atlantic were the peoples of the Iberian peninsula: the small kingdom of Portugal and the several kingdoms of Spain which were unified in 1479 under the Crowns of Castile and Aragon. Partly because it controlled a portion of the Atlantic coastline, and partly because the interest of Aragon lay primarily in the Mediterranean, Castile led the Spanish advance westwards, taking up a position which was later reflected in the application of the name 'New Castile' to an important region of the new world. Spanish overseas expansion began in fact at the end of the fourteenth century with expeditions to the Canary Islands and their partial subjugation. Christopher Columbus's departure from Portugal to seek support in Spain, therefore, was not simply the spontaneous initiative of an ambitious individual seeking a second-best alternative, but a crucial move in the battle of international politics. In the earlier stages, however, Castile had pressing matters of state to attend to at home, leaving Portugal free to initiate her southern advance along the African coasts and to establish staging posts in strategically-placed islands. In the process, the Portuguese gained valuable experience in oceanic seamanship and navigation, as well as a knowledge of the meteorological and hydrographical conditions in the Atlantic which later stood them in such good stead. Indeed they were the first of the new nations to apply astronomical knowledge effectively to solving the problems of sailing the high seas, and their manuals and sailing directions were invaluable to the seamen of other nations who followed in their wake.

Many social, economic and political trends combined to inaugurate this epoch of overseas expansion. Western Europe having emerged from the chaos of the early Middle Ages, the city states of northern Italy, in the full flush of the Renaissance, were developing a wide-ranging, inquisitive attitude to man and his environment, stimulated by the recovery of the learning of Greece and Rome. Their vigorous intellectual life was supported by an extensive commercial system which embraced the markets of southern England, Flanders and Champagne in the north-west and the trading factories on the shores of the Black Sea in the south-east. For a brief spell the Crusaders had held Constantinople and, for a longer period, footholds in the Holy Land and the Levant. Only the southern coasts of the Mediterranean remained firmly under Moslem control, the Moors still holding a bridge-head north of the Straits of Gibraltar, in the kingdom of Granada.

This flourishing commerce was built up on two main types of route. The landways from the Italian plain led northwards over the Alpine passes to the Rhine valley and to central and eastern Europe, and this network was supplemented by the route from the Mediterranean northwards to the great fairs of Flanders. But much of the traffic was seaborne, for the sea often afforded safer passage than the war-tormented land. The merchant fleets of Genoa concentrated in the main on the eastern Mediterranean and the Black Sea. Though Venice also had stations in the East, one of her great enterprises was the annual fleet, the 'Flanders galleys', which sailed through the Straits of Gibraltar, calling at western ports *en route* for Southampton, London and Flanders. Here they encountered merchants from the North, foremost among whom were the Hanseatic men from the cities of the Baltic, and the wool merchants from England.

The contribution of the Italian states to the organization of commerce was thus considerable. An efficient banking system extended through western Europe, financing trade and prepared to support at a price the governments of the rising national states. In seamanship also, adapted to the special conditions of the Mediterranean, they had much to offer the West; the magnetic compass, obscure in its origins, was developed in Italy, and the first marine charts, based on reasonably accurate measurement of direction and distance, were of Italian and Catalan origin. In Italian libraries reposed the manuscripts of the classical authors from which the Renaissance drew its ideas on the nature of the world. Italian bankers, naval commanders, merchants and cosmographers were to be found in many of the courts and ports of maritime Europe; inevitably Venetians, Genoese and Florentines figure prominently in the early history of overseas expansion.

The world within which these explosive forces were accumulating was still restricted. Though the Crusaders had temporarily checked the Moslem advance, a new threat had arisen to the south-east when the Ottoman Turks broke into the Balkan peninsula. The fall of Constantinople in 1453 symbolized the steady decay of western influence in this quarter, and northern Africa was a closed field to European merchants, though trade with the Moors remained important. The Christian states had established treaty rights with the local rulers in North African ports, particularly Honein, Algiers, Bona and Tunis. Traffic in gold, slaves, ivory, ebony and other exotic products came by caravan across the Sahara from the tropical lands to the south, through Moorish and Jewish intermediaries, to meet the demands of the Christian merchants. But for strangers the interior was a hidden, and therefore mysterious, land, save for the sparse and garbled tales which filtered along the caravan routes.

The kingdom of Portugal was well placed to participate in this commercial system. Holding the greater part of the western flank of the Iberian peninsula, from the Minho estuary southwards to the Algarve, the province reconquered from the Moors in 1250, it faced the Atlantic on a long front, broken by several excellent roadsteads and harbours, of which Lisbon and Lagos were to become world-famous. In addition, standing as it did to the north-west of the exit from the Mediterranean through the Straits of Gibraltar, it lay on the important sea-route from southern to northern Europe. As the Portuguese national poet sings: 'If Spain is the head of Europe, Portugal, set at its western extremity, where land ends and sea begins, is as it were, the Crown on the head.'

By 1400, Lisbon was a flourishing and frequented port. Lagos, smaller in size, was well-placed to compete with the rival Spanish centres of Cadiz and Seville. To the west, Cape St. Vincent, the most westerly point of the kingdom, thrust out into the Atlantic; associated with Prince Henry's villa near Sagres, it came to symbolize the Prince and his work. Yet the situation of Portugal was not without its disadvantages. On the east and north her boundaries ran with those of the kingdom of Castile, greater in area and population and richer in natural resources. Spain, like Portugal, was on the road to a vigorous and expanding nationhood. Before the century was over, Castile and Aragon were united, and Granada, the last

Moslem stronghold in the Peninsula, had been reduced. The Spaniards in their strength were not disposed to brook a small and active rival on their flank, particularly one pursuing objectives similar to their own. Portugal, however, had completely thrown off Spanish control at the battle of Aljubarrota in 1385, where a small force of English bowmen contributed to the final victory.

In these conditions there was considerable mingling of Portuguese and Spaniards, especially among the seafarers, and men frequently changed allegiance from one monarch to another without great qualms. The existence of a refuge for the disaffected so close at hand was a constant threat to the stability of the kingdom of Portugal, while the rulers of Portugal, in turn, were not averse to interfering in the dynastic struggles of their fellow monarchs. Since both countries also employed foreign experts, a more specialized manifestation of the ubiquitous *condittore* who fought for the side which paid most lavishly, it was difficult to prevent information passing to and fro, despite the security measures taken by both sides.

The small kingdom, lacking great natural wealth, could not support a numerous population—little more than a million persons— and pressure on the land grew steadily. Thus at an early period she had turned to the sea to supplement her livelihood, and her fishermen and merchant skippers were known as far afield as Ireland, England, Scandinavia and perhaps Iceland. Her connection with Genoa in matters pertaining to the sea had been particularly close, though by the fifteenth century this was slackening. The starting-point in this relationship had been the appointment in 1317 of Manuel Pessanha, a Genoese captain, as Admiral of the Portuguese naval forces with the primary duty of protecting the ocean coast. The terms of his contract obliged him to provide and maintain twenty men of Genoa—'knowledgable in matters of the sea'—whose duty was to serve as officers in the galleys; and, especially significant, they were, when not so employed, to work as commercial agents in Florence or in Flanders. This association continued with some degree of closeness for the next one hundred and fifty years, so that when Columbus, a native of Genoa, sought a career in Portugal, he was merely following in a long tradition. However, the political climate in Lisbon was changing in his day. Foreign specialists were no longer so warmly received, as some had proved unfaithful to their employers, and Columbus himself was to outstay his welcome.

Faithful sons of the Church and firm opponents of the infidel intruders, the men of the Iberian peninsula waged a constant crusade against the Moors. To the Spaniards fell the campaigns on land. The Portuguese, after the re-conquest of the Algarve and with the support of the Papacy, carried on harassing raids by sea, prominent in the fight being the Military Order of Christ, of which Prince Henry was the supreme commander. But, despite their successes and their ardent spirit, the Portuguese were always conscious of their precarious position, a David threatened by more than one Goliath. Their attitude was well summed up by Camoens, when apostrophizing his fellow-countrymen:

'You are a very small part of mankind, you Portuguese, a very small part, even, of God's fold; and yet neither peril nor self-seeking nor lukewarmness in devotion to Mother Church deters you from the conquest of the lands of the infidel. As few in numbers as you are stout of heart, you do not pause to reckon up your weakness. Facing death in manifold forms, you spread the faith that brings life eternal; for Heaven has willed that, few though you may be, you shall do great things for Christendom. So high, O Lord, dost thou exalt the humble.'

Portugal was in fact on the new frontier of Europe, and the frontier was about to move rapidly foward.* This concept has been elaborated by an American economist, Professor C. E. Ayres, in his study of the growth of industrial capital. This takes into account the heritage from Mediterranean civilization, which served as the intellectual springboard, and the influence of 'culture contact'. The tool was the caravel, a combination of the Mediterranean and Viking traditions of shipbuilding, the characteristics of which were a long narrow hull, in contrast to the more stumpy and rounded hulls of medieval times, a high poop, a square-rigged foremast and a second mast carrying a lateen, or triangular, sail. The first mast took maximum advantage of a wind abaft, the other allowed the pilot to beat up wind and provided great manœuvrability in shallow, inshore waters. Without this advance in ship design, it would not have been possible to navigate the African coastal waters so successfully.

While allowing great weight to inherited ideas and knowledge, Professor Ayres also stresses the importance of freedom from traditional restraints. His contention is summed up in this passage: 'The actual experience of the European peoples was that of a community endowed with a full complement of tools and materials derived from a parent culture and then almost completely severed from the

* For this section, see Ayres, C. E.: *The Theory of Economic Progress*, University of North Carolina Press, 1944.

institutional power system of its parent. The result was unique. It is doubtful if history affords another instance of any comparable area and population so richly endowed and so completely severed.'

The Portuguese enter the international stage as participators in the North African trade, and participators also in the frequent piratical affrays, interrupting Moslem communications across the Straits and raiding as far as the eastern Mediterranean. Sailing from Ceuta, inside the Straits, to Tangier, Salee, Massa, and Saffi, along the Atlantic coast of Morocco, they were also learning the craft of navigation, picking up scraps of information about the hidden lands to the south, and embarking, without being conscious of it, on the route to a new world of unexpected dimensions. This interchange across the Mediterranean and its approaches, continuing over centuries, had resulted in much racial admixture with Arab, Moorish and African ingredients. They took, as a consequence, a broader view of colour than did their contemporaries, an attitude which later assisted them in organizing and administering their overseas empire. If one can attempt to characterize a whole nation in a few words, these men were tough and capable of enduring great hardships, personally brave to the point of recklessness, at times capable of great cruelty, and fanatically devoted to their faith. Yet, bound by ties of religion and national pride, they acted with unity and self-discipline in the pursuit of a common purpose. Portuguese historians have contrasted this cohesion with the fantastical, self-willed indidualism of the Spaniard, of which Don Quixote is the supreme example. For this small nation with many calls upon its manpower and in conflict with rivals whose power increased steadily, the pioneer's burden eventually proved too heavy.

During the two hundred years of great activity its policy was directed by the House of Aviz, which provided leaders of the calibre of Prince Henry, Dom Pedro, John II, and Emmanuel, the 'perfect Prince'. To contemporary chroniclers Prince Henry was the embodiment of systematic enterprise overseas. (His somewhat misleading title, 'the Navigator', was bestowed on him by a nineteenth-century English historian, R. H. Major.) He spent much of his time in seclusion at Sagres, tending the affairs of the Order of Christ and directing the African enterprises. His direct interventions in his country's politics were few, and unhappy. His brother, Dom Pedro, on the other hand, was a man of action, involved as Regent in the turbulent politics of the kingdom, a traveller and a scholar.

When Prince Henry initiated the advance southwards, his first moves were directed towards the island groups of Madeira and the Canaries. These were known to the geographers of Greece and Rome and had been visited by Mediterranean seamen during the fourteenth century. Later, Castilians had raided the Canaries but they did not establish firm control until their Portuguese rivals had been beaten off; on this possession of the Canaries Spain was later to base her claim to a sector of the Atlantic in the negotiations leading up to the Treaty of Tordesillas. The Portuguese met with more success in Madeira, occupying that island in 1419 and later acquiring Porto Santo without difficulty. Colonies were then established in the islands which became useful bases for the exploitation of western Africa and the Atlantic.

The Portuguese next found a group of greater importance—the Azores archipelago, some seven hundred miles out in the ocean west of Lisbon, and beyond the meridian of Iceland. These islands had probably been sighted by fourteenth-century sailors, although the evidence for this is confused. As they lie in the belt of steady westerly winds, where heavy seas are frequent, it would have required a determined crew and a well-found ship to reach them on a direct westerly course from Lisbon so that their discovery, or re-discovery, is more likely to have resulted from the sailing conditions off the African coasts. When returning from this area, pilots had to battle with north-easterly winds, and to make headway against them they struck out into the ocean on a north-westerly course, until they fell in with the strong westerlies which then carried them rapidly home. Once this course was generally adopted, it was only a matter of time before a ship sighted these islands, and it is far more probable that they were found accidentally than on a planned voyage of discovery. The date of the first sighting is not certain, but islands approximately in the position of the Azores are depicted on a chart of 1435 with the inscription 'insulle de novo reperte', that is, newly-found islands. Five years later a more accurate representation appeared on the Valseca chart, which assigns their discovery to 'a pilot of the King of Portugal' in the year 1427, one Frey Gonçalo Velho, a knight commander of the Military Order of Christ. In 1439 they were donated by Alfonso V to Prince Henry, who proceeded to colonize them,

While this outpost was being consolidated, pilots on the homeward run from Africa, continuing to traverse Azorean waters, came upon a new oceanographical feature in the Atlantic, which no doubt puzzled and mystified them while stimulating the imaginations of the more perceptive. This was the margin of the Sargasso Sea, the vast area of floating weed which the Gulf Stream and the winds pile up north of the Tropic of Cancer. The name *mar de baga* (*baga*, the floating *Sargassum bacciferum*) which occurs on a Bianco chart of 1436 is generally taken to apply to this phenomenon, which may well have suggested the proximity of land in the west.

The Sargasso Sea is related to the first recorded voyage south-west of the Azores. The commander was a prominent and unruly settler, Diego de Teive, who had with him a Spanish pilot, Pedro de Velasco. De Teive, a man of substance in the new island world of the Portuguese, was a member of the rising class of capitalist-entrepreneurs. A resident of Madeira, he had set up a cane-crushing plant which thrived with the progress of the sugar industry introduced by the Portuguese. When the Azorean island of Terceira was colonized by the Fleming, Jacob Huerter of Bruges, under licence from Dom Pedro, de Teive was among the first arrivals and soon attained a position of authority. In contact with the Portuguese court, he also had a connection with Castile, for his wife was a member of a Seville family. His international affiliations extended even further, for he was also related by marriage to an English resident in Madeira, one Duarte Paym (? Edward Payne). Placed on the economic frontier of Europe, he was thus well equipped to seek new worlds to conquer.

The expedition set out from the island of Fayal, probably in the year 1452, and sailed in a south-westerly direction for about one hundred and fifty leagues. Finding his progress impeded, presumably by westerly winds, de Teive turned back on a course which brought him in sight of the two hitherto unknown islands of Flores and Corvo, the most westerly of the Azores archipelago. (This late discovery is surely evidence that few if any venturers had sailed as far west before him.) After this landfall he continued on a north-easterly course, running before the wind, until he arrived in the vicinity, or on the parallel, of Cape Clear in south-west Ireland. He was still in the zone of the persistent westerlies, but to his surprise, and despite the strong winds, he found the sea tranquil. From this he concluded that he was sheltered on the west by land on a continental scale, for otherwise the sea would have been running strongly. As the season was drawing on, he then abandoned his search for the 'Isle of the Seven Cities', and returned to the Azores.

It is not immediately clear where de Teive's voyage actually took him. A century later, the historian of the Azores, Gaspar Fructuoso, recorded a popular tradition that de Teive had in fact reached the coast of Newfoundland. The evidence, however, hardly supports this claim. There are no charters or other contemporary evidence for the incidents of this voyage, save for the discovery of the two islands; most of what we know of it is drawn from Ferdinand Columbus's Life of his father. To strengthen de Teive's claim it has been argued that 'north-east' should be read as a copyist's error for 'north-west', and that de Teive sailed north-west from the Azores until he sighted land in Newfoundland. This amendment is inadmissible, since in fact Cape Clear is precisely the point at which a north-easterly course from the Azores would arrive. Thus there is no firm evidence that de Teive made a landfall across the Atlantic. On the other hand it is possible that Columbus had heard of the existence of the Sargasso Sea from de Teive's Spanish pilot, Pedro de Velasco, for he kept watch for an island to the south-west of the Azores on his first voyage.

For the next twelve years no further voyage into the western Atlantic is recorded. This was the period when tension between Portugal and Castile was mounting. Local bickering flared up into violent outbreaks. The Castilians, for example, complained bitterly of the conduct of a Portuguese corsair who had seized in territorial waters a vessel belonging to merchants of Seville and Cadiz, which was returning from Guinea, and had ill-treated and mutilated those on board, including a Genoese resident of Seville; the Portuguese counterclaimed that their vessels had suffered similarly at the hands of their rivals.

After this pause, activity in the Atlantic was renewed and optimistic captains continued to seek islands on the horizon. In 1462, João Vogado obtained a royal grant to possess two islands which he claimed to have sighted in the Ocean. Oddly enough, he asserted that they were Logo and Capraria, islands which, if they ever existed, were located in the Azores. Later, another optimist, Gonçalo Fernandes, believed he had seen an island on his return from the fisheries of the Rio de Oro in north-west Africa which lay on a bearing west-north-west from Madeira, but had never been able to recover it. Nothing more is heard of these adventurers.

Interest in western voyages continued spasmodically, but was particularly lively around 1474. In that year, the Infanta Dona Beatriz, as guardian of her young son, the proprietor of the island of Terceira, made over property in the island to two of her servants, João Vaz Corte Real and Alvaro Martins Homem. According to local tradition, written down a century later, this was a reward for having discovered the coasts of Newfoundland. The Corte Real family was associated later with voyages to this area, and it may be that this tradition relates to these subsequent ventures. About the same time, another voyager, Fernão Teles, is mentioned in contemporary documents as having been granted similar rights. This donation is valuable since it specifies with some precision the location of the islands he was seeking. It laid down that they were not 'in the parts of Guinea', that is, not south of the Canary Islands, and they are named as 'the Island of the Seven Cities, or some other populated islands' though elsewhere they are designated as 'populated or not populated'. Whether or not these searches were carried out is unknown, but these references are important, because they show first, that the interest in unknown islands continued, and secondly, that the current name for these elusive targets was the legendary 'Island of the Seven Cities'.

The record, as it has come down to us, of Portuguese enterprise in the western Atlantic before 1492 closes with a relatively well-documented account of preparations for what was clearly intended to be a considerable undertaking. The protagonist was a new type of adventurer, a Flemish immigrant, by name Ferdinand van Olmen, or as rendered by the Portuguese, Fernão Dulmo. Like his forerunners, Dulmo obtained a mandate to seek the Isle of the Seven Cities, an objective later expanded to a search for 'a great island or islands or a coast of a mainland (*terra firme*) presumed to be the island of the Seven Cities'. His grant was made irrespective of whether the islands were populated or unpopulated, and the voyage was planned significantly at the direct order of the Crown (*per mandado del Rey nosso senhor*). He was to prepare two caravels, properly fitted out and manned by competent pilots and seamen, for a voyage of at least six months. The expense involved was evidently too great for Dulmo, for he was obliged to enter into a contract with a merchant of Madeira, João Alfonso do Estreito, who was to provide half the necessary funds in return for any discoveries made in the first forty days. Again, we hear nothing more of the proposed venture, and it is probable that the caravels never set sail. The date of this plan, however, is noteworthy—1486, two years after Columbus, failing to gain the support of Portugal, had moved to Spain.

These early stages in Portugal's advance were not made without opposition from her principal rival, Castile, and clashes at sea were frequent. The Portuguese, in their endeavours to maintain a monopoly of African trade, harassed ships from Seville and Cadiz returning from Guinea, while the Castilians retaliated by attempting to disrupt Portugal's overseas trade. While this feuding continued, both sides sought Papal recognition of their claims to sovereignty. The first round in this contest was won by Portugal when, in January 1455, Prince Henry obtained a Bull, *Pontifex Romanus*, from Pope Nicholas V. By this diplomatic coup, Portugal secured recognition of her African conquests 'extending from Cape Bojador and Cape Naõ [Nun] through all Guinea and passing beyond to the southern parts': the Bull also threatened with excommunication all those who, without licence from the King and his successors, or Prince Henry, entered, navigated or traded in the said 'provinces, islands, ports, and seas'. Three months later, the Bull was proclaimed in the cathedral of Lisbon before a representative assembly which, significantly, included strangers from France, England, Castile, Galicia and the Basque country. The importance of this ceremony does not need to be stressed; Portugal for the first time had secured international recognition as the advance guard of European expansion overseas. The terms of the Bull, however, were loosely drawn, and the phrase 'passing beyond to the southern parts' was capable of wide interpretation. Despite this impressive ceremony, the quarrels did not abate, Spain continuing to maintain her rights in African waters. And inexplicably Portugal chose this moment to concentrate her energies in a new enterprise, rather than to press on southwards. A direct assault was launched on Moorish power when, in 1458, a force was despatched to seize the stronghold of Alcazar el Seguir, near Tangier. Though Castile was not averse to the weakening of Moorish power in this strategic area, the development did nothing to improve her relations with Portugal, and she continued to maintain her claims in African waters.

The long-standing feud between the kingdoms came to a head with the death of Henry IV of Castile in 1474, and the joint succession of Isabella and her husband, Ferdinand of Aragon. In the dynastic war which ensued, King Alfonso of Portugal invaded Spain. Isabella's reply threatened Portuguese colonial plans with disaster, for she despatched two naval expeditions to African waters. One squadron raided the coasts of the Azanegues, the nomad people who dwelt in Guinea. Another seized and devastated Santiago, an island of the Cape Verde group, the Spanish being greatly assisted by the defection of the Governor, Antonio da Noli, a Genoese of standing in the Portuguese service. Elated by this success, Isabella at once organized a more powerful fleet with the object of gaining control of the African trade, and particularly the traffic in gold which centred on El Mina. The Portuguese monarch reacted energetically to this peril; all naval resources were hastily assembled and two powerful squadrons under the command of the ablest officers were sent out to meet the danger. Victory went to the Portuguese. The entire Spanish fleet was captured in the Gulf of Guinea, and the crews sent as prisoners to Portugal.

It now at last became clear to both Spain and Portugal that these diversions of resources from their principal objectives were not profitable to either side. Portugal was anxious to press southwards, with the wealth of the Far East as a glittering prize, while Spain's immediate purpose was the ejection of the Moors from Granada. By the treaty of 1480, Portugal gave up all claims to the Canary Islands, receiving in return unqualified recognition of her rights in the vital southern regions. The treaty secured to her possession of all the other island groups, Madeira, the Cape Verde Islands and the Azores, with all other islands, coasts and lands 'discovered or to be discovered'. Her rights governing trade with these regions was also recognized. South of the Canary Islands, therefore, her position was unchallenged, and she retained in the Azores a springboard for western adventures.

Chapter IV

SOUTHWARD HO! OR WEST ABOUT?

B Y THE mid-fifteenth century much had happened to alter the medieval world picture. The current popular descriptions available to the man in the street, such as that which Cardinal d'Ailly incorporated in his *Imago Mundi*, had changed little, but the merchant, the scholar and the scientist were becoming better informed about the lands on the edge of the known world. The restriction of knowledge arose partly from the fact that, until the invention of printing from movable type, the reports of travellers and seamen had very limited circulation. To discover how far the outlook was changing, it is therefore necessary to bring together the letters, commercial reports, treaties and charts which were known to these men. If this is done with reference to the chain of events which later carried Europe into the Age of the Discoveries, a very illuminating theme can be discerned.

The story begins in or about the year 1425. The scene is set in northern Italy on the occasion of a tour by Dom Pedro of Portugal. A romantic account of his adventures was printed in the following century, in which he is made to visit Alexandria and the Holy Land, but whether these embellishments are discounted or not his authenticated travels must have brought the trade in oriental spices vividly to his mind. After visiting the West, where he received the Garter from Henry VI of England, he was welcomed with great ceremony by the Seignory of Venice, the principal controller of the spice trade in Europe and a source of Portugal's finance. Among the gifts he received was a manuscript of Marco Polo's travels, still the only systematic account of the Far East and its resources available to Christendom, and a large map of the world, of which we have no exact description. After Venice, Dom Pedro proceeded through Pavia to Rome, where he was received by the Pope with the honours due to the representative of a nation which was a faithful supporter of the Church and prominent in the wars against the infidel. In the ensuing negotiations these mutual bonds were strengthened, giving Portugal added support in her fight for independence *vis-à-vis*

Castile. His next sojourn was in Florence where he established good relations with the powerful Medici family. Fifteenth-century Florence was not only a keen rival of Venice in commercial and financial affairs, but was also the intellectual centre of Italy and thus of western Europe. Her citizens were keen to obtain information on lands new and old, but more particularly on the countries of the Orient. In return for financial support, Dom Pedro concluded a commercial treaty which placed Florence on an equal footing with Venice. Equally significant, he made the acquaintance of the scientist and geographer, Paolo Toscanelli, and the chronicler Bracciolini, who was recording the experiences of European travellers in the East. In this way a connection was forged between the new learning and the vigorous nation of seamen in the West, a connection which was to become increasingly stronger.

When therefore Dom Pedro returned to Portugal in 1428, he was a typical Renaissance man, active and bold, cultured and 'much given to study', with a taste for music. His writings included a translation from Cicero and a philosophical treatise, *Tratado da virtuoso benefactoria*, which had a wide appeal for his contemporaries. His horizon had been much enlarged, and he had become imbued with the crusading spirit then reasserting itself in Papal circles. The turbulent period in Portuguese politics into which he plunged, as Regent for his nephew Alfonso V, left him little opportunity to pursue wider aims, and eventually he was slain in the battle of Alfarrobeira. He had, however, been supported in his struggle for supremacy by the rising burgher and merchant classes, who approved his dislike of wild adventures and his interest in trade with Guinea and the islands. And, despite his premature death, the links with Florence were not severed, so that when the Portuguese began to debate the ultimate goal of their overseas voyaging it was natural that they should consult with the Florentines.

A further important development occurred in the 1440's when the Papacy began to plan resistance to the advance of the Ottoman Turks by rallying and reuniting the several Christian communities of the Middle East. Though this effort failed, and Constantinople fell in 1453, the abortive negotiations resulted in new information reaching Europe, particularly through the delegates who attended the Council of Florence, and who were eagerly questioned by Toscanelli and other scientists. Another visitor to Florence at the time was Nicolo di Conti, a Venetian who had spent many years travelling through the islands of the East Indian archipelago and acquiring first-hand information on the trade in spices and other oriental wares. His report, taken down by the chronicler Bracciolini, provided the most authoritative guide since Marco Polo. This fascinating news set Florentine cosmographers speculating on the distance separating Europe from the sources of these legendary riches, and cartographers refurbished their antiquated picture of the world. From this period dates an elliptical world map by an anonymous Genoese or Florentine who incorporated details drawn from di Conti and others. Its title reads, significantly, 'This is the true description of the world of the cosmographers accommodated to the marine charts, from which frivolous tales have been removed'. It depicts, off the extreme eastern coast of Asia, two large islands, Java Major and Java Minor, the modern Borneo and Java, and two smaller islands to the south-east. Their names, 'Sanday et Bandam', have not been satisfactorily explained, but from the associated legend referring to spice and cloves they are probably islands of the Molucca group. This is, therefore, the first delineation of the much-sought-after Spice Islands, a goal which the Portuguese were to spend so much energy, blood and treasure in their efforts to reach. And yet another feature of the map which would have excited interest was the representation of Africa as a distinct continent with a practical sea route round its southern promontory into the Indian Ocean.

In Venice, too, exciting progress in cartography was being made. The celebrated map-maker Fra Mauro, a monk of Murano, was embodying new information in a great world map. But so far as concerting a policy to tap the spice trade at source was concerned, the fall of Constantinople brought matters to a standstill, together with all hope of a reunion of the Churches. Nevertheless the Portuguese were at least aware of these enquiries about an approach to the wealth of the East, and were weighing up the possibilities it offered to their merchant venturers. To support this conjecture there are three pieces of evidence, all from the period of 1457 to 1459. First, Fra Mauro was engaged with his assistant Andrea Bianco upon a great circular map of the world, a well-preserved copy of which can be seen today in the Biblioteca Marciano Nazionale in Venice. The important point is that during these years he was receiving payments made on behalf of the King of Portugal for work on this world map. The Royal copy was despatched to Portugal in 1459, and the map now in Venice was completed shortly after Fra Mauro's death in 1460. The former has been lost, but there is no reason to suppose that there was much difference between the two.

There is one feature of Fra Mauro's map in particular which would have especially stimulated the imagination of Portugal. Since the African section was compiled with Portuguese help they had nothing to learn from that, but in the representation of the Far East they had plenty to ponder. Java Major and Java Minor again appear, with an important inscription: 'Java Minor, a very fertile island, in which there are eight kingdoms, is surrounded by eight islands in which grow the finest spices. And in the said Java grow ginger and other fine spices in great quantities, and all the crop from this and the other islands is carried to Java Major where it is divided into three parts, one for Zaiton [Changchow] and Cathay [China], the other by the Sea of India for Ormuz, Jidda and Mecca [in other words for Europe] and the third northwards by the Sea of Cathay.' A legend refers also to Java Major as 'a very noble island, placed in the east in the furthest part of the world in the direction of Cin and to the east of Zaiton . . . the island is full of delights and very fertile, producing many things such as gold in great quantities, aloes, spices and other marvels'. But, most intriguing of all, to the north of Java Major is an island, Zimpagu; though small and erroneously placed, this is the island of Cipangu (Japan), over whose riches Marco Polo had rhapsodized so eloquently, and the goal for which Columbus so persistently strove.

For the second piece of evidence we must return to Florence. This is a note in the manuscript papers of a contemporary, Francesco Castellani: 'In 1459, I record that in July I loaned to Andrea Bochacino, for Master Paolo of the family of Dominico da Pozo Toscanelli, my great historical *mappemonde* complete in every way. . . . And he was to restore it to me, except it was agreed that he should have it for several days and show it to certain ambassadors of the King of Portugal; and so the said Andrea and the said Paolo promised to restore it to me.' Much later, after Toscanelli's death, he added a note, 'Received from Master Ludovic, nephew of the said Paolo, February 2, 1484, the said *mappemonde* somewhat damaged and worn by handling.' This *cri de cœur* establishes, in a very human way, that, at the time when the King of Portugal had commissioned a world map in Venice, his envoys in Florence were in conference with the cosmographer Paolo Toscanelli, but also consulted another world map.

The third point associates Toscanelli and the Portuguese to an even closer degree, on evidence provided by Columbus himself. At some date, probably in 1483 or 1484, the Admiral copied out on the flyleaf of Pius II's *Historia* a letter in Latin bearing the date 1474 and addressed by Toscanelli to a Canon Fernão Martins as representing the King of Portugal. This document establishes that Toscanelli had made representations to the King about the route to the 'Indies' some years earlier, and had then been asked to illustrate his views by a map. This earlier communication is dated only by the phrase 'before the wars in Castile', that is, before 1464. As Toscanelli was talking with Portuguese envoys in 1459, it is clear that his letter was part of the same transaction. In effect, what he was then saying to the Portuguese was: 'If you wish to reach the Indies, you are making a great mistake in concentrating your efforts on sailing southwards along the African coast. As you will see from my map, the most direct and shortest route to eastern Asia is due west from Lisbon across the Ocean.' How the Toscanelli letter came into Columbus's hands is not known, but this gap in our knowledge does not destroy its importance in the antecedents of the Age of Discovery.

The Portuguese had been given excellent advice but were beginning to draw profits from the African trade and continued intermittently to push to the south, ignoring Toscanelli's opinion. By the time that Prince Henry died in 1462, his men had discovered the Cape Verde Islands, were trading on the coast south of Sierra Leone, and were even about to sail into the Gulf of Guinea. This change in direction must have raised their hopes that they were about to pass round the continent of Africa and sail towards the elusive Indies.

Chapter V

COLUMBUS: THE PURSUIT OF AN IDEA

IN THE year 1484, a Genoese merchant, some thirty-three years of age and lately resident in Madeira, presented himself in Lisbon. 'The Admiral was well built and above average height with a long face and rather prominent cheekbones, and neither stout nor thin. His nose was aquiline, his eyes light and twinkling. In his youth his hair was fair, but by his thirtieth year it had turned white. In eating and drinking, and also in his apparel, he was restrained and modest. His manner with strangers was affable, with his servants courteous but modest and pleasantly grave. In matters of religion he was most observant, so that in his habit of fasting and reciting the whole canonical office one might have thought he had taken religious vows. He was so averse to swearing and blasphemy that I wager no one ever heard him use a stronger expression than "By San Fernando". When parting with one who had angered him, his reproof was "Go with God".'

Having obtained an interview with King John II, he requested royal patronage for a scheme to reach eastern Asia by sailing westwards across the Atlantic and, even more surprisingly, demanded extraordinary rewards and privileges in the event of the success he was convinced would be his. For the man, Christopher Columbus, this was the first great stage in his career, and firm in his own mind as to the practicability of his plans, he endured with suppressed resentment the arguments and objections with which he was assailed. He appeared such a persistent petitioner for the excellent reason that he had acquired an obstinate faith in his destiny.

There is no serious reason to doubt that Christopher Columbus was born in Genoa between August and October 1451 to Domenico Columbus, a weaver, and his wife Susanna Fontanarossa. The family had been established in the city and its neighbourhood for two centuries. One branch had settled at Cogleto about 1400, and it was from this that Columbus was descended. Like many self-made men, he was given to boasting that his ancestors had been men of substance, distinguished in their country's history, who had been reduced to 'want and poverty' by war and party strife. The truth or otherwise of these assertions is of little consequence, though they provided chroniclers with material for much fanciful speculation. For Columbus the hard fact was that his family was low in the social hierarchy, and was not in a position to give him a good start in life. The future Admiral was to keep silent on this subject, though he never repudiated his connection with Genoa, the city 'whence I came and where I was born'. His natural son and biographer, Ferdinand, did not deny outright his father's humble origin, though he refers to possible distinguished ancestors and attempted to show, unconvincingly, that he had received an academic training.

At the time of Christopher's birth, Domenico, aged about thirty-three, had been working as a weaver for twelve years. His family was to grow eventually to three more sons and a daughter. Like most Italians striving to make their way in the world, they displayed strong family loyalties, and Christopher, the eldest, always had their interests in mind. Bartolomeo, some ten years younger, joined his brother in Lisbon where he worked as a map-maker and later held an office of importance in Hispaniola. His youngest brother, Giacomo (known in Spain as Diego), made less of a mark in the world. After working as a weaver, he too moved to Spain after his brother's triumphal first voyage, returned with him on the second voyage, held public office for a brief spell, and finally entered the Church. Nor did Columbus neglect sundry cousins and sons of neighbours, none of whom achieved great distinction.

In these early years Domenico met with some little success in business and took a small part in the affairs of the city. In 1440 he was able to purchase a piece of land in the Vico dell'Olivella in the eastern quarter of Rione di Portoria, and in 1447 and 1450 was warden of the neighbouring city-gate. Four years later he is recorded as taking the lease of another property in the suburbs. This may mark the peak of his success, for the next we hear of him is in 1470, when Christopher, then scarcely twenty years of age, was obliged to rescue him from debt. About this time he moved with his family to neighbouring Savona but later returned to Genoa where he died at some time between the years 1495 and 1500. This sojourn in Savona, as it turned out, gave Christopher his first opportunity to break out into the wider world. Domenico remains a shadowy figure in his son's background—of his mother, Susanna, even less is known; though he

died at a respectable age after his son's name had spread throughout
Europe, his reactions to this fame are unknown.

Christopher had little choice but to start life in his father's trade,
and was accordingly apprenticed as a wool-carder. What education
he received is unknown. His son Ferdinand asserted roundly that he
had studied at the University of Padua, but this claim cannot be
substantiated, and on the face of it is most unlikely. In his later years
there is no suggestion that he had any pretensions to scholarship in
the strict sense of the term. His knowledge of Latin was not of a
high standard and his acquaintance with Latin authors was largely
through popular compendiums. The language in which he ordinarily
wrote was Spanish which he acquired from 1486 onwards, with
traces of Portuguese idioms. This is not surprising in view of his
position as a high officer of the Crown in daily contact with Spaniards. In a letter to Their Catholic Majesties he claimed that for many
years he had been, with God's help, a student of the sciences: 'And
in this my desire I was greatly favoured by God, from Whom I had
received a spirit of intelligence. He made me very knowledgeable in
Navigation, sufficiently so in Astrology, and similarly in Geometry
and Arithmetic. He gave me the ingenuity and the skill to design
this sphere, on which are placed cities, mountains and rivers, islands
and ports, all in their correct positions . . .'

It will be noted that he places navigation first. This, unless it
stands for astronomy, was not then taught in schools or universities.
He also adds cartography to his accomplishments, another skill which
was not ordinarily found in the academic curriculum. The tenor of
the whole passage is that he had acquired his knowledge over the
years—navigation at sea and cartography in the workshop—and, as
he believed with increasing fervour, through divine beneficence.

Columbus in fact started from scratch. When precisely he abandoned wool-carding for the sea has not been established, though he
said of himself that he had followed the sea from a very tender age.
For an intelligent lad growing up in Genoa and anxious to better
himself, the step was not a surprising one. Though past its zenith
and outdistanced by its rival Venice, Genoa was still among the
great commercial and shipping centres of Europe, linked to the ports
of the Mediterranean world and to the countries of the Atlantic
seaboard beyond.

The extent of Columbus's voyaging in the Mediterranean before
he arrived in Portugal is not clear, but it included a voyage to Chios
and the Levant in the employ of the trading and banking houses of

Genoa with which he was afterwards associated. This was a decisive moment in his career. He was making contact with one source of the products which contributed to the wealth of Genoa, contact also with a new insular environment—and islands, mythical and actual, were to be his concern throughout his life. These first impressions were constantly in his mind when he sailed West Indian waters.

The voyage to Chios has been identified with that organized by the firm of Spinola and Di Negri in 1474. Its purpose was partly trade and partly to relieve the islanders who were threatened by the Turks. On board was a party of weavers from Savona, which may explain Columbus's presence, though he was probably employed in a commercial capacity. For him the voyage had two important results: relations with a firm which had considerable interests in Portugal, and the realization that, with Christendom in retreat in the East and trade languishing, opportunity for expansion must be sought elsewhere. These experiences may also account for that crusading spirit which he displayed at intervals, but never decisively, throughout his career.

On returning from Chios, the ships refitted at Noli for a conventional trading voyage to the ports of the West as far as southern England, on which a number of Savonese, including Columbus, again embarked. *En route*, the squadron was attacked off Cape St. Vincent by a French corsair, de Cazenove (also known as Colombo, a fact which has greatly confused historians). In the ensuing fight several Genoese vessels were sunk, including the *Bechalla* in which Columbus was sailing. With other survivors he swam ashore, and eventually reached Lisbon.

The Genoese were not easily diverted from their projects by such disasters. Another fleet was despatched from Genoa with orders to pick up the survivors and proceed to England. Columbus claimed later that in 1477 he had visited Iceland and had sailed a hundred leagues beyond. Although it has been ascertained that 1477 was a very open year, this purposeless extension seems dubious. As he also referred to the trade between Bristol and the far northern island, a more plausible explanation is that he accompanied the Genoese fleet to Bristol and there learnt details of this trade from English skippers. One piece of evidence in support of his having made the voyage himself is his statement elsewhere that he had visited Galway, a likely port of call on the Iceland run. Like many of his claims, however, it is a curious mixture of the possible and the improbable.

The next firm date in his career occurs about a year later, when he was a witness in a lawsuit at Genoa. In his deposition he stated that he had been sent by the Di Negri firm to Madeira on business relating to a cargo of sugar destined for Genoa. A hitch in the transaction had led to the lawsuit. He also deposed that he was returning to Lisbon the following day. This, incidentally, is his last recorded visit to his native city. He was now clearly engaged in business as an agent of Di Negri, voyaging between the Madeira group and Lisbon.

At this time he was joined by his brother in Lisbon and in that city he married Felipa Perestrello e Moniz. This marriage is another event which has given rise to a deal of controversy. Those who deny his Genoese origin argue that no Portuguese family of standing would have permitted a daughter to marry an obscure Italian trader. The Perestrello family was certainly of some standing, though its fortunes were perhaps on the decline. Felipa's father had been the first Captain-General of Porto Santo, the island neighbouring Madeira, and in his youth a squire to Prince Henry. The family was also of Italian origin, an ancestor having migrated from Piacenza to Portugal a century earlier. This may have inclined the balance in favour of the stranger at a time when marriage between enterprising young foreigners and high-born Portuguese girls was not altogether unusual—a well-known, and contemporary, example was that of Martin Behaim of Nuremberg and the daughter of the Captain-General of Terceira. It is also likely that Felipa was illegitimate, for genealogists have been unable to place her firmly in the Perestrello family-tree, an indication that her family may have been less strict over her suitor than they might otherwise have been. The marriage, traditionally the result of love at first sight, took place in Lisbon, and in 1480 a son, Diego, the second Admiral, was born to them at Porto Santo.

Columbus was now in contact with the main line of Portuguese expansion. Ferdinand relates that Columbus's widowed mother-in-law, seeing his interest in this movement, allowed him access to her husband's library. No doubt the family connection with Prince Henry also stimulated his imagination. Thus the plan which eventually materialized as the enterprise of 'the Indies' began to form in his mind, though in the beginning it is unlikely that it embraced eastern Asia or a route to the Indies as an objective. This emerged when his strong imagination grasped the trend of the age and turned it into a powerful tool for his own advancement. He himself was in no doubt as to this being a turning point in his career.

QUEEN ISABELLA OF CASTILE
The portrait by Bartolome Bermejo.

(*left*) AN IMAGINATIVE SKETCH OF THE ISLANDS DISCOVERED BY COLUMBUS IN 1492

From the edition of the First Letter published in Basel, 1493.

(*below*) THE TITLE PAGE OF THE FOUR LETTERS OF AMERIGO VESPUCCI, FLORENCE, 1505-6

This is a 'reverse' of the block used for the first edition of Columbus's Letter published in Barcelona in 1493—the first graphic representation of American Indians.

Twenty-five years later he wrote: 'From the age of twenty-eight I served in the enterprise and conquest of the said Indies', a statement which places its inauguration in the year of his marriage.

As a young man of natural intelligence, determined to make a career for himself and beginning to cherish a sense of mission, he was conveniently placed in that part of western Europe from which there opened out splendid vistas of future advancement. He had continual contact with the Portuguese skippers, foremost among the navigators of the day, who had learnt their skills the hard way by boldly venturing out into the Atlantic to find the most expeditious route to and from their West African footholds. He was learning also of the wealth which these new lands yielded to Portugal and to his own compatriots, and the system by which this trade was conducted. And around him were the retailers of stories about islands out in the western Ocean, searched for but never found, and pilots and sailors who had taken part in these ventures. At the same time, he was aware of the Portuguese design to establish a monopoly in the African trade and the growing hostility towards foreigners. It is hardly surprising that in the mind of a young, ambitious man at that time and in that place the conviction grew rapidly that here was his great opportunity to play a notable part in the advance of Christendom across the world. The infidel might effectively bar the way in the Levant and the further East, but here in the West the Ocean offered an open path to final victory. And so the concept of the westward voyage grew and, according to Ferdinand, he began to collect details of natural phenomena tending to show that in the world ocean there must exist islands, and perhaps continental lands, which others had so far failed to find—signs which were the common talk of the seamen who frequented the waters of the eastern Atlantic. There were the great exotic canes which drifted ashore along the European seaboards, and the 'pines' picked up in the Azores, particularly on the islands of Graçiosa and Fayal. These branches and tree-trunks, significantly, came drifting in before the south-westerly winds. Even more stimulating to his imagination were the vestiges of man and his works which were washed up in the same way: the two corpses, very broad faced and un-Christianlike, found on the shores of Flores, and the empty canoe stranded on an African beach. Such evidence suggested that all the islands sighted but never found were not necessarily chimerical.

Finally there were the tales of those who had ventured in search of these elusive islands. From passages in the *Journal* of the first

Voyage of 1492, it can be gathered that Columbus had particularly
in mind the voyage of Diego de Teive, some forty years earlier,
which Ferdinand recounts in greater detail than any other voyage
to which he refers. As de Teive had been a merchant in Madeira,
some account of his experiences was likely to have been preserved
by his family or was embodied in local tradition. Alternatively
Columbus may have heard it from de Teive's Spanish pilot, Pedro
de Velasco. When the nature of his achievements was challenged in
the early years of the next century, a popular stick with which to
belabour the dead explorer was the story of the 'unknown pilot'.
This individual was alleged to have been succoured in his last days
by Columbus, to whom in gratitude he imparted an account of a
western discovery, supported by an appropriate chart: an example
of the romantic treatment which Columbus's career was to undergo.
In one sense there were dozens of pilots who assisted him in his
plans, though in less fanciful ways. If however there is to be one
pilot singled out for the distinction, it was probably de Velasco. And,
in any case, it was during this period that Columbus began his somewhat superficial reading of the medieval cosmographers.

Between his business voyages Columbus passed his time in
Madeira and Lisbon. His married life was not destined to last long,
for Felipa was dead by 1488, the year in which he finally approached
King John with his plan. From his own statements he made two
voyages at least to West Africa. The sights he witnessed during them
frequently recurred to him in his West Indian years, and his writings
are made more vivid by his comparisons and contrasts with what he
had seen in Guinea. He states positively that he had voyaged to El
Mina, the trading-post set up by King John on the Guinea Gulf,
near a profitable source of alluvial gold. If this was so, that was the
moment when, stimulated by the Portuguese success, Columbus
acquired that passion for gold which was to influence him for the
rest of his life and which, combined with the argument that, since
the Portuguese had struck gold richly in this part of the Tropics,
it was logical to suppose that other tropical areas, hitherto unknown,
might prove to be equally well-endowed with this treasure, was a
principal driving-force behind his actions.

In another passage he says that he sailed to Guinea on the ship
which carried the celebrated astronomer, José Vizinho, who was
sent by King John to carry out observations for latitude so that the
sailing directions for the coasts beyond the Equator might be
improved. He tells us that it was his practice to watch and note the

work of the pilots on these voyages, and on occasion to carry out similar observations himself. One specific instance he gives is not very convincing, when he claims to have verified the length of a degree on the earth's surface. He certainly obtained the result, 45⅔ miles, which he wanted for his argument, but this was much lower than the current, and correct, Portuguese figure. The fact seems to be that his astronomical knowledge was acquired not as a navigator responsible for the conduct of a voyage, but as an observant traveller during his four voyages.

When Columbus finally obtained access to King John with proposals for his western enterprise, he found that monarch in an unreceptive mood. Having added 'Lord of Guinea' to the royal titles, the King was firmly pledged to the southern and eastern route to India, in which he had invested much capital, particularly in the establishment of the outpost at El Mina. The future of this policy appeared very bright at the time: when Diego Cão returned in 1484 after reaching the estuary of the river Congo, it was widely believed that the long, frustrating route down the western coast of Africa was at last coming to an end and that, at a short distance to the south, it would commence to trend eastwards and open the way to the Indian Ocean. This at least was the tenor of the 'Oration of Obedience' delivered at the Papal court by the royal representative, Dr. Vasco Fernandes de Lucena: 'We have', he declaimed, 'the well-grounded hope of exploring the Arabian Sea, where kings and peoples known but uncertainly to us practise conscientiously the Holy Faith of the Saviour, of which peoples, if experienced geographers may be believed, Portuguese navigation is within a few days' reach. In fact our men, having discovered an enormous part of the African coast, last year came near to the Prassus Promontory, where the Arabian Sea begins. All rivers, beaches and ports have been explored from Lisbon for forty-five hundred thousand paces [4,500 miles]. They have been enumerated with exact observation of the sea, the land, and the stars.*

What had Columbus to offer, in competition with these achievements and prospects?—stories of branches and dead bodies washed ashore, of islands in the western Ocean, sighted but never found; the assertion that the eastern coast of Asia was but a very short distance across the sea from Spain; the expectation of great wealth from fabulous lands and cities, to be brought under the rule of the Crown of Portugal as the representative of Christendom.

* Sanceau, E.: *The Perfect Prince*, p. 229.

And what did he demand in return?—privileges which the Crown had never before promised or granted to such adventurers: rights over all his discoveries, not merely one or two islands but all lands, islands and seas, with the status of a Viceroy and the title of Admiral, and in addition, for himself and his descendants in perpetuity, a share in all the wealth accruing from the new lands. Over and above these future rewards, the Crown must equip and man a well-found expedition of several caravels and place it at the disposal of this foreigner.

King John had no reason to hesitate long before rejecting such pretentious demands, apart from the fact that he was contemplating fitting out just such an expedition to follow up Cão's second voyage to southern Africa. Besides, the proposals held little that was novel to him and his advisers. They were aware of these tales of fugitive islands and these signs of other lands. As to voyages in search of them, the Crown had licensed several in recent years, and they knew precisely what they had, or had not, achieved. The short sea voyage to Asia, that, too, was an old story, and one discredited by his astronomers and navigators.

In fact, twenty-five years before, similar arguments had been advanced by Toscanelli and his colleagues in Florence to the envoys of King Alfonso V, and only ten years ago they had been repeated, at the very time when King John himself had taken over the direction of the African adventure.

On the second occasion, Toscanelli had, as has already been noted, written to Fernão Martins, as representing the King of Portugal. The letter, accompanied by a chart, is known from three versions: the copy, generally accepted as in the handwriting of Columbus, written on the flyleaf of one of his books; an Italian translation in Ferdinand's biography, and a Spanish version contained in Las Casas's history. These versions, though differing in phrasing, clearly have a common origin and expound similar ideas. Las Casas comments that he had found the document and the accompanying chart among the Admiral's papers. There is no incontrovertible evidence, however, that Columbus himself had corresponded directly with the Florentine. Ferdinand in fact states that Toscanelli's views 'came to the notice of the Admiral, very curious in such matters'. It is true that he states that his father then wrote to Florence and received a letter in reply, but since this is simply a copy of the 1474 one, this seems implausible. The transcript made by Columbus is headed 'Copy sent to Christopher Columbus by Paul the physician, with a map of navigation'. This endorsement, however, is not in the same hand as the body of the letter, and was added later, although not by Columbus.

If all these circumstances are weighed up the conclusion is reached that Columbus, either through friends at court or an Italian colleague, had sight of papers relating to the earlier Portuguese-Florentine negotiations. For their part, the Portuguese had simply maintained their previous position and given preference to the African route over the western. Columbus in fact, on his first voyage, kept within the framework of the Toscanelli concepts, though this in no way detracts from the merits of his achievements. At a late stage in the evolution of his plan he had found in the Toscanelli correspondence, not the germ of the whole idea, but welcome confirmation, within certain limits, of his own arguments. Moreover, he had outdone Toscanelli by reducing still further the estimated distance from western Europe to eastern Asia.

The chart, according to the details in the correspondence, displayed all the coasts from Ireland to southern Guinea, with all the known oceanic islands.* Opposite were all 'the end of the West' and the regions of India, alternatively described as 'the beginning of the Indies'. These coincided with the eastern and south-eastern coasts and islands of Asia, inserted in case the expedition was driven off-course. The map also showed the very splendid port of Zaiton, Quinsay, and the island of Cipangu.

The breadth of the dividing ocean is given as '26 spaces', or 6,500 miles. (This would place the coast of Asia almost in the position of California.) The position of the island of Cipangu, the objective of the first voyage, is not explicitly stated. Contemporaries placed it some 1,500 miles off the Asian coast. Allowing for this, Columbus contemplated a voyage of at least 5,000 miles. This alone would have been sufficient to damn the project in the eyes of the Portuguese, for contemporary ships or equipment could not be relied on for an unbroken voyage of this distance, though it might be conceivable if islands suitable as staging posts were discovered on the outward voyage. It may even be that the island of Antilia was regarded as a possible half-way point. When, therefore, John curtly turned down Columbus's proposition, he had adequate scientific grounds for doing so; but what was undoubtedly the major consideration was the fact that all the resources of Portugal were invested in the African route to the Indies. For his part, Columbus at once decided to try

* See Appendix, p. 201 ff.

his fortune in Spain, transferring his services to the other protagonist in the contest for the command of the seas. We are told that a favourite saying of King John's was: 'A fool thinks that he is able to do anything, but in the end he does nothing at all.' If he thought of Columbus in this way, he was right up to a point. The Genoese would never reach Cipangu, but, aiming for the treasures of the East, he hit America—an excellent example of the advantage of setting one's sights high.

Some historians have given a highly romantic account of Columbus's 'flight' to Spain, accompanied by his infant son, and of his troubles before the Sovereigns, Ferdinand and Isabella, accepted his proposals. Much of this is exaggeration or local gossip, in some instances collected later by his detractors. There is little doubt that Columbus was for part of the time in straitened circumstances, and may have supported himself by drawing charts. On the other hand, he did not arrive in Spain as poor and as friendless as he had been when he first reached Lisbon. His whole attitude towards King John was in fact ambiguous. His son tells us that he left Portugal in fear and stealthily, so detesting the country and the people that he resolved to take his 'secret' to Castile. John had endeavoured, Ferdinand wrote, to test Columbus's ideas by sending a caravel secretly to the Cape Verde Islands with orders to make a reconnaissance westwards. But, says Ferdinand, her captain, 'lacking the knowledge, constancy and character of the Admiral', returned with the report that it was impossible to find any land in those seas. (This may be a confused reference to the Dulmo expedition then fitting out in the Azores.) But this reaction on the King's part seems implausible. If he had firm reasons for believing that there were accessible lands in the western Ocean, or for thinking that there might be some foundation for Columbus's ideas, it is improbable that he would have allowed him to take them to his rivals. However, the exact relationship between the King and the explorer is unclear, as not very long afterwards Columbus applied for, and received, a safe-conduct to visit Lisbon. This was granted by King John who is made to refer to him as 'our especial friend in Seville' and to thank him for 'his good will and affection'. This may of course be merely the conventional language of diplomacy, but perhaps the two were not completely estranged.

The departure for Spain undoubtedly coincided with a time of great personal strain for Columbus: his project had been summarily rejected, and his wife was dead, leaving him alone with his young son Diego. In the circumstances it was not surprising that he went first to Palos where relatives of his wife were living. In case he should meet with no greater success than in Portugal, he also reinsured himself against a second failure by sending his brother Bartholomew, 'judicious and practised in affairs of the sea', to treat with King Henry VII of England.

No record of Bartholomew's stay has been found in contemporary English records, though twenty years later Francis Bacon made a short reference to it. Nor does his nephew Ferdinand give much detail in the *Historie*. Bartholomew, though having no Latin, was instructed in cosmography and a skilled maker of globes, charts and instruments. Having fallen a victim to pirates on his journey, he was reduced to poverty and barely supported himself by his professional work. Nevertheless he obtained access to the King and presented him with a world map now unknown. This was inscribed with a set of interesting Latin verses: 'This drawing will teach conveniently whomsoever wishes to learn of the shores [outlines] of the world according to the tenets of Strabo, Ptolemy, Pliny and Isidore, but not all after the same fashion. On it is depicted that torrid zone, formerly unknown to men, but which through the Spaniards is now well known to many.' Below this was inscribed: 'Genoa is the country and Bartholomaeus Columbus of Terra Rubra is the name of him who made this map in London in the year of Our Lord Fourteen hundred and eighty-eight, the thirteenth day of February. Let praises to Christ be sung abundantly.' Ferdinand adds, rather intriguingly, that he was quoting the verses, not for their elegance, but for their antiquity. The term 'Spaniards' was often used to include the Portuguese, so the reference is to Portuguese exploration in West African waters, of which Bartholomew would have knowledge. Of interest also are the authorities he quoted. The reference to Ptolemy implies that he had available a contemporary copy of the Alexandrian geographer's world map, and the emphasis on the previously unknown torrid zone and the early medieval cosmographer Isidore of Seville points to his also having a zone map of the hemisphere showing the climates. Here the possible significance of the date should be noted, for from 1480 onwards the men of Bristol were voyaging into the Atlantic and their efforts were intensified at the end of the decade. It would perhaps be too much to affirm, on the evidence now available, that this world map had a direct influence on them, but if King Henry studied it, his interest in Atlantic exploration would surely have been aroused.

While his brother met with no success in England, Columbus himself seemed at first fated to fail in Spain as he had failed in Portugal. When he arrived, the country was emerging from an even tougher period of social and political strain than Portugal had undergone. Though regional rivalries had been reduced through the union of Aragon and Castile by the marriage of Ferdinand and Isabella, the disorders accompanying the transition from a medieval society to a bureaucratic state were still fermenting. The old chivalry had served its purpose in driving the Moors from the peninsula, and among its ranks there was the feeling that the great days of old were passing away and that they were living a purposeless existence in a harsh and cruel world. This strain of melancholy and unhappiness is reflected in the work of contemporary poets, most forcibly perhaps in Jorge Manrique's poem on the death of his father:

> 'Thus through life ever labouring . . .
> We die to find our happiness,
> After long strain and bitterness
> To attain it.'

But even the most melancholic could not bring themselves to renounce completely the world around them in all its beauty and mystery. They turned once more for refreshment of spirit to the heroes of knightly romance and sought to emulate their achievements in love and war. Through the popular romances floated the contrasting theme of a marvellous land beyond the seas, calling out to the adventurous. In the 'Romance of Count Arnaldos', as the knight strolled along the beach with his falcon, he saw a wondrous galley with silken sails and the finest ropes seeking the land. As it drew near the captain began a song; immediately the wind dropped, fish were attracted from the depth of the sea and birds in flight perched on the mast. To the knight's request for the song, the captain replied, 'I do not tell this song save to those who come to me.' This combination of adventurousness and high courage with a fatalistic, savage despair animated many of the *conquistadores* of the New World, and goes far to explain those actions which appear so unaccountable to modern commentators. But this faith in the virtue of the individual warring against 'the four corners of the world in arms' led to the belief in his ability to affect dramatically the destiny of the age, that the real might be changed into the ideal. This sentiment was influential in shaping the empire in the Americas. It lay at the root of the ejection or forcible conversion of the Moors and later of the 'Indians' to the Christian faith, and, allied to the rigour of Church discipline, contributed powerfully to the establishment of a 'universal rule' over the continent by Spaniards, the people whom God especially favoured. There were Spaniards who looked forward indeed to the achievement of world hegemony under the Emperor Charles V. Another soldier poet, Hernando de Acuna, apostrophizing his monarch, announced the approach of '*la edad gloriosa*', when there would be one flock and one shepherd in the world, or less metaphorically, 'One Monarch, one Empire and one Sword'.

The two monarchs who moulded Spain into the dominant European power of the sixteenth century strikingly represent these two strands of the national character: an overriding universalism and beneath it a multiplicity of individual characters, the eccentrics (in the eyes of outside observers) who live in the pages of *Don Quixote*. Isabella of Castile was the universalist, in de Madariaga's phrase 'deeply possessed by the responsibility as the minister of God on earth', and Ferdinand of Aragon the politician *par excellence*: 'astuteness was his method as much or as more than force'. Between them, Their Catholic Majesties broke the power of the grandees, remodelled the constitutions of the towns, reformed the Spanish Church, defeated and ultimately banished the Moors, and expelled the Jews—believing that the essential aim was unity of faith. To achieve this, they forged two instruments of government, a centralized civil service, efficient, controlled by checks and counter-checks, strictly accountable and animated by a professional *esprit de corps*: and secondly a first-class professional army—both unique in the Europe of the day. Until the constant drain on manpower, the inflation following the influx of Peruvian silver, the decline of agriculture, and the decay of intellectual liberty as the intolerance of the Spanish Church increased, had undermined the social order, no rulers in Europe possessed a more finely tempered instrument of government.

The civil unrest which plagued Spain before Ferdinand and Isabella restored and strengthened the position of the Crown was notorious throughout Europe, as was the harsh rigour with which the laws were administered and the general callousness. The traveller Arnold von Harff commented tersely: 'Item, in Spain they administer very strong justice. The evil doer is bound against a lofty pillar sitting on a wooden stick with eyes uncovered, and they mark his heart by a piece of white paper. Then the criminal's nearest relation has to shoot first, then the other next of kin, with a crossbow until he is dead. Further they hang women criminals by the neck on a gallows or a tree. The clothes are tied below the knee. We saw many such hanging beside the road after this manner.' The strength of Ferdinand and Isabella's position and their ability to carry out large-scale reform sprang from the general recognition of the plight from which they had redeemed the country. The feeling was powerfully expressed by Francisco Ortiz in the year 1492, when Columbus was preparing to sail: 'You received the royal sceptre from the Most High in very perturbed times, when all Spain was being shaken by dangerous tempests, when civil wars were at their height and the laws of the realm, already in abeyance, were about to be destroyed. None held his property fearlessly without danger to his life; there was general distress, and everyone took refuge in the cities; remoter parts were full of bloodshed by robbers. Arms were not prepared for the defence of Christian frontiers but in order to wound the vitals of our own country. The domestic foe gorged himself on the blood of fellow-citizens; he who was strongest and most resourceful in malice was the most favoured and praised among us, and thus all things were outside the reign of justice, disordered, restless and chaotic. To whom did the highways offer safety? To very few indeed; the oxen were stolen from the plough, towns and cities were occupied by the more powerful ... Already the venerable majesty of the law had veiled its face; all hope had departed.'

At first sight a country undergoing so violent a revolution would seem unlikely to offer much scope for an Italian with a debatable project for reaching the treasures on the further side of the world, a project already turned down by the active maritime country of Portugal; and Columbus had indeed to wait seven years for approval and adequate support. But from a wider point of view the times were not unpropitious; a great head of national energy was about to explode in the peninsula and this could be diverted overseas. Indeed, Castile was not new to the idea of overseas expansion, and had already a footing in the Canaries. The stranger's scheme was precisely of the kind to appeal to Castilians in this mood, the opportunity to undertake a world-embracing mission, to continue under the banner of the Faith across the seas their crusade against the infidel, and perhaps to find in the mysterious East that terrestrial paradise which had haunted the medieval imagination. These were the aspects which appealed most strongly to Isabella the Catholic; for her husband Ferdinand, practical considerations were uppermost. His was the world of European politics, of dynastic marriages, of Papal diplomats and Italian bankers, of shrewd calculations and involved manœuvrings—the world of a man who knew how to bide his time and to exploit opportunities when they arose. If his cousin of Portugal was concentrating on imperial expansion in one direction, then the time would no doubt come when he could find an opening in another. Meanwhile, between them, they were forging a weapon admirably suited in the circumstances of the times to bring half the globe under their control.

On his side, Columbus had certain advantages which he had not enjoyed when pursuing his plans in Portugal. He had the experiences gained on trading voyages to and from Madeira and the West African coast, a knowledge of the profits which accrued to the Portuguese and the methods employed in opening up traffic with the native populations, the kind of wares which appealed to them, the manner in which the Crown controlled the trade, in fact, the 'know-how' necessary and valuable to a country wishing to step out along the path of overseas expansion.

Secondly he was known to his compatriots in the commercial and banking world with whom he had worked for a number of years, and also as one whom the Portuguese authorities had been willing at least to hear, if not to support. If his friends in Lisbon had done little to advance his plans, the reason was to be found in the firm refusal of the King and his advisers to allow foreign interests to exploit the regions under their control. But given the patronage of the Spanish Crown, might not the Italian commercial houses be prepared to put up the necessary, and to them modest, capital he so urgently required for his plan and all its exciting possibilities? His plan was prompted, after all, by the intense desire of the Italian traders to find some way round the Turkish monopoly of the Eastern trade which struck at the vitals of their prosperity. In the event, he was successful when, after years of protracted negotiations with the royal councillors, the Genoese and Florentine bankers arranged the necessary credits. In the third place, he had acquired practical and theoretical arguments for the existence of land-masses not prohibitively far across the ocean which, though rejected by the Portuguese, could be shown to have had the approval of eminent Italian scholars.

Nevertheless, the six years he spent in Spain prior to 1492 were frustrating and seemingly penurious. Apart from all the *pros* and *cons*, King Ferdinand and Queen Isabella, engaged in the final conflict with the Moors, were no more prepared than the Portuguese monarch to finance directly the speculative plans of a visionary stranger, even if they had possessed the funds to do so. Though he was not without friends in high places he failed to win over the royal advisers to his side. The ecclesiastics and scholars did not go so far as to deny that the earth was a sphere; rather they appear to have deduced from this dogma a number of counter-assertions, for instance that the return voyage could not be made 'uphill', that is, against the rotundity of the sphere, or that antipodes could not exist below the Equator. Supporters of Columbus replied that, since the Portuguese had demonstrably sailed south of the Equator and had found the tropics inhabitable, such arguments were nonsensical. The argument that there were multitudes of benighted peoples beyond the ocean waiting to be won over to the Christian faith was not one at that particular moment to commend itself to the politicians of the Spanish Church, then fully occupied in dealing with infidel Moors and heretical Jews—however much the idea might appeal to the pious Queen Isabella.

It was a weakness of Columbus's case that he had not completely cast off all ancient concepts. When his opponents argued against his assertion that a short voyage would take him to eastern Asia, it was they who were in the right—but it was his contention that ocean-going voyages were practical, and that the proportion of land to sea on the earth's surface was high, which ultimately led him to success. That he and those of his way of thinking were unable to explain how, given the existence of populous islands isolated from the known world, the inhabitants could have sprung from a single human stock, was a problem for future theologians to resolve, and one indeed which was to occupy them for many years to come.

These arguments marked the deep division between the land-bound scholars, resting their arguments on the writings of the Fathers of the early Church and contemptuous of the unlettered laymen, the rebellious citizens, the active merchants, and the practical seamen—who were challenging authority in the expanding world of the fifteenth century, and who felt that, if the scholars and churchmen maintained that it was impossible to return from a voyage south of the Equator, so much the worse for them. In addition, the Spanish Church was known for its conservatism; its general attitude was similar to that of those who feel today that governments and scientists would be better advised to concentrate on problems of the world, rather than devote so much of their resources to placing men on the moon.

Too much attention should not be paid to this academic wrangling. The disputants never seem to have come to a clear-cut decision. Columbus was first told that the Sovereigns were not prepared to sponsor the project, but that at a more favourable time they would reconsider it. Columbus then took the only course open to him, and there are various rather vague hints in his papers that he contemplated submitting his plan to other monarchs, in particular to the King of France. Naturally, when he had achieved success under Spanish patronage, he played down the incidents in this period of his career, harping upon his long years of service to the Crown before his first voyage, and claiming that he had rejected offers from France.

The upshot was a second approach to Their Catholic Majesties late in 1491. As Columbus represented it, he was, while staying at the Monastery of La Rabida, near Palos, contemplating leaving Spain for a more sympathetic environment, when he was persuaded to give up this plan by the priest Juan Perez. Perez was confessor to Queen Isabella and no doubt the possibilities of winning many souls to the Christian faith appealed strongly to him. However, the second negotiations arranged by him were no more successful than the first. The Queen was no doubt sympathetic to the missionary aspect of the project but the decision did not lie with her; the problem was now primarily a financial one, and the wary and devious King Ferdinand, deeply committed in other directions, was not prepared to find the sum required.

In the true Columbus tradition there then followed the well-known incident of the rebuffed 'discoverer' leaving the royal camp at Santa Fé and setting out on the road to France, his being overtaken in the first few miles by a royal messenger with word that the Sovereigns had accepted his proposals, and his return in triumph to the Court.

What in reality had happened was markedly different. The Court had certainly not experienced a 'moment of truth'. No sudden revelation of the correctness of his cosmographical arguments had flashed into their minds, nor had the certainty of untold wealth at last dazzled the cautious Ferdinand. The fact was much more prosaic. The decisive blow had been struck by the Treasurer, Luis de Santangel, for it was he who came forward at this critical moment to provide what had so far eluded Columbus, the funds necessary for the proper equipment of the expedition.

All this leads to a consideration of the share of the city of Seville, and particularly of the Genoese merchants there resident, in the financing of the discoveries. The Genoese commercial colony, from small beginnings in the thirteenth century, was flourishing and influential, having doubled in numbers in the half-century after 1450. Its leading members had prospered, become naturalized citizens, and had married into the highest families of Spain. Though continuing to engage in commerce, they were financiers rather than merchants, co-operating with Court officials in floating royal loans. In touch with the banking institutions of Italy and western Europe and drawing on the profits of widespread commercial enterprises, they were in a position to raise loans quickly and to arrange foreign credits as required. One of their prominent members was Francesco Pinelli, whose services to the Crown were later recognized by his appointment as chief factor of the Casa de la Contratación in Seville, the official institution which from 1504 organized and controlled trade with the Indies. In moving from Lisbon to Seville, therefore, Columbus had placed himself in the one centre where, with his Genoese connections, he could hope to find really adequate financial support for his project. At an early stage he was in touch with the powerful Duke of Medina Sidonia, a great landowner in the neighbourhood with extensive shipping interests. The Duke later asserted that he had at first considered subsidizing a western voyage himself but, concluding that it was too momentous an undertaking for a subject, however powerful, had brought Columbus to the notice of Queen Isabella. Of equal significance, Medina Sidonia had business contacts with Francesco Pinelli, and when the second voyage was being undertaken he advanced a considerable loan which was guaranteed by the financier. On receipt of the Duke's letter, Queen Isabella had placed the matter in the hands of Luis de Santangel, the royal Treasurer. Santangel, a converted Jew, whose family had suffered much persecution, was particularly concerned with relations between Aragon and the Republic of Genoa, and had already worked in close cooperation with Pinelli; together they were responsible for the accounts of a powerful corporation, the Santa Hermandad, charged with maintaining civil order. The books of this organization reveal the method of financing the enterprise after royal approval had been obtained, for early in May 1492 there is recorded a credit of 1,140,000 *maravedis** furnished to Their Highnesses for the des-

* S. E. Morison gives the value of 1,000 *maravedis*, if paid in gold, as equivalent to 6·95 U.S. gold dollars (pre-1934). This sum would therefore amount to approximately $7,000.

patch of Cristoval Colón, Almirante, a title later amplified to 'Almirante de las Indias'. Thus the royal contribution was raised by a loan through the agency of Pinelli and guaranteed by him. The abrupt intervention by Santangel immediately following the second rejection suggests a certain lack of co-ordination at the critical moment, or the occurrence of an event which finally resolved Pinelli's doubts. As for King Ferdinand, with a guaranteed loan, he had nothing to lose and much to gain.

This method of financing the expedition explains other hitherto obscure points. The gossip that Columbus had sought in vain the aid of his native city may well be based on rumours of prolonged negotiations with Genoese bankers, while the fact that after the discovery the glory was focused on King Ferdinand, while Queen Isabella's part was virtually ignored, becomes more intelligible when the immediate impetus is seen to have come from Aragon, not from Castile. The source of the balance of the funds remains obscure. Columbus claimed that he had put up one-half of the total, which seems unlikely in view of his circumstances when he arrived in Spain. In later life he was closely associated with Genoese and Florentines in dealing with his financial affairs, so that they may have advanced his share, if any.

An incident occurred after the return of the first fleet which throws an interesting light on these obscure dealings, and links them with the Toscanelli correspondence. In June 1494, the Duke of Ferrara wrote to his envoy in Florence in these terms: 'Understanding that the late Master Paolo dal Pozo Toscanelli, physician, made a note, while living, about some islands in Spain which appear to be the same as those now re-discovered, according to intelligences we have received about those regions, we have become desirous of seeing these notes, if it is possible, and we wish you to find at once a certain Ludovico nephew of the late Master Paolo, to whom it appears that he left most of his books and to pray him . . . to give you the exact note of all he may have in his possession regarding these islands . . .'

From this we can infer that it was fairly widely known that Columbus had successfully carried out a plan similar to that put forward by Toscanelli. Thus this association is clearly established for three well-defined periods: in the Portuguese phase, in the year 1459, when their envoys in Florence were discussing a westward voyage with Toscanelli directly; in 1474, when that scientist sent his version of what had passed between them to Canon Fernão Martins in Lisbon; and in the Spanish period, shortly before 1494, when interest in the plan had again revived.

It is therefore legitimate to examine the bearing of this revival of interest. It is hinted by Ferdinand Columbus that a Florentine merchant, Zuanoto Berardi, had some part in bringing Columbus into touch with the Toscanelli correspondence. It is significant, however, that the Duke of Ferrara does not mention Columbus by name. There is a strong possibility, therefore, that, before finally deciding to back Columbus, the Italians in Spain had made efforts to check his proposals with Toscanelli's papers. Having done this, they acted through the agency of Santangel with decision. Some such series of events would explain the sudden and dramatic *dénouement* at Santa Fé.

Events, then, moved rapidly in the early months of 1492. Granada fell in January, and Columbus witnessed the triumph of Their Catholic Majesties. Later in the same month, his proposals were rejected for the second time, but shortly after came the longed-for acceptance. Another decree against the Jews was issued in March. The Capitulations, the agreements between the Sovereigns and Columbus, were signed in April. Santangel was busy transferring the necessary funds in May. Four months later, Columbus set sail for the west.

The clauses of the Capitulations are, though of great importance, relatively brief but comprehensive; they set out the broad outlines and avoid niggling details. Columbus is appointed Admiral 'in all those islands and mainlands which by his labour and industry shall be discovered or acquired in the said Ocean Sea during his life and, after his death, his heirs and successors . . .' He is also to be 'Viceroy and Governor-General in all the said islands and mainlands'. The first of these clauses gave him jurisdiction over the seas. His was not in the strict sense a naval appointment, the title of Admiral implying juridical and administrative powers over the seas. The second established his authority over the territories he might succeed in possessing. The limits of this authority are specified in surprisingly vague terms. The portion of the Ocean Sea allotted to Columbus is presumably that part north of the parallel of the Canary Islands, excepting the waters of the Azores, as agreed by the Treaty of 1479. This is made more clear in the *Titulo*, the conditional grant of titles and honours, which states specifically: 'And we forbid the said Christopher Columbus, or any one else who sails in the said caravels, to go to The Mine [the Portuguese post, S. Jorge da

Mina, on the Gold coast] or engage in the trade thereof, which the Most Serene King of Portugal, our brother, holds. For it is our pleasure to abide by and enforce the terms which we agreed upon with the said King of Portugal on this matter.'

'Islands and mainlands' is of purpose non-committal. No island names—Antilia, Cipangu—are inserted, nor is there any reference to Cathay or Asia. This omission led many to suppose that Columbus had no intention of reaching eastern Asia; nevertheless the evidence to the contrary is strong. It was also understood that he might be in contact with civilized communities, for he was furnished with blank letters of credence from the sovereigns, the terms of which show that the Asia of Marco Polo and the early travellers was in their minds: 'We have learned with joy of your esteem and high regard for us and our nation and of your great eagerness to be informed about things with us. Wherefore, we have resolved to send you our noble Captain, Christopherus Colón, bearer of these, from whom you may learn of our good health and prosperity, and other matters which we ordered him to tell you on our part . . .'

The next group of clauses defines the concrete rewards to which the Admiral shall be entitled. The wording runs: 'Of all merchandise whatsoever, pearls, precious stones, gold, silver, spiceries, and other things and merchandise of whatever kind, name or description that may be bought, bartered, found, acquired or obtained within the limits of the said Admiralty, Your Highnesses grant to the said Don Christopher, and decree that he take and keep for himself the tenth part of the whole after all expenses have been deducted, so that of all that remains free and clear he may have and take the tenth part for himself, and dispose of it as he pleases; the other nine parts remaining for Your Highnesses.' In any disputes arising from this assignment within the limits of his Admiralty, Columbus or 'his representative, and no other magistrate', is to have jurisdiction. Furthermore, he is to have the right to contribute the eighth part of the expenses of equipping any ship which may in the future engage in this trade, in return for a similar proportion of the profits.

Control of the administration of the newly-won lands is to be shared between Columbus and the Crown: 'For the government of each and every one of them he [Columbus] may name three persons for each office, and Your Highnesses may take and choose the one most suitable to your service, so that the lands will be better governed.'

This is a comprehensively drawn agreement with all the appearance of resulting from hard bargaining. Columbus is to enjoy the traditional rights of the High Admiral of Castile, and these are to be hereditary in his family. He is also appointed Viceroy and Governor-General, but nothing is said about this office being hereditary. As to the control of any disputes which may arise, this is not specifically assigned to his heirs in perpetuity, though it is stated to pertain to the office of High Admiral.

These terms show that, by the time they were negotiated and agreed, the 'enterprise of the Indies' was conceived largely as a commercial undertaking, midway between the 'donations' issued by the Portuguese kings and the joint-stock ventures of Tudor times. The hand of the Italian financiers seems apparent, for it was they who were putting up the risk capital, and they required a high return on it. It is noticeable that, among the products detailed, specific mention is made of pearls, precious stones, and silver. These had not, like gold and spices, been obtained from West Africa, but were traditionally associated with the East—additional evidence that the Cathay of Marco Polo was in the minds of those who drafted the terms.

The Capitulations were signed by the Sovereigns on April 17; the *Titulo*, which spelt out the terms a little more fully, was signed on the 30th. On the same day, the people of Palos, a small port near Huelva, were ordered, as punishment for certain misdemeanours, to provide two of the three caravels required by Columbus for twelve months. As these were criminal offences, the Santa Hermandad comes into the picture again, and its hand is also apparent in the decree which offered immunity from legal actions to those volunteering as members of the crews. The number availing themselves of this offer, however, was small, five in all. The town was warned not to procrastinate, and to place the vessels at Columbus's entire disposal. He, on his part, was to advance the crew four months' pay at the recognized rates. Almost four weeks passed before this order reached Palos on May 23. At the same time general instructions were issued to the province of Andalusia to assist without delay in fitting out the fleet by supplying the necessary workmen and furnishing equipment and stores at reasonable prices. Local officials were also ordered to abstain from taxing the purchase and transport of materials and stores.

The *Santa Maria*, the flagship of the fleet, was chartered from her owner, Juan de la Cosa. There was a certain reluctance among owners and seamen to undertake what promised to be a hazardous voyage. Columbus himself had made a special request for the offer of immunity for any offenders who might be persuaded to join, and later complained of the condition of the ships and the half-heartedness of the crews. Stories later became current that, but for the intervention and support of Martin Alonso Pinzon, an experienced skipper and a man of some standing in the town, Columbus would never have put to sea. This difficulty was strongly emphasized in the proceedings during the legal contest which started forty years later in 1511. No doubt there was some resentment on the part of the seamen at being forced to engage in a voyage which promised to be lengthy and dangerous, under a foreigner with fixed ideas of his own. But behind the Admiral was the authority of the Crown, and there was nothing they could do but make the best of it. Pinzon undoubtedly played an effective, though independent, part in the voyage, but the attempt to build him up as a rival to Columbus—even to present him as the true discoverer of America—has little foundation. In the event, Pinzon took command of the *Pinta*, with his youngest brother, Francisco, as pilot; another brother, Vicente Yañez, was in command of the *Niña*, and a cousin was among her crew. Thus the Pinzon family was certainly fully committed to the expedition, and must have assisted Columbus considerably in the preparations.

In the lawsuit, witnesses were produced by the Crown to testify that Martin Alonso was already interested in Atlantic exploration, and had, while on a visit to Rome, examined relevant charts. It was also asserted that Columbus had promised him a half-share in the venture in return for his help. Martin may well have been interested, like so many of his compatriots, in the tales of islands in the western Ocean, but there can have been little reason for him to wait for a visit to Rome to inspect charts, when these would be available in Palos, a centre of maritime activity. As for his material support, it is not unlikely that he had assisted Columbus in a moment of temporary embarrassment, but a half-share is another matter. As the documents quoted above demonstrate, the expedition was now a Royal undertaking with powerful backing, and Columbus was not in the position of needing to seek assistance by mortgaging the future, even if the Crown was ready to let him do so. The most telling point against the claim for the Pinzons was, however, that the Crown, having brought it forward at the outset of the proceedings, dropped it suddenly and completely during the course of the lawsuit. Martin Alonso's reputation still stands as that of an intrepid and experienced seaman, though the rôle played by Juan de la Cosa, ship-owner, pilot, and chart-maker, who was captain of the *Santa Maria*, should not be overlooked.

The final composition of the fleet was: the flagship, the *Santa Maria*, on which the Admiral sailed, owned by La Cosa, who sailed as master with two pilots, Sancho Ruiz and Bartolomeo Roldan. She was a three-masted, square-rigged ship of about fifty tons, with a crew of approximately forty-five. The two caravels, the *Pinta* and the *Niña*, were provided by the town of Palos: the *Pinta* was owned by two local men, Gomez Rascon and Cristobal Quintero. Her master was Martin Alonso Pinzon, with his brother, Francisco, and a Portuguese, Cristobal Garcia Sarmiento, as co-pilots. Smaller than the flagship, she carried a crew of twenty-five, and was the best sailor of the little fleet, much to Columbus's anger and apprehension. The *Niña*, the property of the Niño family, was smaller again than the *Pinta*; Vicente Yañez Pinzon was captain with one of her owner's family, Pero Alonso, as pilot. When the *Santa Maria* was eventually shipwrecked, Columbus transferred to the *Niña*, returned home in her and employed her again on exploration during his second voyage. The men of Palos clearly kept firm control of the two vessels they were forced to provide.

Much has been made of the fact that Columbus started his western voyage from the Canary Islands and sailed directly to the Caribbean, as though, it was said, 'he had the key of the chamber in his pocket'. It has also been argued that he must have had previous experience in the western Atlantic to have made such good use of the wind system. His choice can be explained less speculatively. In the first place, he was serving Their Catholic Majesties, and the Canaries were their most westerly possessions. It was impossible in all the circumstances for him to have started from the Portuguese bases in the Azores or Madeira. He was probably fortunate in not sailing from the Azores, since he might well have failed, as had others before him, to make head against the south-westerlies. As the conduct of his voyage shows, one of his objects was to search for islands to the south-west of the Azores, and these could be more conveniently approached from the Canaries in the south. This parallel was the generally accepted line between the Spanish and Portuguese 'zones of spheres of interest', and it was important to know the relation of any discoveries to this line.

Secondly, one of his distant objectives was the ports of Zaiton and Quinsay. On maps of the period, Zaiton is shown as being on the same parallel of latitude as the Canaries. Columbus believed, therefore, that he had merely to sail due westwards, keeping as close to the parallel as possible, for a relatively short distance, and behold, the riches of the East would open before him.

This approach to Zaiton, as it happened, fell in very neatly with a standard practice of contemporary navigators. This was known as 'running down the latitude'. The method was to sail southwards to the parallel of latitude on which the port or coast of your destination lay and then to sail along it until you made a landfall. Whether you could then establish your position as being north or south of your destination depended upon recognizing a prominent landmark from a description in your book of sailing directions, though this obviously did not apply in the case of the first voyage.

The navigational methods were not very complex, or very 'scientific'. There was a large element in it of 'By guess and by God'. Few instruments were carried, the principal being the mariner's compass and the lead line. The compass was not observed continuously; from time to time, the pilot stood over it with upraised arms and then brought them down sharply in the direction the needle was pointing. Everyone then had an idea, very approximately, of where the north lay, and could determine, and if necessary adjust, the ship's course. Speed was estimated either from experience of the ship's sailing qualities, or by throwing small objects over the bows and timing them as they floated past. With the instruments available, the astrolabe or the quadrant, it was extremely difficult or impossible to take a sighting from the decks of the small ships except in calm weather. Columbus claimed to have made a number when on Cuba and Hispaniola, but the figures he records are extremely suspect. On the outward voyage there was no need, even if it were possible, to determine the latitude. What he had to do was to keep as close as possible to a westerly course. On the return voyage, after the great storm, everyone on the *Niña* was concerned in identifying the landfall, and no one was very sure of their position, until it was established that they were off the Azores.

The return voyage presented more difficulties. In his voyaging with the Portuguese Columbus had learned a good deal about the winds of the eastern Atlantic. He knew that at the start he could rely generally on following winds. He also knew that further north, in the latitude of the Azores, strong south-westerlies prevailed for most of the year, and that if he could get into this zone, they would carry him rapidly back to Spain. So when he left Hispaniola for home his first thoughts were to make as much northing as possible, to pick up these winds.

The course which Columbus took both on the outward and homeward voyages derived from his belief or 'hunch' that the wind system of the western Atlantic could be deduced from what had been observed in the eastern sector. In other words he was following the sound scientific technique of arguing from observed facts about one half of the ocean to a general principle applicable to the whole. This is the true foundation of his achievements on the high seas. It was a bold decision to take—and it paid off handsomely. Whether or not he was a skipper in the sense that he directed the actual handling of the ship at sea is open to discussion. In any case, it may appear that in the conditions of the outward voyage—the generally fair weather and following winds—Columbus was extremely fortunate; but he had made the big decision, and fortune favours the brave.

Chapter VI

ACROSS THE ATLANTIC
AND AMONG THE ISLANDS

THE THREE vessels crossed the bar of Saltes on the morning of Friday, August 3, 1492, and took the established course southwards to the Canary Islands. Four days out, the *Pinta* was in trouble with her rudder. This gave Columbus some anxiety, but he reflected that Martin Alonso Pinzon was 'a man of real power, and very ingenious'. He aimed to make the island of Lanzerote, but found himself, as the result of calms and variable winds, near Grand Canary. Here he decided to leave the *Pinta*, still handicapped by her damaged rudder and making water, while, in the hope of procuring another caravel to replace her, he endeavoured to reach the island of Gomera. But he again failed to make a landfall, and returned to the *Pinta* which had been beached at Grand Canary. With the assistance of Pinzon and the crews, he repaired the *Pinta* and, by changing her rig from lateen to square, greatly improved her sailing qualities.

The squadron then proceeded to Gomera on September 2, Columbus noting volcanic activity on Tenerife as he passed. While stores were being taken aboard, he heard from people from the nearby island of Ferro (Hiero) that every summer they saw appearances of land to the west—the result of atmospheric conditions frequently encountered in this area. Like most episodes in Columbus's career, this delay at the Canaries has been a source of speculation, but there is little or no reason to suppose it was occasioned by anything but the necessity for repairs.

On the morning of September 6, a month after leaving Saltes, they sailed from Gomera. They were warned by a passing caravel that three Portuguese ships were cruising off Ferro with intent to intercept them, so they sailed to the north of the island. For the rest of that day and the following two days, they lay becalmed near Gomera but did not sight the Portuguese. It is clear that, while he was in the vicinity of the Canaries, Columbus experienced the variable winds associated with seasonal conditions on the North African land-mass. On the night of September 8, the north-easterly trades resumed, a westward course was set, and the trans-oceanic crossing began in earnest.

The second day out, Columbus had to chide the seamen for steering badly, allowing the *Santa Maria* to fall off course. In case the men should be discouraged by too long an outward voyage, he decided to underestimate the daily run and to keep two distinct reckonings. Thus for September 10 he reckoned the run at sixty leagues but announced it as only forty. This behaviour was quite contrary to contemporary practice. A Portuguese manual translated into Spanish in 1519, allowing that estimates of the distance made good each day by the pilots must vary owing to the approximate character of the method, recommends that the largest estimate should always be accepted for safety's sake, so that land is not reached unexpectedly.

The following day they sighted a large mast floating in the sea but were unable to take it aboard. On September 13, the compass needles were observed to vary to the north-west and in the morning a little to the north-east. For a long time it was held that, by these observations, Columbus was the first to discover magnetic variation and to cross the meridian of zero variation. But it has been shown that they were made on the North Star by pilots to check their instruments and revealed the diurnal rotation of that star, but had nothing to do with the variation of the compass. Columbus, however, was continually on the watch for phenomena of this kind as signs that he was approaching a new world. In this mood, he began to note a series of observations which he took to signify his squadron's approach to land, and which had an important influence on the course of the voyage. They began with a report from the *Niña* that they had seen a tern and a boatswain bird, birds, Columbus believed, 'which never depart from land more than twenty-five leagues'. A feeling of great expectancy then spread among the crews. On the night of the 15th, another sign of their nearness to a strange world was seen in the fall from the sky of a 'marvellous branch of fire into the sea at a distance of four or five leagues from them' (obviously a meteor). The next day, they encountered an even more exciting phenomenon, for they began to see 'many tufts of very green seaweed which, it appeared, had not been long torn from land'. From this evidence they concluded that they were near land from which the weed had drifted. This, the Admiral thought, was not the

Asian mainland—'for the mainland I take to be further on'. It was indeed.

They had in fact reached the margin of the Sargasso Sea, the probable limit of de Teive's voyage, and from then on were generally in sight of varying quantities of weed. Everything now pointed, or was thought to point, to the proximity of land. A live crab, 'not to be found eighty leagues from land', was taken from the weed. 'The water was less salty than it had been' (they thought they might be nearing the estuaries of fresh-water rivers; the waters of this part of the Atlantic are not less salty than those off the Canaries). The sea was very smooth, 'like the river at Seville', and the breezes were softer. Dolphins were seen and the boatswain bird, 'which is not accustomed to sleep on the sea', again appeared; 'it was a great delight to enjoy the mornings, and nothing was lacking except to hear the nightingales'. This somewhat surprising reference to the nightingale shows that Columbus had very much in mind the stories of the Orient in which that bird, the scent-laden air, and the exotic trees figure prominently—the nightingale had for him become the symbol of the lands he hoped to reach. Another set of observations on the North Star added to his conviction that they were entering a new world. Accordingly, 'they all went on their way greatly rejoicing, and as to the ships, she that sailed fastest went ahead, in order to be the first to sight land'.

*

They were now running fast before the north-easterlies, the *Pinta* in the lead, with runs of fifty leagues on the 17th and fifty-five leagues on the 18th. On that day Pinzon hailed the Admiral to tell him that he had sighted a great flock of birds flying westwards, and a great cloud-bank was seen in the north which was presumed to be over land. Pinzon then sailed ahead eagerly in the hope of making a landfall that night, but his hopes were disappointed.

On the 19th, they were becalmed in a drizzle of rain, and Columbus decided that he would not delay beating to windward in order to make sure that there was land in that direction, although he was certain that there were islands to north and south, between which they were passing. His intention was to press on to the mainland: 'The weather is favourable, wherefore, God willing, on the return voyage all will be seen.'

The pilots now worked up their dead reckoning from the Canaries.

The *Pinta*'s pilot made it 420 leagues, the *Niña*'s pilot 440 leagues, and Columbus's pilot on the *Santa Maria* 400 leagues. This last figure is extraordinarily accurate. Admiral McElroy, of the United States Navy, working systematically through the observations, has calculated that they were then 390 leagues from the Canaries. Amusingly enough, Columbus's deception with his faked distances had achieved nothing.

September 20 was calm with very variable breezes, and the course was generally west by north or west-north-west, and the weed thicker. The calm continued overnight, and they made only thirteen leagues. A significant change was then made in their course, and for the next two days they sailed to the north-west. This marked an important stage in the voyage. The decision was taken when the fleet was precisely south-west of the Azores, at a distance of approximately 1,200 miles. The new direction was the same as the one on which de Teive had sailed from the Azores in 1452, although he had apparently taken it for 600 miles only. The discrepancy in the distances does not disprove the theory that Columbus had knowledge of this Portuguese voyage, nor that he was seeking in this area for something de Teive thought he had seen before turning back. This was 'Antilia or the Island of the Seven Cities', which appeared on maps like that drawn by Ruysch in approximately this position, though these specific names are not used in the *Journal*. All this evidence establishes Antilia as one of the Admiral's subsidiary objectives.*

The behaviour of the crews at this point, as recorded in the *Journal*, strongly confirms the view that this was indeed a critical point. The Admiral accused them of conduct which he considered amounted to mutiny. The timing of this expression of feeling suggests that they regarded the search for Antilia as the main object of the voyage, and that when it had failed, they were anxious to return to Spain without more ado. Such behaviour on long voyages was not uncommon: a well-known instance occurred when Bartholomew Diaz, having rounded the Cape of Good Hope, was obliged by his crew to restrict further progress to a few days' sail, and to turn back without penetrating far into the Indian Ocean.

The *Journal* version does not contradict this interpretation. The calms were now troubling the crews, and they were asking the question: if the sea was so smooth in this area, after steady north-east

* For the history of Antilia, see Cortesão, A. Z.: *The nautical chart of 1424*. He argues that Antilia represents a landfall on the American continent.

winds, would they ever find winds blowing in the contrary direction
when they sought to return? Later in the *Journal* (the entry for
February 14, 1493) Columbus referred to these 'difficulties with seamen and people whom he carried, who all with one voice were
determined to return and to mutiny against him, making protests,
but the eternal God had given him strength and courage against all'.
After these protests—mutiny seems too strong a word—his men
were astonished to observe that the sea was then running strongly
from the south-west, although there was no wind from that direction.
This appears to have satisfied their qualms about the return.
Columbus welcomed this incident as a sign of divine favour at a
critical moment: 'that high sea was very necessary to me, because
such a thing had not been seen save in the time of the Jews, when
those of Egypt came out against Moses who was leading them out of
captivity'.

On September 24, abandoning the search for islands, he resumed
his westerly course. Many petrels were again seen and the westerly
course was continued on the next day; it was very calm at first, and
many of the sailors seized the opportunity to take a swim. Later, the
wind strengthened.

The Admiral consulted Pinzon about certain islands depicted on
a chart which he had sent over to the *Pinta* three days earlier, when
they had discussed their position. Pinzon agreed that the ships were
in the vicinity of the islands, and Columbus thought they had not
sighted them because of the northerly set of the current, and because
the pilots had overestimated the distance made good. Columbus, like
his contemporaries, had no means of ascertaining the direction of a
current, and this is merely a reference to the strong sea setting from
the south-west, which had pleased him earlier. The pilots had not
overestimated the course; the difficulty arose from their having no
accurate details of the position of the islands they were seeking.
Columbus then asked Pinzon to return the chart on a line, and set
to work with his pilots to plot their position.

At sunset on September 25, Martin Alonso Pinzon, in great
excitement, shouted to the Admiral from the poop of the *Pinta* that
he had sighted land, and claimed the promised reward. At this the
Admiral fell on his knees to give thanks to God, and the crews sang
the *Gloria in excelsis*. The men of the *Niña* climbed into the rigging,
and they all declared that it was land. The Admiral thought it was
twenty-five leagues distant and promptly altered course to the
south-west, maintaining this throughout the night. But, with the

morning light, they saw that the supposed land was only a cloud-bank; disappointed, Columbus set course again for the west. From September 27 until October 2, the calm weather and light breezes continued, allowing for short daily runs westwards which averaged twenty-four leagues. 'The air was very sweet and savory . . . The only thing wanting was to hear the nightingale, and the sea was smooth as a river.' Columbus noted, on seeing a man-o'-war bird, that 'it does not alight on the sea or depart twenty leagues from land . . . There are many of them in the Cape Verde Islands'.

The trade wind was gradually strengthening again; from October 3 to 5, the average run was fifty-five leagues, that on October 5 being the longest day's run on the outward voyage. On October 1, the flagship's pilot had calculated that they were 578 leagues west of Ferro. He had hit the bull's-eye again, for Admiral McElroy puts the correct figure at 575 leagues.

On October 6, Pinzon again suggested a change of course, to south-west-by-west. The Admiral was not sure what prompted this advice, but did not think it was because Pinzon believed they were near the island of Cipangu. He himself was for continuing west-wards, straight to the mainland—they could look for the islands later. These 'islands' were undoubtedly, in Columbus's mind, the hundreds scattered throughout the seas off south-east Asia on most contemporary world maps; as it happened, he was still 12,000 miles away.

By October 7, the tension was mounting again and everyone was on the look-out for land. At dawn the *Niña*, who was in the lead, hoisted a flag at her masthead and fired a lombard, the prescribed signal for a landfall. But the hours passed and by evening no land had been sighted. Nevertheless, they saw great flocks of birds flying from the north towards the south-west, and deduced acutely that they were fleeing the northern winter. The Admiral recalled that most of the islands which the Portuguese held had been discovered through observing the flight of birds. This time their deduction was correct. They were no longer watching stray sea-birds which could give no certain indication of land, but were in fact crossing the path of migratory flocks from Bermuda to the West Indies at precisely the right season.*

At this impressive sight the Admiral again changed course from

* See the note on p. 61 of Morison: *Journals* (contributed, with many others, by the late Ludlow Griscom, Curator of Ornithology, Harvard Museum of Zoology).

Secretary, read a proclamation taking possession of the island in the name of Their Highnesses. To the island, which was small and low, Columbus gave the name of San Salvador. The party then fell upon their knees and gave thanks to God. Tears of joy at long-delayed success ran down Columbus's cheeks as the men crowded round to acknowledge him as Admiral and Viceroy.

The appearance of the 'Indians', as they were soon called, was surprising but reassuring. Most of those Columbus first saw were young males, 'very well built, of very handsome bodies and fine faces: the hair coarse, almost like that of a horse's tail, and short. The hair they wear over their eyebrows, except for a hank behind that they wear long and never cut . . . They are of the colour of the Canary Islanders, neither black nor white.' In another passage, he compares their complexions to those of Spanish peasants burned by the sun.

Immediately, after recording the landing, Columbus proclaimed his intention of establishing good relations with these natives, believing that 'they were a people who could better be freed and converted to our Holy Faith by love rather than by force'. What he proposed to free them from is not clear. He also noted that they were not warlike—'they bear no arms, nor know of them . . . They have no iron'—and at first sight appeared to have no greatly developed material culture; save for small ornaments of thin beaten gold, they were stark naked. Later reconnaissances into the interior of the islands brought the Spaniards into contact with a social organization of some complexity, but in these early days they were dealing with the least sophisticated Arawaks on the margin of their cultural area. Later, when coasting northern Hispaniola, they met more advanced tribes with a well-established hierarchy, large settlements, and organized agriculture.

Columbus was struck by the natives' friendliness and their readiness to trade cotton, parrots, small pieces of beaten gold, and many small objects for trifles such as glass beads and little bells. To remain on friendly terms and to win their confidence, he gave orders to his own men forbidding outrageous cheating, but these were not rigidly enforced for very long. His additional intention in this was to keep the collection of gold under his own control.

The sailors were impressed by the native canoes, skilfully hollowed out of the trunks of trees, which were of all sizes, accommodating from one to fifty-five persons. Columbus was also intrigued by the behaviour of some of the older men who, on seeing the strangers, would leap into the air crying out: 'Come and see the men from the sky; bring them food and drink.' And whenever his scouts visited a settlement of any size, although the whole population would immediately take to their heels at first sight of their visitors, they would later return, hospitably supply them with food and escort them courteously and merrily back to the ships.

Watching them with an approving eye, Columbus's thoughts were turning to the future: 'they ought to be good servants and of good skill . . . I believe they would easily be made Christians . . . because it seemed to me that they belonged to no religion.' Within two days of the first landing, he had noted a secure site for a fortress.

Columbus soon convinced himself that these peoples were subjected to raids by more warlike tribes, coming from the south-east, who carried them off as slaves, and practised cannibalism. These enemies he identified as Caribs, though he never on this voyage came into contact with them. It was certainly unfortunate, but understandable, that when news of the discovery spread through Europe the popular idea of the inhabitants of the Caribbean islands was that they were naked savages, and mostly cannibals. Columbus eventually decided to carry six of them back to Spain, so that they might be taught to speak Spanish, as he says he had often done with the negroes of the Guinea coast. These earlier experiences made him careful to include a proportion of women in the party. Some of the Indians seized suitable opportunities to escape; others, however, did not take exception to this treatment, were happy on board, and performed useful services as interpreters for the rest of the voyage.

From the first contacts, Spaniards and Arawaks soon learned to make themselves understood, largely by signs. As time went on, knowledge of each other's language grew, though not without much confusion. In his search for spices and gold, Columbus had provided himself with suitable specimens which he hoped the Indians would recognize. With the aid of signs this method was fairly effective, but he came to recognize that misunderstandings were occurring, and wished that he could overcome this obstacle. Over one item, however, there was common ground among the natives—and that was gold. Whenever questioned as to its source they would emphatically indicate that large supplies were to be found away to the south-east, though it was not always clear to the Spaniards whether or not this was merely a device to encourage the visitors to move on as quickly as possible. One cause of confusion was that Columbus, having the islands of south-east Asia in mind, and seeing that he was un-

VESPUCCI
DISEMBARKS
IN THE
NEW WORLD

*The engraving by
J. Stradano for
Americae retectio.
A sixteenth-century
idealisation of the
contact between the
two civilisations;
nature confronts
science.*

INDIANS COMMANDEERED AS PORTERS BY THE CONQUISTADORES
One view of the Spanish presence in America, engraved by T. de Bry

doubtedly sailing through an archipelago of some size, interpreted any name raised in connection with the whereabouts of gold as being that of an Asian island. All in all, however, he collected a good deal of information on a subject that was to become an obsession with him, and on the whole this information was surprisingly accurate. Apart from the misunderstanding about islands, much of the native information directed him to the only regional source of gold in any quantity—the Cibao area in north-central Hispaniola. The concept of 'mainland' was not so easy to convey to the native mind; it was difficult to tell whether, when questioned on this point, their answers referred to the mainland, or simply to a large island to the west. Columbus, his mind preoccupied with trying to reconcile what he saw with his notions on the geography of Asia, was always prone to hear what he wanted to hear.

The small islands he sailed among in his first days in 'the Indies' were not, however, calculated to arouse unbounded enthusiasm. They certainly gave no suggestion that they held the wealth of the Orient, but as he sailed on, his spirits rose, encouraged by frequent reports of gold close at hand, and by the discovery of Cuba and Hispaniola. Before he left for Spain in January, his descriptions are glowing and eloquent; he was convinced, or had convinced himself, that he was on the threshold of the East.

His course was not a complicated one on this first visit, and there is no need to follow it in detail here. It has been carefully traced and the coastal features identified by Admiral Morison who has sailed over the greater part of the Admiral's routes in the Caribbean. Of more interest in the present context is the record of the primary contact between Europeans and aboriginal Americans.

On October 28, Columbus sighted the northern coast of Cuba ('Juana', after Prince Juan, son of King Ferdinand) and, in pursuance of his cosmographical theories, sailed westwards along it for some thirty miles from Bahia Bariay to Puerta Gibara, his limit in this direction. The squadron lay there, in the shelter of the Puerto de Mares, and the ships were careened. Believing that he had at last hit the Asian mainland, the Admiral sent two men, Rodrigo de Xeres and Luis de Torres, a converted Jew who was reputed to know Hebrew, Aramaic and a little Arabic, to reconnoitre the interior. They returned four days later with three Indians (who decamped that night), having after twelve leagues reached a large village of one thousand inhabitants. They had been received in a friendly way and had understood that there were pepper, cinnamon and other spices to the south-east. It was plain, however, that this was no resort of wealthy merchants. The Admiral, still believing that this island was part of 'a very big continent that trended far to the north' and fancying that 'the king of that land made war with the Grand Khan', was nevertheless constrained to turn on his track. He had gathered from Indians that there was much gold in a large island in the south-easterly direction which they called Bohio (Haiti). While on this coast he had encountered contrary winds which were continuing, and he had also noted a fall in the temperature. He therefore decided that it would not be wise to attempt to make discoveries in the north during the winter. Accordingly, despite his earlier conclusion that 'it is certain that this is the mainland and that I am before Zaiton and Quinsay', the Admiral followed the golden trail to the south-east.

He was, in fact, in a quandary as to his actual position. If he was really in the parallel of Zaiton then he was in a higher latitude than 40° north. But, given his route across the Atlantic, he must have known that he could not be in a higher latitude than that of the Canaries, which he took to be about 30°. He claimed in his *Journal* to have made three observations of latitude on this voyage. Two produced the extraordinary figure of 42° north; the third was more reasonable, 34° north. No navigator of any competence could have made repeated errors of these dimensions; the probable explanation is that, believing that he was off Zaiton, he simply read the latitude of that port from his map and passed it off as an observation. That he was more than ten degrees out of the position assigned to the expedition by dead-reckoning he no doubt attributed to the fact that he was in a 'new world', where marvels were to be expected. (Later in life this conviction grew strongly upon him; he came to hold the notion that in the west the surface of the earth had the shape of a pear, thus contradicting the 'authorities'.) When he recorded these latitudes, he was in cold fact in approximately 21° 20' north latitude.

For all these reasons, he chose to turn southwards—a highly momentous decision. After beating back and forth, and two fruitless attempts to reach Babeque (Great Inagua Island), another spot reputedly rich in gold, Columbus passed Cape Alpha and Omega (Cape Maysi, the termination of Cuba) and negotiated the Windward Passage. The name given to the Cape symbolized his belief that he was now at the 'beginning of the East' and the end of the West. A landfall was made on Cuba at Cape Saint Nicholas on December 5.

Meanwhile the Pinzons on the *Pinta*, impatient at the time wasted in these waters, and tired of the talk of oriental marvels and of the great port of Zaiton, had sailed off on their own to find Babeque. If Columbus had informed them that they were in latitude 42° north, they no doubt repudiated the idea contemptuously, and resolved to seek the rumoured gold alone. They were not to meet again until January 6, when Columbus, shaken by the experience of shipwreck, was in no position to enforce disciplinary measures.

On the evening of December 24, the *Santa Maria* and her consort were off Cape Haitien, in calm water, and progressing slowly eastwards up-wind. Taking advantage of the fine weather and pleading that he had had no sleep for two days and a night, Columbus felt secure enough to go below and turn in. The crew, including the steersman, promptly followed his example, leaving a small lad at the tiller, despite strict standing orders to the contrary. The current steadily carried the *Santa Maria* on to a reef over which the sea was breaking noisily. According to the Admiral's account, he awoke immediately, rushed on deck and sent off the boat to put out an anchor astern. The boat did put out but promptly made for the *Niña*. The *Santa Maria* was now lying broadside on, with the tide running out. In an attempt to get her off, Columbus ordered the mainmast to be cut away, but this did not lighten her sufficiently, and her seams began to open. The Admiral and the crew were then taken off by the *Niña*'s boat, where he remained until morning.

With the ready assistance of the Indians, everything was then brought ashore from the *Santa Maria* without loss, 'because she remained whole as when she set sail, except that she was cut and razed to get at the jars of water, oil, etc.' Columbus put the blame on the treachery of the master, Juan de la Cosa, and the crew for not carrying out his orders, and then on the men of Palos for not providing him with a proper ship for the voyage. No attempt was made to repair the wrecked *Santa Maria*. Why La Cosa should have behaved as abjectly as Columbus says is difficult to understand. He was after all part-owner of the flagship and an experienced sailor. Ferdinand Columbus in his summary account says that La Cosa in fact returned to the ship but was beaten to her by the *Niña*'s boat. It was certainly late in the day, after a successful crossing, to blame the men of Palos for their negligence. It was, however, for Columbus a time of great strain, and there was possibly some bad feeling still between commander and crew. The Admiral had yet to find a profitable source of gold and there was always the prospect that Pinzon had reached it before him. In the end he reacted to the crisis in a characteristic manner. He recognized that 'Our Lord had caused the ship to run aground there in order that he might have a settlement there'. 'And in addition to this,' he says, 'so many things came to hand, that in truth it was no disaster but great luck; for it is certain that if I had not run aground, I should have kept to sea without anchoring there . . . Nor on this voyage should I have left people there or, had I desired to leave them, could I have given them good equipment, or so many weapons or supplies, or materials for a fortress. And it is true that many people of those on board have asked and made petition that I grant them permission to stay. Now I have given orders to erect a tower and fortress, all very well done, and a great moat, not that I believe it to be necessary . . .'

Although Columbus endeavoured to gloss over the shipwreck, it was very nearly a disaster for the expedition. He was left with two crews and one vessel on a strange coast hundreds of miles from home, without having reached the much-sought-for gold, and with a hazardous return voyage before him. Fortunately, the prospect of immediate gain influenced the bolder members of the crew, otherwise he might have had trouble in persuading any to remain behind. However, again with Indian co-operation, La Navidad, the first, though short-lived, European settlement in the New World, was rapidly established. Some forty men, mostly from the crew of the wrecked flagship, but also some from the *Niña*, were fitted out as a garrison.

The man who emerged in the most favourable light in this situation was the great cacique, Guacanagari, the ruler of the province. On learning of the wreck, he came immediately to comfort the weeping Admiral and to offer all the assistance in his power. He also presented him with several small gold objects and promised to bring him many more. They dined together ceremoniously on the *Niña*, parting on very friendly terms. While they were dining again on the following day, news arrived that the *Pinta* was lying further along the coast to the east, and a sailor and an Indian were immediately sent off in a canoe with a placatory letter to Pinzon. Though in his predicament he was prepared to temporize with the deserters, Columbus continued to complain that Pinzon's action, with all the evil and inconvenience that flowed from it, had prevented him from completing the discovery. The messengers returned without finding the caravel.

The Admiral's anxiety was redoubled, for it was now not unlikely that Pinzon was on the way home and would be first with his version of the discovery for Ferdinand and Isabella. Preparations for the return were speeded up, and on January 4 Columbus weighed anchor and left the harbour of La Navidad, sailing eastwards. Two days later the *Pinta* came sailing briskly down-wind from the east. Martin Alonso Pinzon had many excuses, the main one being that he had been compelled by force of circumstances to leave the Admiral. Columbus treated him calmly, though he did not accept his excuses, regarding him as actuated by greed, insolence, and disloyalty.

It appeared that Pinzon had been lying-up in a river mouth some fifty leagues east of La Navidad for twenty days, during which time he had collected a quantity of gold. This was the nearest point on the coast to the Cibao deposits of placer gold, and was later known as the 'Rio de Martin Alonso Pinzon'. Pinzon also brought with him the first nuggets of gold which the Spaniards had seen, and since he had had sufficient time to make the fifty-mile journey to the deposits, at least one authority has concluded that he did in fact make this journey inland.

All this caused Columbus great anxiety, and the reconciliation with the Pinzons did not last long. 'Lewd fellows devoid of virtue', he calls them. The *Journal* entry of two days later has more complaints of Pinzon's conduct. As Columbus was clearly not in a position to impose his authority, and was still convinced that Pinzon would set off on his own at any moment, he finally decided to sail, hoping to arrive in Spain first with the information on the position of the gold-mines. This decision was made in spite of the fact that he had been considering whether it might not now be safe, in company with the *Pinta*, to continue the exploration of Hispaniola. Finally, on January 16, the two vessels stood out to sea on a north-easterly course with a favourable wind.

During his three months in the Caribbean, Columbus, as the *Journal* shows, was very observant of the daily life of the Arawaks. Second only to his obsession about the gold of Cipangu, it forms the principal interest of its pages. His descriptions and comments, it is true, are scattered and brief, but assembled together they form a comprehensive survey. Supplemented by the accounts of other keen observers like Las Casas, they give the first documented account of a New World culture—a landmark in field enthnography. The basis of Arawak life was the South American root culture—*yuca* and sweet potatoes, which Columbus, thinking of his West African days, called yams. These roots were grown in great mounds, and once planted required little attention, though in parts of Hispaniola irrigation was practised. Professor Sauer has calculated that two acres of these mounds produced sufficient food for a year for as many as one hundred persons. The principal stable was the bitter *yuca*, known to us as manioc, which, grated and drained of juice, was baked into an unleavened bread with a high starch content—'very white and very good', remarks Columbus. Fish was also an important article of diet, as well as birds—pigeons, doves and parrots—and small animals, iguanas and varieties of rodents. Barkless dogs, kept as pets, were also eaten on occasion. Several varieties of vegetables and fruits supplemented the diet.

Despite Columbus's emphasis on their nakedness, the Arawaks collected much cotton from small trees, about the size of peach-trees, from which short cloaks, other small garments and mats were woven. Body paints, red and black, were obtained from a variety of shrubs—it has been suggested that the term 'Red Indian' was derived from this habit. They were also expert wood-workers, considered by Sauer to have been unrivalled in this craft by any inhabitants of the New World.* Their ceremonial canoes, often lodged in elaborate boat-houses, their carved seats and benches, attracted the admiration of the Spaniards, and they were also expert in working thin gold plates into ceremonial belts, masks, and small personal ornaments, nose- and ear-rings.

Their houses also fascinated the Spaniards, as the Admiral's description of one interior shows: 'He came to two houses which he thought were those of fishermen who had fled from fear: in one of them he found a dog that did not bark, and in both houses he found nets of palm fibre and ropes and fish hooks of horn, and bone harpoons, and other fishing tackle. There were many fireplaces within, and he believed that many people lived in one house.' They dwelt in fact in large communal houses (*Bohios*), some apparently circular and constructed from palm branches, which accommodated ten to fifteen families each. As many as a dozen of these constituted a village: these 'gave the appearance of tents in encampments without order of streets, but one here and another there'. The interiors, with woven partitions, beds and hammocks, were well-swept and clean. Under the high roof there was space for preserving the remains of ancestors. One seaman found in a house 'a man's head in a basket, covered with another basket and hanging to the post of a house, and they found another of the same sort in another village. The Admiral

* For this section, see Sauer, C. O.: *Early Spanish Main*, chapter 3.

believed that they must be those of ancestors of the family.' Some-where near the centre of the village, before the cacique's house, was a rectangular space for assemblies, festivities, and games, which included dancing and the ball game which the Spaniards called *pelota*.

The Admiral's attitude to the Indians was markedly ambivalent. He appreciated their orderly behaviour and helpfulness, their cour-tesy and 'civilized' manners, and their peaceful disposition; at the same time he constantly noted in them what he considered to be their timorous and unaggressive character, their anxiety to please, and their absence of warlike qualities, even their lack of weapons. With an eye to the future, he increasingly emphasized the latter point of view until he was suggesting their complete subjugation.

As to what precisely he had discovered, Columbus, as a close study of the *Journal* demonstrates, was torn between two contra-dictory theses. Though somewhat shaken in his belief that he had in fact reached the vicinity of the Asian mainland, he continued to maintain, as the *Letter* proves, that he had achieved what he had set out to do. In taking this standpoint he was aware that the main argument against him was that of distance. Yet he was also anxious to show that the archipelago he had explored was not far from Spain. The relevant passage occurs shortly before he left on his return, and arises from an observation that there was a considerable amount of weed in the Bay of Samana: 'There was much weed in that bay of the kind that they found in the gulf when he came upon the dis-covery; whence he believed that there were islands directly to the east where he began to find the weed; for he holds for certain that that weed grows in slight depth near the land, and says that if it is so, these Indies were very near the Canary Islands, and for that reason he believed that they were less than 400 leagues distant.'

He is here harking back to the hypothetical island groups which he thought he had passed through on the outward voyage and for which he proposed to search, although he did not do so, on the return. The importance he attached to them arose from a desire to find conveni-ent staging-posts on the 'route to the Indies'. This conception is clearly displayed in one of a group of small cartographical sketches formerly attributed to Bartholomew Columbus but now believed to have been drawn about 1525 by the Italian cartographer Alessandro Zorzi to illustrate Bartholomew Columbus's ideas.

*

On the return voyage, the Admiral's task was to make sufficient northing to pass through the belt of north-easterly winds which had carried him out from the Canaries, since it was impracticable to attempt to beat back in their teeth. From the experience of Portuguese sailors in the Azorean area he knew that if he made a sufficiently high latitude he could count on the strong westerly winds to carry him to that island group, or beyond it to the Iberian coast. Except for the stormy weather he met with off the Azores, the return voyage was no more eventful than the outward. For this reason, enthusiasts have seen in the homeward route a proof of his exceptional ability as a navigator, crediting him with the discovery at the first attempt of what immediately became the standard return route for sailing-vessels from the West Indies. But he had, in fact, no alternative. To attempt an easterly passage would have been impracticable, and a southerly route even more so, apart from the fact that he had been forbidden to sail in southern waters under Portuguese control, and the immediate hostility it would have aroused among the crews, whose one desire was to reach home as soon as possible. One curious fact in this connection has gone unnoticed. He soon turned back from his voyage along the north-west-trending coast of Cuba on the grounds, among others, that he did not wish to venture northwards during the winter months. Yet in January he was ready without apparent hesitation to set off across an unknown tract of ocean on a northerly course.

The *Journal* of the homeward voyage, as summarized and edited by Las Casas, is fundamentally different from that of the outward. The navigational detail is considerably reduced: a large part of it is a vivid account of the Azorean storm, a demonstration of Columbus's superiority over the other pilots as a navigator, and a lengthy, almost hysterical declaration of Divine assistance at a moment when all seemed lost. This imbalance is doubtless due in part to Las Casas as editor, for he had his own reasons for representing the voyage in this light.

The required parallel—that is, of the Azores—was reached almost without incident. Columbus complains once more of the condition of the ships, which were making water, and speaks disparagingly of the want of seamanlike qualities in the crews. Provisions were running short, and on one occasion they feasted on the flesh of a large shark. The Indians were unperturbed by their experiences, and taking advantage of a calm enjoyed a swim. The Pinzons again come in for criticism: the *Pinta* sails badly when close-hauled to the wind, and her mast and hull are defective; if they had not been so intent on seeking and collecting gold, they could have given more time and attention to refitting their caravel.

While running down the latitude of the Azores, they were hit by a severe storm which raged for three days, and before which they were obliged to run. During this crisis, contact was finally lost with the *Pinta*. As they approached the islands it became imperative to establish their position as accurately as possible. On February 10, the pilots of the *Niña* concluded that they had passed the meridian of Santa Maria Island, and were heading for Madeira. Columbus, however, disagreed with them, arguing that they were considerably short of that position—by about 150 leagues—although on the same parallel. Late on the 14th the weather cleared, and after sunrise next morning land was sighted. A keen discussion then broke out; according to Columbus, the pilots, on the basis of their estimate of the 10th, declared that the landfall must be on Madeira or even on the coast of Castile. He asserts that his own estimate placed the ship among the Azores archipelago. Beating up and down in a heavy sea, it was not until the 18th that they were able to anchor off an island, which to his satisfaction they certified was Santa Maria.

In recording these incidents, Columbus makes a statement which throws a rather strange light on his abilities as a navigator. It reads: 'The Admiral admits that this navigation of his had been very exact, and that he had laid his route down well (for which should be given many thanks to Our Lord) although he had made it somewhat further on; but he held for certain that he was in the area of the Azores and that this was one of them. And he says that he pretended to have gone further than he had in order to confuse the pilots and seamen who pricked off the chart, in order to remain master of that route to the Indies, as in fact he remained, since none of them was certain of his course, hence nobody could be sure of his route to the Indies.'

It is difficult to believe that Columbus really thought that the pilots were so confused, or that he could prevent the details of his route becoming general knowledge. At this particular moment they had completed the voyage out and home as far as the Azores; the pilots had proved themselves highly competent, as is witnessed by the accuracy of their dead reckoning on the outward voyage; and then there was Martin Alonso Pinzon, ahead and, for all the Admiral knew, nearing Spanish shores. If Columbus deluded himself to this extent at the time, Las Casas might charitably have omitted this passage—but then he was almost as convinced as Columbus that the feat was unique, and divinely inspired. Certainly the Admiral did not long remain master of that route.

Their reception by the Governor of the Azores was distinctly unfriendly, and for part of the time members of the crew were imprisoned ashore. The Portuguese at first suspected, not without reason, that they were interlopers coming from West African waters, but after much argument and threats from both sides the prisoners were released. They informed Columbus that the Governor had told them he had strict orders to arrest him when an opportunity arose. With all this commotion, it was not until the 24th that the *Niña* sailed from Santa Maria on the last lap. After weathering another storm on the route to Cape St. Vincent, Columbus was blown off-course to the north and sought refuge in the river Tagus.

That Columbus should have landed on his return at Lisbon and not at Palos has raised much controversy. Looking at all the circumstances, especially the manner in which he was received by King John II, this debate seems pointless, and as things turned out he had no necessity to regret the turn of events. After parleying with local officials, Columbus received a courteous reply to his letter to the Portuguese king. He was permitted to continue up to Lisbon to obtain whatever he required, and was invited to the Court, then at Val de Paraiso, some miles north of the city. There his reception was correct but, understandably, not over-cordial. A story circulated later that some courtiers suggested to King John that the easiest solution would be to have the unwelcome foreigner murdered. John however played his hand with dexterity. The Admiral gave an account of his discoveries, explained that his Sovereigns had expressly forbidden him to enter African waters recognized as under Portuguese control, and stated that the gold he had brought with him came, not from Guinea, but from 'the Indies'. The King was naturally interested in all that he heard, however much he may have doubted whether Columbus had reached Asian waters, and suggested that the discoveries lay in the Portuguese zone. That business, however, could be settled amicably in the course of the current negotiations between the two countries. Columbus repudiated the suggestion that he had been in Portuguese waters, and denied any knowledge of negotiations.

John II was clearly anxious to remain on good terms with Spain and not to jeopardize his own African and Indian projects. The negotiations to which he referred were to conclude with the Treaty of Tordesillas of 1494. If Columbus gave him a detailed account of his voyage, he was justified in thinking that part at least of the discoveries lay in the Portuguese zone, on the basis of the parallel of the Canaries being the dividing line. It is not unlikely that Columbus, to counter this argument, insisted that the extreme northerly point he had reached was in latitude 42° north. If he did, it is equally likely that John expressed his disbelief. At that particular moment, however, the Admiral was not in a position to be other than diplomatic, for he had yet to receive his Sovereigns' instructions.

After further courtesies, Columbus returned to the *Niña* and sailed for Palos where he arrived on March 3, after an absence of six months and eleven days. Some hours after the Admiral had been rapturously received, Martin Alonso Pinzon in the *Pinta* also dropped anchor in the harbour—a dramatic conclusion to the enterprise. He had weathered the Azorean storm and, like Columbus, had been driven far out of his course, taking refuge in Bayona del Mino, a small port in Galicia, to the north of Portugal. He had at once written to the Court at Barcelona for permission to present himself with news of the discovery, but had been told that the Admiral was the commander of the expedition, and he must rejoin him immediately. A worried and sick man, suffering either from the hazards of the return voyage or perhaps from some illness he had picked up in the Indies, he died shortly after, and was buried in the neighbouring monastery of La Rabida. This was not, however, the last of the Pinzon family in the story of discovery.

Chapter VII

TRIUMPHANT RETURN

O N HIS arrival in Portugal, Columbus immediately sent off a despatch to the Sovereigns. This took the form of a *Letter*, copies of which were also addressed to various court officials, including the invaluable Luis de Santangel. This *Letter*, the first account of the discovery to be made public, was handed to a Barcelona printer about the beginning of April 1493 and was soon circulating widely. Within a month a Latin translation appeared in Rome and this was reprinted at Antwerp, Basel, and Paris in the same year. A versified translation into Italian appeared in June 1493, and a German translation at Strasbourg four years later.

The importance of the *Letter* is obvious: whatever may be written about Columbus's early life, the nature of his plans, or where he thought he had been, we have in this small pamphlet a reasonably clear statement of what he reported and what was accepted by Court and public a month after his return.

Though the emphasis differs slightly—Columbus is putting his case as persuasively as he can—the general picture is in accord with that drawn in the *Journal* as summarized by Las Casas. Cuba is the 'province of Cathay', 'the continent over there', in other words in the west, belongs to the Great Khan, but the island of Cipangu, and the ports of Zaiton and Quinsay are not mentioned, though the terms Indies and Indians are used. It was force of circumstances which obliged him to abandon the exploration of the north-trending 'Cathay' coast. He himself had seen no monstrosities, though he had heard of an island peopled by men with tails, and at the entrance to the Indies he had been told there was the Island of Women. As for the islands he had discovered: Hispaniola is full of marvels, with beautiful trees, many spices and great mines of gold. The inhabitants are 'wondrous timid', go naked except for small cloths, are unarmed, without iron or steel, intelligent, and good boatmen. In an island larger than Hispaniola there are men without hair. All the islanders he had seen are uniform in race, language and culture. On the second island at the 'entrance to the Indies', he was told, there is a people 'who are regarded in all the islands as very ferocious and who eat human flesh; they have many canoes with which they range all the islands of India and pillage and take as much as they can ... They are ferocious towards these other people who are exceedingly great cowards, but I make no more account of them than of the rest.'

Future policy is pretty clearly indicated. He has established, equipped and provisioned 'La Villa de Navidad' near a great gold-mine and is on good terms with the king of that province who treated him as a brother. Even if this king were to change his mind and offer insult to the garrison, 'neither he nor his people know the use of arms and they go naked as I have already said, and are the most timid people in the world, so that merely those whom I have left there could destroy all that land; and the island is without danger for their persons, if they know how to behave themselves'. With a little help he can give Their Highnesses as much gold as they want, not to speak of spice, cotton and gum mastic, and last but not least 'slaves as many as they shall order, who will be idolaters'. With God's help, he has accomplished what many regarded as the impossible. The King and Queen, with all Christendom, should rejoice at this great opportunity to turn 'so many peoples to our holy faith, and afterwards for material benefits, since not only Spain but all Christians will hence have refreshment and profit'.

The Sovereigns received this news with the greatest enthusiasm, and instructions were sent to the Admiral then in Seville to present himself at Court with the utmost speed. On his arrival he received a reception almost regal in its pomp. At the first audience Ferdinand refused to allow him to do obeisance, and seated him by his side on the royal dais. In public progress through the city streets the King rode with the Infante John on his right hand and the Admiral on his left. The titles and privileges conferred conditionally by the earlier Capitulations were confirmed, the proposals for the next voyage were approved, and orders issued for the assembly and equipment of the fleet. Ferdinand and Isabella might be vague as to where precisely their Admiral had been, but were in no doubt of the value of his achievements to the Crown. By this dazzling, if somewhat mysterious, stroke he had revealed a potentially powerful means of containing, if not outdoing, the advance of their ambitious and able cousin of Portugal, with his growing colonial power and his hopes of vast wealth. As the Queen wrote to the Admiral: 'Every day the import of this affair becomes greater. You have rendered an immense service.'

The monarchs, indeed, were beginning to act as if they were responsible for the whole affair. By reference to the Spanish gains in the Canaries, the western venture was represented as a continuation of a national policy for the conversion of the heathen. Forgotten were the early rebuffs and the difficulties Columbus had experienced in obtaining funds and ships. He continued to enjoy royal favour and, when he was in dispute with those fitting out the fleet, Ferdinand intervened on his behalf. But plainly the affair was moving out of his control into the realms of international politics.

The first moves were made in Rome, where the missionary theme was strongly pressed. (The six Indians had been christened and given high-sounding titles, Don Diego, and so forth.) The Pope, Alexander VI, had recently been elected to the Chair of Saint Peter with the influential support of King Ferdinand. A Spaniard by birth, whom Ferdinand had patronized to an extent excessive even for that period, and a diplomat seeking allies for his foreign policy, Alexander offered little resistance to demands for the immediate recognition of Spanish sovereignty in the western Ocean and beyond, and of her future rôle as bearer of the Christian faith to the naked savages revealed by Columbus to an astonished world. The Spanish policy was underlined for all the world to read by Bernardino de Carvajal, the ambassador in Rome, in a sermon preached the following June. Grandiloquently, he proclaimed: 'Christ has subjected under them [the Castilians] the Canary Islands, whose fertility has been proved marvellous, and he has lately given them other unknown islands towards the Indies, which may fully be regarded as the most precious things in the whole world, and it is expected that they will shortly be prepared for Christ by royal emissaries.' Carvajal makes no reference to the Africans who had been prepared for Christ by the Portuguese, and the Pope himself was prepared for the time being to play down their services to the Faith and to his predecessors. But Ferdinand and Isabella had not forgotten their intelligent, active and determined opponent, John II. Indeed it was he who was mainly responsible for all these diplomatic flurries.

King John, who had taken as his device a pelican piercing her breast to feed her young, and the motto, 'For the law and for the people', was now in unchallenged command of his virile though small nation. He had survived several conspiracies plotted by unruly nobles, and governed his people wisely but with a certain disdain, likening them to sardines, for they were in his eyes 'numerous, small and cheap'. He also held several strong cards in the current negotiations. He had secured the Portuguese footholds on the African coasts and in the islands, had organized a prosperous trade in the exotic products so much in demand, and established a fortress and factory at El Mina on the Gold Coast. As a consequence, his exchequer compared favourably with that of the needy Ferdinand. All this strength was based upon virtual command of the adjacent seas, exercised through a first-class navy, superior to that of any neighbouring power. He could count as well on a body of experts in cosmography, and in the science of navigation, acknowledged by contemporaries to be more effective than any which Spain could muster. And then he had two invaluable assets in the current bargaining, the strategic bases of Madeira and the Azores from which he could sever with impunity the tenuous line of communication between Spain and the Canaries and, more ominously, that with the newly-found islands in the west. He had, in fact, fashioned an admirable instrument with which to prise open the door to the wealth of the Orient, and after the slow patient labour of years was almost across the threshold, for his captain, Diaz, had rounded the Cape of Good Hope and shown the way into the Indian Ocean. For these reasons he, like his protagonist, had every reason to proceed cautiously in the western affair—the last thing he desired at this crisis was a first-class row with Spain.

Diplomatically, his position was not without strength. His predecessors had received Papal recognition of their sovereignty over African waters and he himself in the Treaty of 1479 had extracted an agreement from Spain which gave him a free hand south of the parallel of the Canaries while leaving the area to the north, with the exception of the Azores, to the Spaniards. In retrospect this was seen to have left little scope to the Spaniards, for it was concluded before the western areas were under discussion. It was therefore quite natural in the altered circumstances for Spain to wish to amplify the understanding.

John played his hand with coolness and skill, aided by an efficient intelligence service. He had men of standing at the Spanish Court, never identified, in his pay, and through a well-organized system of relays of couriers he was kept up to date with proceedings there, so much so that he would astonish his counsellors by saying that on such and such a date Their Catholic Majesties would say or do this or that, and events would prove his accuracy. In this way he was able to provide his envoys with appropriate and carefully-designed replies for the right moment, and unperturbed he dealt with the

Spanish moves as they materialized. At the audience he had granted to Columbus on his return, he had declined to discuss questions of sovereignty, and claimed that the new discoveries lay in his sphere as delimited by treaty. In this claim John had considerable justification. If Columbus gave him any accurate account of his course across the Atlantic at all, he would perceive that this must have taken the discoverer a certain distance south of the Canaries parallel. This conclusion would be further reinforced if Columbus repeated the Indian stories that richer islands, and even mainland, lay further to the south. But John tapped further sources of information. The Indians in the Admiral's train were induced to arrange a handful of beans to illustrate the relative positions of the islands; if these included Matinino and neighbouring isles, John can have had no further doubts. He was well-prepared therefore to meet the Spanish moves, quietly suggesting that 'each should have what belonged to him'.

The next eighteen months were occupied by the three-cornered tussle between Barcelona, Rome and Lisbon. At first Ferdinand played mainly for time until Columbus should be safely at sea, *en route* to occupy the islands systematically and to push further west, 'over toward the Indies'. With little difficulty he extracted four Bulls from Alexander conferring far-reaching rights upon his country. The first, *Inter cetera*, dated May 3, recites how 'our beloved son Christopher Columbus, navigating in the Ocean Sea in the western regions 'as it is said, toward the Indies, had found certain most remote islands and also continental lands which up to that time had not been discovered by others'. The Pope therefore assigns to Their Christian Majesties 'all and singular, the said lands and islands unknown and up to this time discovered and to be discovered' on the condition that 'the legal rights of no Christian Prince shall be understood to be taken away or ought to be taken away from him'. The Bull concluded with the pronouncement that 'since some Portuguese kings under Apostolic concession have acquired other islands similarly in the regions of Africa, Guinea and The Mine of Gold [S. Jorge el Mina]', the Spanish monarchs are to enjoy similar rights 'in the islands and lands discovered by you and to be discovered'.

This was certainly a solution of the problem, but one reached, from the Portuguese point of view, by ignoring the question at issue. Vaguely drawn, it made no distinction between the Portuguese and Spanish zones. What had happened, for instance, to Portugal's share of the ocean south of the Canaries parallel? Were Portuguese skippers in future barred from voyaging from the Azores in search of other islands? Was not Portugal entitled, as Spain was doing, to extend her zone to the west? The casual reference to the rights of 'some Portuguese kings' over unspecified islands was not calculated to lessen John's apprehensions.

The Spaniards, undaunted, went one better. If the Portuguese wanted a dividing line then Spain was ready with one. The second Bull refers to discoveries 'in the sea where hitherto it has not been navigated'. This is viewed as extending not only towards the Indies but to 'whatsoever part' Spanish captains may penetrate, vaguely lying in the west and south. But the crowning insult was the delimitation of a line which would virtually confine the Portuguese to African coastal waters, for the Bull defines a meridian extending from Pole to Pole 'towards the west and south, establishing and constituting a line from the Arctic Pole, that is to say from the North, to the Antarctic Pole, that is to say to the South, including the continental lands and islands found and to be found which are towards India, or towards whatever part it may be, which line may be distant from whatsoever one you may wish of the islands commonly known as the Azores and Cape Verde Islands one hundred leagues towards the west and south. And so we do give and assign in perpetuity ... all the islands and continental lands found and to be found, discovered and to be discovered, from the said line towards the west and south not actually possessed by any other Christian king [before 1494].' This Bull, it is true, offered some concession to Portugal by recognizing her existing rights, but over large portions of the globe the Spaniards were given a free hand. A third Bull, issued on the same day, though reaffirming in general the earlier assignments, did something to allay Portuguese suspicions.

But Spain was clearly determined to start negotiations with Portugal at a most extreme position, from which she could retire gracefully if necessary. Four months later, the fourth and last Bull practically threw the whole globe open to Spanish exploitation: 'Since it is possible to happen that your envoys, captains and subjects navigating west and south may direct themselves to the eastern parts [of Asia] and may find islands and continental lands which were or had been there known, We ... extend and enlarge our donation ... to all and singular islands and continental lands found and to be found, discovered and to be discovered, which in navigation or journeying towards the west or south in this way may be ...

existing either in the western regions, or in the southern and eastern regions or in India . . .' It then stated that the Spanish monarchs had the right of 'defending these against any obstructing persons whomsoever' and went on to hint broadly who these obstructors might be—'notwithstanding . . . whatever donations by us or by our predecessors to kings or princes or Infantes . . . even if by chance at some time those to whom donations and grants of this kind had been made, or through messengers, had navigated to those regions'. The sting is in this final phrase, clearly aimed at Portugal.

However prepared he was for this move, John must have experienced some qualms when it materialized. At the moment when he was planning the last stage of his progress round Africa, his rivals were claiming that if they reached that goal by the western route they were authorized to seize and hold it against Portugal or any other nation, thus depriving him at a stroke of the fruits of his country's endeavours through half a century. But, on consideration, his mood would change to one of slightly bitter hilarity. He knew from reports of his agents that he was indeed on the threshold of success. Within a reasonable time his ships would be in the Indian Ocean—the maritime link between the Spice Islands of south-east Asia and the markets of southern Europe. He had only to seize one or two strategic ports in order to tap one of the great contemporary world routes, and in due course no doubt his captains would reach the very source of all this wealth. He also had a shrewd idea that several thousand miles of ocean, supposing it were not in fact blocked by continental lands, still lay between the Spaniards in the western islands and the Spice Islands, the title to which they were now claiming to hold.

In John's eyes, these Bulls might once have been simply the repetitive fantasies of a 'mere Italian boaster' but, now that they had become the official policy of Spain, they could not be ignored in view of the magnitude of the stakes. Accordingly he applied himself with skill to his tortuous diplomacy. Early in the contest he had spread the rumour that he was preparing a fleet under one of his greatest captains, Francisco d'Almeida, to assert his rights in the western islands. With a show of moderation, he now agreed to postpone its departure for seventy days, but continued his war of nerves. Soon there were more rumours of four caravels having left Madeira for the west, and John hinted that he had knowledge of mysterious lands in the southern Atlantic. After nine months of these diplomatic exchanges, that astute monarch gained much for which he had worked when he and Their Catholic Majesties signed the Treaty of Tordesillas—'to preserve the love and kinship existing between them'.

John's protests and threats, backed by the necessary naval power to carry them out, had had a marked effect. The Spanish retreat from the extravagances of the Bull *Dudum siquidem* was precipitate. Their envoys were instructed to reach an equitable solution of the differences between the two countries, and, more remarkably, were given a free hand to determine a mutually agreeable boundary between their zones. The vital words were: 'You can leave to the said King of Portugal all the seas, islands and lands which shall be, and might be, within any boundary and demarcation of coasts which shall be fixed and established. And moreover we give you the said authority in order that . . . you can agree . . . with the said King of Portugal and with his ambassadors that all the seas, islands and lands that shall be or might be within the boundary and demarcation . . . which shall remain for us and for our successors, and for our dominion and conquest, shall belong to our Realms and our successors therein, with those limitations and exemptions which you shall approve.'

The Portuguese negotiators received similar instructions, and the formal part of the treaty-making was concluded with rapidity. Adopting the idea of a meridian as a dividing line, the commissioners agreed that 'there shall be made and marked out through the said ocean, a mark or line straight from Pole to Pole, from the Arctic Pole to the Antarctic Pole, which is from north to south, which mark or line and indication may be drawn and must be drawn straight as is said, at 370 leagues from the islands of Cape Verde to the West, by degrees or by another manner, as it can best be most quickly drawn, so that it will not include a greater distance. And all that which up to the present may be found and discovered, and which from now henceforward shall be found and discovered by the said King of Portugal, or by his vessels, islands as well as mainland, from the said line above, drawn in the form aforesaid, going by the said Eastern side within the said line to the East or North or South, from it, so long as the said line is not crossed—That this may be and remain and belong to the said King of Portugal, and his successors for ever after.' All the rest, 'going by the said western side, after having passed the said line', shall remain to Their Catholic Majesties.

Having Columbus's second voyage in mind—he was then in the Indies—the Spanish envoys secured a temporary concession; if within twenty days of the conclusion of the agreement, islands or mainland should be discovered within the first 250 leagues, they were to go to Portugal as agreed, but lands between this limit of 250 leagues and the meridian at 370 leagues were, if discovered in this period, to become the property of Spain.

The first effect of the treaty was to substitute a north–south dividing line in place of the previously accepted east–west parallel. The establishment of the line at a distance of 370 leagues from the Cape Verde Islands recognized Portugal's pre-eminence in the southern Atlantic, and removed the possibility of any threat to her route via the Cape to India. Moreover, by abandoning the large claim to the Indian, that is, East Indian, islands set out in the Bull *Dudum siquidem*, Spain had obtained for herself freedom to develop the 'other world' to which Columbus had blazed the way, beyond the line to which he liked to refer as 'the beginning of the east', or with equal justification, 'the end of the west'. Neither side showed any concern at this juncture with the Antipodes, and the treaty makes no mention of the complementary meridian dividing the other hemisphere. This was not at the moment a matter of practical politics. Portugal with her advanced knowledge of cosmography no doubt had a shrewd idea of its course, but Spain was more concerned with securing the western islands.

It has been argued that John stood out for the meridian at 370 leagues from the Cape Verde Islands because he had knowledge of the existence and approximate position of the South American continent and wished to stake his claim. The discovery by Cabral of the Brazilian coast in the year 1500 is held to strengthen this view, but it is a conclusion governed by hindsight. The line was fixed primarily to restore Portugal's position in the South Atlantic, and her chief gain from the treaty was the acknowledgement of her goal eastwards of the line, in the approaches to, and in the coasts of, the Indian Ocean. There is no direct evidence that it was drawn to include part of Brazil.

The treaty also contained an agreement on the method of demarcating the meridian, but it was soon recognized that this would be impossible where it ran through the open ocean. By common consent the two Powers later agreed to inform each other of the position of any new discoveries in their respective spheres and to proceed accordingly. The precise course of the meridian assumed importance only when it became necessary to establish a boundary on the South American continent. A major problem also arose when, to establish the division of sovereignty in the Moluccas (the Spice Islands), the course of the counter-meridian through the archipelago had to be determined; this particular difficulty was finally resolved by Spain selling her claim outright to the Portuguese. The treaty, however, admirably achieved its main object, the peaceful settlement of the relationship between the colonial spheres of Spain and Portugal, and its importance for the future development of the Americas was immense.

While these negotiations were in train, Columbus was occupied with preparations for a second expedition which, in view of the reactions to be expected from Portugal, was to leave without delay. To the Admiral, newly confirmed in his titles, its object was primarily to secure possession by occupation of the new lands, and thus to establish a stable base for further exploration to the west and south, whether or not Hispaniola was indeed Cipangu. But before pressing further westwards he was particularly anxious to examine Matinino* and neighbouring islands, which had been indicated by the natives as a rich source of gold, and which, in his scheme of things, stood at the 'beginning of the east'. It was in these islands that he made his second landfall, having followed a course west by south from Gomera in the Azores.

But, associated with settlement and exploration, was the systematic organization of the traffic in gold in the interest of the Crown and of himself as Viceroy. In his proposals of April 1494 he put forward the figure of two thousand colonists, to be settled in three or four towns. All those who wished to try their luck in the 'gold rush' must obtain royal licences and for the first year surrender half the gold collected. A tax of one per cent was to go towards the expenses of the Church in its work for the conversion of the Indians. The export of gold was to be strictly channelled through Cadiz, which would become the staple for the trade. In contrast to his general desire to keep any discovery under his own control, Columbus proposed that those searching for new lands should be encouraged by the promise of at least twenty per cent of the profits of the voyage; no doubt he hoped that he might receive this proportion in place of the eighth share under the original agreement. His proposals were generally endorsed by his Sovereigns, but in their replies there was a distinctly different emphasis. The proposals for the missionary work are placed first, and Father Buil, a Catalan, and another friar

* Martinique. This island was associated by Columbus with classical legends about 'islands of women'.

must go with the fleet. The Admiral is strictly enjoined not to permit the ill-treatment of the natives. The replies also made it quite clear that Hispaniola was to be Crown territory; it was laid down, for example, that all commissions issued in the colony to magistrates and other officials were to be publicly proclaimed in the Sovereigns' names.

The second fleet, in size, manpower, and equipment, was commensurate with the importance of the plans. After some difficulties seventeen vessels of various types and tonnage were assembled, among them craft of shallow draught for inshore reconnaissance, the lack of which had handicapped Columbus the previous year; among them was the staunch little caravel, the *Niña*, rechristened the *Santa Clara*. Room was eventually found for fifteen hundred people, the majority in the pay of the Crown. The military contingent included twenty horsemen, whose animals were to strike terror in the Indian warriors. Columbus's personal staff included his young brother Diego, 'a virtuous young man, very reserved, pacific and well-intentioned rather than maliciously silent, who was accustomed to go very plainly dressed, almost in clerical garb' according to Las Casas, and Antonio de Torres who was to command the return fleet, 'a man of standing, prudent and well-fitted for the post' and brother of the Donna Juana, governess of Prince John and a close friend of the Admiral.

Unlike the first venture, when he had to deal with skippers, pilots and unwilling or obstreperous seamen, Columbus was now accompanied by men of some distinction—civil servants and well-bred though impecunious adventurers. Francisco de Peñalosa, a member of the Queen's circle, was in command of the troops, and others on board were Melchior Maldonado, formerly Castilian envoy in Rome, Bernal de Pisa the treasurer, and Diego Marquez, an hidalgo from Seville, the inspector-general. Two other men were suspected of having been sent to keep an eye on the Admiral, Mossen Pedro Margarit, a distinguished Catalan knight, and the priest, Father Buil. Of less immediate note, but of interest for the future, were Pedro de Las Casas, father of the future historian and 'apostle of the Indies'; Michele de Cuneo, a Genoese of some culture whose father had had business dealings with Domenico Columbus, who went on the voyage for the fun of it; Guillermo Coma, an Aragonese, and Dr. Diego Alvares Chanca the medical officer. To the last three we owe firsthand accounts of the voyage and the proceedings in the Indies. In their letters we see not only the islands and their peoples but also the Admiral and his officers in action as they appeared to observant and educated men of the Renaissance, who for the most part had no axes to grind. Several less distinguished men were later to achieve prominence in the Indies; among them Juan Ponce de Leon, the discoverer of Florida, and Alonso de Hojeda, the ardent youth who was to cause the Admiral much anxiety. Juan de la Cosa was also there, evidently pardoned for his alleged responsibility for the loss of the *Santa Maria*. He was now, however, serving as official cartographer and was well on the way to a successful career as an explorer-trader in his own right.

This impressive roll-call is striking evidence of the fundamental change which the whole enterprise had undergone; no longer was it the dream of a self-made man, a stranger of low birth, but a powerfully-backed national campaign. Columbus was surely well aware of this change and the extent to which control was passing from his hands, but his self-confidence was as yet unshaken. Nevertheless, when the fleet sailed out of Cadiz on May 29, 1493, he was a sick man confined to his cabin, loaded with responsibilities, worn out with the bickerings of the outfitting Commission and suffering from his earlier exertions.

The departure, as described by Guillermo Coma, could scarcely have been in greater contrast to the almost unnoticed start in the early morning ten months before. 'The customary religious rites having been celebrated by the sailors, last embraces were exchanged. The ships were dressed with bunting, pennants fluttered from the rigging, and the poops were gay with royal standards. The flutes and zithers held entranced the Nereides, Galatheus, even the very sirens themselves, with their tuneful notes: the strident sounds of the trumpets echoed from the shores, and the roar of cannon reverberated over the waves. By chance some Venetian galleys who had been trading in the British Sea had sailed into the harbour and did not disdain to emulate the Spanish ships, joining with equal heartiness in the cheers of the sailors and imploring blessings on the ships setting sail for the Indies.' Assuming that this juxtaposition was not simply a piece of rhetoric, it was certainly an historic moment: the Spanish fleet, intent on reaching the Indies to deprive Venice of her monopoly of the spice trade, is cheered on its way by the crews of Venetian merchant ships.

Chapter VIII

SECOND VOYAGE AND TROUBLES
IN HISPANIOLA

THE SECOND fleet reached La Navidad on November 27, 1493, having *en route* examined the lesser Antilles from Martinique to St. Croix, and Puerto Rico, but without finding the reported gold. This return to La Navidad, the first settlement in the new world, graphically described by Guillermo Coma, provided a severe shock to the Admiral's self-confidence. 'They entered the harbour late at night. When none of the Christians garrisoning the fortress on shore answered their signals, poignant grief and sorrow overcame them all, for they suspected rightly that the comrades whom they had left there had been completely wiped out. At about the tenth hour of the evening, while they were torn with despair and fearful anxiety, an Indian canoe put off from the shore and sped towards the ships ... As soon as an opportunity for speaking had been afforded, the Admiral first made solicitous enquiries about Guacanagari and then asked eagerly for news of the Christians. They replied that Guacanagari was sick from a wound and that all the Christians had been slain. [The next day] they related how the men had met their death: they had been killed by Coanabo, a powerful ruler of warlike spirit and varied talents, who was universally feared ... Bad feeling had arisen and had broken out into warfare because of the licentious conduct of our men towards the Indian women, for each Spaniard had five women to minister to his pleasure ... Although they had resisted strongly to the last, our men were unable to withstand the close-order attacks of the enemy very long, and they were at length ruthlessly cut down. The truth of these words was demonstrated both by Guacanagari and by the corpses of ten Spaniards, which had been found by our men miserably deformed and corrupted, smeared with dirt and foul blood, and hideously discoloured, for they had lain out in the open.'

This was indeed a miserable start to the Admiral's efforts to establish stable government in Hispaniola, for it prejudiced his hopes of good relations with the Indians. He had already failed on the voyage out to prevent a party from raiding an island, and one Spaniard had been killed in a slight affray. More sinister was the carrying-off of some thirty Caribs. Columbus was able however to retain the friendship of the cacique Guacanagari, who remained a faithful ally throughout the ensuing years—one of the brighter spots in the dismal record. The next step was to construct a new fortified base, for the memories of La Navidad were too painful. The site selected for Isabella lay forty leagues to the east, near the mouth of Pinzon's river and on the route to the only considerable source of gold in the island. Otherwise, it had little to recommend it—it was ill-supplied with water—and was in fact soon abandoned. Nevertheless, in his excitement to reach gold, the Admiral drove the work of construction forward, designing the first European town in the western hemisphere on ample lines, a long, straight main street intersected by numerous cross-roads with a stone-built church, where the first Mass in the new world was celebrated, a governor's residence and a fortress to dominate the sea-front, all fitted in the founder's eyes to receive the visit of a monarch. The labourers were put to work at once, thus producing the first crop of complaints. Others made a start at cultivating small gardens with the grain and vegetable seeds which they had brought out. Columbus had enthused over the prospects of the settlement becoming self-supporting, but in fact these early efforts were half-hearted and the seed corn was soon being ground to meet the need for flour. The settlers stuck as long as they could to their accustomed bread and wine. When these ran short they supplemented their rations with native produce, but it was a considerable time before they took to this with any enthusiasm.

After the voyage, when they had been crowded together in the small ships, and faced with the strangeness of life in a tropical environment, the men were in poor condition, dysentery was rife, and morale low. The root of the trouble was the great contrast between what they had expected to find in Hispaniola and the stark reality. Adventurers, more than could be easily accommodated, had flocked to the ships, excited by the prospect of gold in the new lands and of a quick and easy fortune to be won. That they would be obliged to earn their keep by steady labour, helping to found a permanent colony, can have occurred to few if any of them. The absence of women of their own race also resulted in deteriorating relations with the Indians.

Since sickness and death had reduced the available labour-force, the Admiral gave orders that everyone, irrespective of rank or standing, should take a share in the work. The grumbles of the ordinary men were as nothing to the indignant protests from the minor nobility who scorned such demeaning work. All these difficulties and grievances, however, were only the background to the fundamental crisis which threatened Columbus and eventually brought about his fall. Technically he was Viceroy in Hispaniola with the powers defined in the Capitulations, and all were obliged to render obedience to him. But there was one powerful group which challenged his position—the officials of the Crown, both those appointed before the departure and, ironically, those appointed by Columbus in Hispaniola. It had been stipulated that the commissions of the latter should be proclaimed in the names of the Sovereigns, but it was not clear whether their immediate loyalty was to Columbus or to the Crown.

There was also plenty of scope for bickering over the control of the traffic in gold, fanned by the resentment felt against Columbus as a fortune-seeking foreigner.

As the prospects of sudden fortune faded and hardships grew, faith in the Amiral's credibility vanished and it was easy for the disillusioned Spaniards to believe that they were being ill-treated, oppressed, and mercilessly punished by a stranger, and one of plebeian origin at that, for his own profit and glory. In these circumstances they came to feel that their lot was little better than transported criminals, and longed to leave for home. That intelligent observer de Cuneo put his finger on the main cause of the unrest when he wrote: 'No one wants to live in these countries.'

As soon as some sort of order had been established at Isabella, the Admiral turned his attention to what had become his obsession, the search for gold, sending Alonso de Hojeda with a small party inland up the Yaque river towards Cibao, where the Indians had told him the principal source of their gold lay. Hojeda returned with a few small nuggets, and the inevitable reports that if the strangers would only push on just a little further, into someone else's country, they would find all the gold they wanted. This was sufficient for Columbus: at last, after all those years of labour, despised and rejected, he was about to reap the tangible reward which God had ordained for him. This was the crisis of his career, and he marked it by an unusual decision. Up to that time he had never, while in the Indies, ventured more than a short distance from the shore; now he would lead the expedition to the 'gold-mines' himself. This was a bold decision to take, for signs of a revolt were evident and there were rumours of a plot to seize a ship and sail for Spain. That he took this step is further proof of all this venture meant for him. Having made up his mind, he acted with unusual decisiveness. Bernard de Pisa, the reputed leader of the dissidents, was arrested and confined aboard ship, all valuable supplies and equipment were placed in the ships under a strong guard, and young Diego given command at Isabella. As for the rank and file, their hardships were momentarily forgotten, for all were just as eager as the Admiral to reach the 'gold-mines'.

When the column of horse and foot (500-strong, according to de Cuneo, for every available man had been rounded up) marched out in battle array, with banners flying and trumpets blowing, it was more than a brave show to impress the natives. To Columbus it was the prelude to a long-delayed triumph which would vindicate his reputation and secure his future, and he had staked much upon it.

With the active help of friendly natives, particularly in transporting materials for a fort, and in crossing the rivers, the outward march was uneventful, though it was noted that as they passed by the Indian villages the inhabitants fled or shut themselves up in their huts, while the 'loyal' Indians, imitating the white men, plundered as they pleased. Later, as they marched further inland, large numbers flocked to see the great lord and his following, bearing small gifts of the gold which so inexplicably fascinated them. The route took the column through the fertile and well-watered plains of the Yaque—Columbus commemorated their promise by naming them the Vega Real (royal meadow)—and up into the foothills of the central cordillera, a country of broken granitic ridges much scarred by ravines and scattered with trees. Here, as their supplies were running short, a mule-train went back for bread and wine. The rough track then narrowed and the horsemen were obliged to dismount and lead their animals. Soon there was little inclination to push further into this inhospitable country of Cibao, especially as there was evidence of gold in the stream-beds and on the boulder-strewn hillsides. Columbus accordingly chose a site for a small fort on an isolated hill washed by a tributary of the Yaqui. This he named Fortaleza San Tomás, as a rebuke to the many doubters in his train. The journey of twenty-seven leagues had taken five days. Columbus, uneasy and no doubt disheartened, gave the command of the fort and the garrison of fifty men to Pedro Margarit, with orders to organize the working of the placer deposits, collect nuggets and overawe the cacique of the province. This post was evidently uncongenial to the

Catalan noble who had qualms about the treatment of the natives, for in a short time he was back in Isabella and, indeed, on the high seas for Spain. Columbus himself wasted no time in further exploration and hurried back to the coast. The return journey, except for the passage of the swollen rivers, was as uneventful as the outward, and the expedition was back in Isabella in less than three weeks.

Very little success attended this all-out effort. When other forts had been built in the Vega Real the quantity of gold collected increased temporarily and the Spanish hold was a little firmer, but these improvements can scarcely have appeared to Columbus as the triumphant success he needed so desperately. Ferdinand Columbus and Las Casas make no attempt to estimate the amount of gold collected, in itself a criticism of the affair, and the only other report comes from de Cuneo who was distinctly unenthusiastic: the weather was terrible, the food bad, and the drink worse. He estimated that a total of gold equivalent to about ten thousand dollars had been obtained at San Tomás, but one-third of this had been acquired clandestinely by the men. His concluding comment reveals the general low state of morale. In addition to the official dealings, he wrote, 'there were also exchanged in secret against the rules and our own agreement to a value of about one thousand castellanos. As you know the devil makes you do wrong and then lets your wrong be discovered; moreover, so long as Spain is Spain, traitors will never be wanting. One gave the other away, so that almost all were exposed, and whoever was found guilty was well whipped, some had their ears slit and some the nose, very pitiful to see.'

Such punishment, not severe by Spanish standards, did little to increase the Admiral's popularity at a time when failure seemed imminent. These native villages, however neat and prosperous they might appear, were clearly not the cities of the Great Khan, and Columbus himself could only suggest that perhaps this was the land of the Queen of Sheba, or the Ophir of the Bible. That he should have decided, despite the evident risk and his categorical statement to the Catholic Sovereigns, to embark at this juncture upon a voyage of exploration is a measure of his disappointment, even his desperation. Before he could sail, however, a disturbing series of incidents occurred, in which Las Casas saw the beginning of the bloody trail of conquest across the Americas. To relieve the force at San Tomás, which reported that attacks were threatening, and to remove some of the discontented from Isabella, he sent Hojeda once again with a force into the Vega Real. A series of petty misunderstand-

ings developed into open conflict with the natives, in which several
were killed and two caciques taken prisoner. The Admiral was about
to execute these unfortunates when a friendly chief interceded on
their behalf, and they were reprieved. However the harm had been
done. This was the first severe clash, and it occurred on the vital
route to the interior. That the Admiral still persisted in his plans for
discovery serves to underline the importance he attached to continuing his search for Cathay.

This second voyage was an attempt first to restore the prestige
lost in the island and to a lesser extent at home, and secondly to
satisfy his increasing lust for gold. As he declaimed at the end of his
life as an explorer: 'The Genoese, the Venetians and everyone who
has pearls, precious stones and other things of value, they all carry
them to the ends of the earth to barter and convert into gold. O
most excellent gold! Who has gold has a treasure with which he gets
what he wants, imposes his will on the world, and even helps souls
to Paradise.' Both these aims would be achieved if only he could
reach the treasury of the East which he was convinced was located in
the islands and mainland of south-east Asia, the regions to the west
and south which the Pope had been willing to grant to Their Catholic
Majesties. If the Indies were not in fact the islands of his first discovery, then 'Forward' must still be his watchword.

Urged on by the thought that he might still be on the verge of a
sensational success, and having established a measure of order, he
placed Diego in charge, embarked in the *Niña* and, accompanied by
two other vessels, set a course for the west. He sighted the southern
coast of Cuba at Cape Alpha and Omega (shown on Ruysch as 'C.
fun d' April', the date of the sighting)* and coasted it as far as Cape
Cruz. He then decided to seek the island of Yamaye (Jamaica) of
which he had heard reports when first in Cuba and which as usual
was alleged to be particularly rich in gold. As he sailed its northern
shores he was met and followed by large numbers of canoes manned
by natives more energetic, pugnacious and persistent than the placid
Arawaks. At one point a sharp engagement took place, in which a
dozen natives were killed by Spanish cross-bows and five others by
the ships' lombards. According to de Cuneo, this affair had an
astonishing effect on them, for they abandoned their aggressive
behaviour and engaged busily in barter for toys and petty articles and
bells, which they hung from their noses and ears. Encountering
contrary winds, Columbus then set a northerly course for the Cuban

* See Appendix, p. 210.

coast with the intention of determining whether it was island or mainland. To his son Ferdinand there was a much wider objective, for he states that the Admiral proposed, by continuing his westerly route, to circumnavigate the globe and return to Spain from the East. This somewhat surprising statement is supported by Andres Bernaldes, who had many conversations with the Admiral on his return.

Back on the Cuban coast, the ships sailed through the maze of islets, banks, reefs and channels lying inside the line of cays beyond Cape Cruz. These islands, clothed with luxuriant vegetation and in calm sunlit waters, so impressed the Admiral that he gave them the poetical name of 'Garden of the Queen'. As he sailed through them westwards, his hopes of entering the promised land constantly flared up. But when they entered the Gulf of Batabano conditions deteriorated. Navigation through the more intricate maze of shallows, banks and reefs was laborious: the vessels were frequently aground and had to be hauled off, while food supplies and water were running out. Added to these privations were the frequent tropical storms and the least congenial weather he had so far experienced in the Tropics. All this produced growing discontent among the crews. Despite his obstinate belief, therefore, in the proximity of the Golden Chersonese and other oriental enchantments, he was obliged, when within less than a hundred miles of the western end of Cuba, to recognize that the means he commanded were insufficient for the navigation of this difficult coast. But before he put about he made an effort to wrest some advantage from his frustrations—an effort which, like many of his actions, was to bring upon him charges of trickery and harshness, and the derision of his opponents. On his instructions, his public notary, Fernando Perez de Luna, caused all responsible members of the crews to sign a declaration that they firmly believed that Cuba was not an island but a peninsula, and that, having so declared, they would never repudiate this opinion. As a matter of maritime procedure, such a declaration was merely the extension of the practice of consulting with the officers at critical moments of a voyage. What was unusual was its extension to the majority of the crew, the demand that they should never alter their views, and the penalties for so doing. The action shows how desperately he needed to bolster his claim that he was on the way to the Indian Sea: everyone must believe implicitly that the peninsula that figured on his map was part of the Asian mainland, in proximity to the celebrated port of Zaiton in Cathay. Thus each deponent was required to declare: 'that he had never heard of, nor saw, an island which could have 335 leagues on one coast from west to east, and which extended still further; and that he saw now that the land turned to the south-south-west and to the south-south-east'.

The men evidently signed out of weariness with the voyage. Indeed de Cuneo states that few believed in their hearts that the Admiral was right, and persisted in thinking they were off a great island. Apart from any other consideration, the stated length of the coast was twice the correct figure. De Cuneo does not refer to the incident but records at this point that the Admiral was still governed by his desires: 'We returned to the WSW, and sailing for about sixty leagues, saw land. This we thought must be mainland. Then sailing NW in order to find Cathay, according to the opinion of the Admiral, we found that this was a gulf. Seeing it we turned around and went back on our course.'

No action in fact was taken against any doubters who later changed their opinion. The most famous of these was Juan de la Cosa, the official map-maker, who five years later depicted on his map the large island of Cuba.

Columbus himself was now a sick man, tired and anxious about events in Hispaniola. As he wrote to the Sovereigns later, à propos of the rotten biscuit and the carafe of wine which was now their daily fare: 'I too submitted to these privations. May it please Our Lord that all this may be to His holy service and to that of Your Highnesses. As to what I have suffered, I have never undergone greater labours or dangers. Not a day passed that I did not think that we had all come to the ends of our lives.'

In this mood he did not continue beyond the Isle of Pines, which he called Evangelista. On the return he carried out two further pieces of exploration—the southern coasts of Jamaica and of Hispaniola—before he reached Isabella after five months' absence. The mapping of Cuba on the Ruysch map exactly reflects the results of the voyage, the southern turn of the coastline beyond Evangelista being particularly notable. This was not a great deal to show for his labours and it was no doubt for this reason that, back at Isabella, de Cuneo tells us, he planned an immediate voyage to the Cuban north coast. During his absence his brother Bartholomew had arrived in Isabella; reaching Spain from France too late to join the second fleet he had come out on Torres's second voyage, and it was to him that he proposed to entrust the new voyage. De Cuneo, aware that his correspondent was a friend of Bartholomew's, writes:

'He [Bartholomew] had to depart with two caravels and one *fusta* which had been built in the island of Hispaniola during the whole month of April, and had to go discovering to the north. If in that direction no more will be found than we had found in our voyage, I am much afraid he will have to abandon everything . . . We are somewhat sure that when Master Bartholomew will have sailed northwards 500 leagues, he will find land; but he will also find greater storms and fouler winds than we ourselves have found.' Although there is no other evidence that this voyage took place, it is interesting to learn that Columbus was still debating whether to direct his attention once more to the north. The passage is also significant as it expresses the disillusionment produced by the failure of the second voyage either to make an important discovery or to find gold. If Bartholomew could not do better, then the whole enterprise was in jeopardy. Columbus's contribution to the mapping of Cuba therefore remains as on the Ruysch map, a triangular outline with the apex towards Hispaniola, and the northern coast running away to the north-west.

De Cuneo has one other interesting detail to add: an argument between the Admiral and a certain Abbot, a man of learning and of wealth, who had arrived in the island merely to satisfy his intellectual curiosity. This man, rather a surprising character to find in Hispaniola at this early date, is described as Abbot of Lucena, astronomer and cosmographer, but unfortunately he is known only from this mention by de Cuneo. The dialogue between him and the Admiral would make good reading, the latter maintaining that the extent of the coastline he had just returned from exploring proved that Cuba must be the mainland of Asia, with the Abbot pouring scorn on the proposition, holding it to be only a very big island.

During his five months' absence, Diego Columbus, advised by Pero Hernandes Coronel, the military commander, and Father Buil, was in charge of the settlement. Diego was not the man to hold the conflicting interests in check, and the intrigues against the Columbus party came to a head when Buil left for Spain with a list of grievances. With him went Margarit, the original commander at San Tomás. This was what the Admiral had feared, but when he returned from the Cuban voyage all he could do was to endeavour to prevent others from following their example, for he well knew the kind of report that the cleric would present. For five months at this critical period he was a sick man, and his position would have been exceedingly precarious but for the support of Bartholomew. From then onwards Bartholomew, appointed Adelantado, was his brother's chief executive and, during his illness or absence, the *de facto* Viceroy—another development which rankled with the Spanish officials. Meanwhile the Admiral was steadily losing his grip on affairs, and the stronger his feeling of betrayal and persecution grew, the wilder and more fantastical became his illusions.

But, for the moment, there were more practical matters to be dealt with. Another supply crisis was impending and the Spaniards were ravaging the countryside for the once-despised local foodstuffs. This crisis was warded off by the timely arrival of further stores from Spain, and Columbus's attention could be turned to future policy. In view of the deteriorating state of the interior—even San Tomás had been abandoned—it was resolved to overawe the native population by making an example of Caonabo, the resolute and unsubdued cacique of Cibao. In this policy can be seen the hand of Bartholomew, for this was the kind of solution to which he was later very partial. The task of seizing the chief was allotted to Hojeda who had given proof of a headstrong courage. With a handful of horsemen he kidnapped the unsuspecting chief and carried him off to Isabella where, after being placed on public exhibition, he disappeared into oblivion. This coup, however, had little effect on native morale for by the end of the year they were in open revolt, the Spaniards losing ten men in one incident.

In a fresh burst of energy the Admiral resolved to put into effect the scheme which he had proposed to Their Catholic Majesties after his first voyage: the establishment of a number of strong-points throughout the north-east of the island to which the natives would bring gold regularly and systematically, on the lines of the Portuguese factories in West Africa except for the important difference that, instead of the natives obtaining barter goods in return, the gold was to be levied as a tribute.

Mustering all the force available, as well as the support of his old friend and ally Guacanagari, Columbus and Bartholomew rapidly overran the north-east of the island, meeting no effective opposition from the supreme cacique, and built new forts in the Vega Real. The lesser caciques were then ordered to bring in quarterly a given tribute in gold, calculated according to the number of their people over the age of fourteen. This was a heavy blow to the native way of life, already shaken by the assault from outside. Many of their natural leaders were dead or in hiding, and their nicely-balanced economy was disrupted by the strangers, just as the great trains of porters accompanying nineteenth-century African explorers were to prove too great a burden for local food-economies to support. But above all, even with the greatest goodwill, this tributary system was beyond the caciques' powers to carry out. Before the coming of the Spaniards, gold had played little or no part in their economy except as an ornamental accessory on ceremonial occasions. For this purpose the small nuggets collected haphazardly or the small deposits of dust found in river-beds were sufficient. These supplies were not inexhaustible, and the natives were without the techniques for working the major deposits systematically. Moreover, in the apathy accompanying the break-up of their social structure, they had no incentive, other than the avoidance of punishment, to meet the incomprehensible demands of their new masters.

The difficulties which all methods of obtaining the gold encountered also affected the morale of the Spaniards, already at a low level. The stricter control of its collection removed the hopes of the rank and file that they might somehow win personal fortunes, and with these hopes also vanished their readiness to risk their lives on war-like forays into the interior. All they desired was to get out of what Columbus himself described as 'hell'. Their attitude was summed up in Las Casas's remark that their favourite oath was 'As God may carry me back to Castile'.

Meanwhile the reports of those who had returned to Spain were disturbing the authorities, who were also finding the need for the constant despatch of supply ships increasingly irksome. To obtain a first-hand appreciation of the situation, the Sovereigns decided to send out Juan Aguado, who also carried instructions to the Admiral to effect economies in the administration and to reduce the pay-roll. Columbus, recognizing the danger-signal, determined to forestall Aguado's report by presenting his own case to the Sovereigns. The ever-willing Bartholomew was once more put in charge of the enfeebled colony, and proceeded to show himself, against all the odds, a more successful administrator than his brother. The settlement of Isabella, despite the high hopes entertained at its foundation, had proved to be badly-sited and without an adequate water-supply. It was therefore gradually abandoned, and Bartholomew set energetically about building a new city, Santo Domingo, on a fine site on the south-east coast. He also brought some order into the lines of communications, opened up new sources of alluvial gold, and began for the first time to extend Spanish influence into western Hispaniola, where he instituted friendly negotiations with the caciques. His conciliatory approach was less successful in Cibao, where he had to repress another revolt with severity.

When the Admiral arrived at the Spanish Court in 1496, he found his affairs in hardly a better state. His Sovereigns, still honouring him as their Admiral of the Ocean Sea, were becoming increasingly doubtful of his capabilities as Viceroy in the Indies. The great wealth which he had dangled before their eyes had yet to flow into their treasury, and men and ships were urgently needed in the pursuit of other policies. At this juncture, indeed, it was possible that 'the enterprise of the Indies', hovering on the brink of chaos, might be abandoned altogether, a prospect which the Admiral could not for one moment contemplate. Apart from having left his brothers with little support to cope with the fractious colonists, his career up to that point had been a continuous struggle against obstacles far more daunting than those which now confronted him, sick in body as he was, and he still held his royal privileges largely unimpaired. Another, and successful, voyage directed to the right quarter and tapping a really rich source of gold would completely restore his position; he must therefore combine exploration with a relief expedition to Hispaniola.

There could only be one answer to the question of where it should be directed to. As he thumbed through his summaries of classical authors, he eagerly noted the references to the wealth of the tropics and the perennial theme of the universal superiority of southern over northern lands. He recalled, too, the continual reports, vague but insistent, of the gold-bearing islands in the south, a theme supported by the lack of gold in Cuba and the relative poverty of Hispaniola in this respect. That there was land south of his discoveries he had little doubt. The Scriptures were emphatic that the greater part of the globe was covered by dry land, and on the principle of symmetry, so fundamental to the thought of cosmographers from the Greek philosophers onwards, it was almost more than a certainty that a great mainland across the Atlantic in the west must balance the continent of Africa. Must this not also contain resources comparable to those flowing into the coffers of the King of Portugal? Was it not common gossip that the late King John had come to a similar conclusion, and that this had governed his conduct of the Tordesillas negotiations? Before that treaty, Spain had been precluded from expansion to the south, but now, beyond the line of demarcation, half the globe was open to her enterprise. Accordingly Columbus planned to make his next approach on a course nearer the Equator.

The period from June 1496 to May 1498, when he embarked on his third voyage, was as wearisome as any in his career. To his persistent demands the Sovereigns replied encouragingly, but action was slow to follow. Finally he obtained six small vessels, three for discovery and three for supplies to Hispaniola. The latter he accompanied as far as Gomera from where he despatched them on the course he had followed in 1493. His own point of departure was the Cape Verde Islands, where the Portuguese officials treated him with friendly courtesy, with no suggestion that they regarded him as about to poach on their preserves. We know a little of the circumstances of this crossing, for we have an abstract of his *Journal* edited by Las Casas, although more summary and with fewer direct questions than that of the first voyage. It was uneventful, apart from the great heat which the men had to endure—conditions of which the Spaniards had less experience than their Portuguese rivals. Nevertheless, it is curious that Columbus, who claimed to have voyaged to El Mina, should have been so impressed by it. Perhaps it set him thinking of the 'zone uninhabitable through heat' of the older cosmographers. On July 13, it is recorded: 'The wind failed and he came into such great, vehement, burning heat that he feared lest the ships catch fire and the people perish. So suddenly and unexpectedly did the wind cease and the excessive and unusual heat come on, that there was no one who would dare go below to look after the casks of wine and water which burst, snapping the hoops of the pipes; the wheat burned like fire; the bacon and salt meat roasted and putrefied. This heat and fire lasted eight days.'

They were then relieved by cloudy weather and rain, and he decided to run for the west for several days into a temperate zone (this was a reflection of his notion that beyond the Azores there was a dramatic change in the natural environment), and then to turn southwards, which was the course he wished to follow, at a point approximately south of Hispaniola. Some days later, he saw flocks of birds flying towards the north-east, the old, sure sign of land. As water was running short, he changed his mind again, and set a course north by east, with the intention of picking up Dominica or some other Caribbean island, in other words, of abandoning his southern exploration. At midday on July 31 his servant, Alonso Perez, saw from the crow's-nest land at fifteen leagues to the west— three hills still called the Trinity Hills. In accordance with a vow he had taken, he named the discovery 'The Land of Trinity' (Trinidad). For some reason which is not set out in the *Journal*, but which probably arose from his growing belief that he was divinely guided, he regarded this landfall as 'a great miracle', as great as the discovery of the First Voyage. In reality, however, the abandonment of the intention to turn south and the change to a northerly course was, at this stage, of little importance. A southerly leg would sooner or later have struck the South American coast somewhere in the vicinity of the main Orinoco estuary. In his then state of mind, caused by anxiety over the deterioration of the supplies for the colony, it is probable that this would not have had any sensational result, for he would then almost certainly have coasted northwards. But it is just possible that he would have recognized in the Orinoco one of the Rivers of Paradise, and have either explored it or continued on his southerly course.

Coasting along southern Trinidad, refilling his fresh-water casks, and mistaking the land to the south for an island, he reached its western end at Punta del Arenal. There he sent the crews ashore to rest and divert themselves. Beyond the point, he entered a narrow channel where the out-flowing stream and the incoming ocean-swell clashed with such a great noise and discord that the crews were terrified, and the ships tossed wildly about. This passage he accordingly named 'The Serpent's Mouth' (Boca de la Sierpe). Sailing northwards across the Gulf of Parias ('Gulf of the Whale'), he examined the northern shore-line, sending a party ashore to take formal possession of the new land. Owing to illness—he was complaining about his eyes—he did not accompany them, and so missed the opportunity of being among the first to land on South American shores. Still harping on the necessity of getting the stores to Hispaniola and proposing to send back Bartholomew to continue the discovery, he made a hazardous passage through the northern exit from the gulf. He feelingly recorded the experience: 'Reaching the said mouth at the hour of terce, he found a great contest between the fresh water seeking an exit to the sea and the salt water of the sea seeking an entrance into the Gulf: and it was so furious and violent that it raised a great tidal bore with a very high crest, and with this the two waters raised from east to west a noise and a thundering, very great and terrifying, with a wave, succeeded by four other waves, one after the other, with conflicting currents. Then they thought they would perish no less than in the Boca de la Sierpe off Cabo del Arenal as they were entering the Gulf. But the peril was now doubly what the other had been, for the wind which they hoped to carry them out died down, and they would have anchored, which would have given some relief, though not without danger on account of the conflict of the waters; but they could not hit bottom, for the sea was very deep at that point. When the wind fell they feared lest the fresh water or the salt cast them on the rocks by their currents, and there they would have no hope. It pleased the goodness of God that from that very danger sprang safety and liberation, for the same fresh water, overcoming the salt, swept the vessels out without a scratch.'

Believing the northern shores of the Gulf were an island, he turned westwards to ascertain the source of so great a flood of water, and whether in fact it had its origin in rivers as his men asserted. In his opinion they were wrong for 'he knew that neither the Ganges, nor the Euphrates nor the Nile carried so much fresh water'. He then goes on to write that he had not seen lands large enough to supply rivers of this size—unless the land were continental. This seems to be the germ of his idea that he was approaching the terrestrial Paradise, set by the early Christian Fathers in the East, where four great rivers welled up and flowed on their separate courses through the world. This notion also chimed in with his belief that the meridian of Dominica was 'the beginning of the East'. Search failed to resolve this problem, and his mind then turned to the possibility that, after all, this 'river' must flow through continental land, and from this to another, even more exciting thought—the land he was coasting was not part of the Asian continent. He had found 'another world'. But even this prospect was not sufficiently alluring to detain him longer. At this point, worn out with his exertions, lack of sleep, and his affliction of the eyes, he took to his bed again. Lacking his supervision, their course, he writes, departed from the land northwards sooner than he had intended. The *Journal* as edited by Las Casas is full of other excuses for discontinuing exploration and sailing to Hispaniola. Whatever the truth of the matter, the final landfall was made on the islet of Alto Vela, midway along the south coast of Hispaniola.

On arrival in Santo Domingo, the Admiral's first action was to compromise with a rebellion which had broken out shortly before. The leader was Francisco Roldan, the chief justice in criminal affairs, who, ironically, had been picked out for promotion by Columbus. He had proved a thorn in the flesh of Bartholomew, for he had denied the Admiral's right to delegate powers to his brother without reference to the Crown, having aspirations to the command himself. Columbus's excuse for giving way in this pusillanimous fashion was that Roldan had unexpectedly received recruits from the supply ships which had missed their way. No doubt, also, his reception in Spain had taught him to avoid offending the royalist faction. Roldan, for his part, was equally unwilling to come to blows. After an angry quarrel, his followers were allowed to settle in some of the best areas of the Cibao, a concession which foreshadowed the introduction of the *repartimiento* system. What eventually happened to Roldan is obscure: there were reports that he was drowned at sea on the return to Spain, but others suggest that he was later indicted in the courts for his behaviour in Hispaniola.

The chief rebel had now been removed, and the Admiral could give his energies to his last effort to put the economy on a sounder footing. In his predicament, despite the disapproval expressed by the Sovereigns, he turned to organizing the slave trade on a commercial basis. All pretence that it was for the good of their souls, or that they were cannibals and therefore deserving of their fate, was abandoned; contracts were made with the captains of returning ships, and the simple, timorous people were ruthlessly crowded into the holds. With his usual unbalanced burst of optimism, and contending that there was a large unsatisfied market for them not only in Spain but also in the Mediterranean countries, he calculated a financial return which would bring a handsome revenue to the Crown and at the same time put the island régime on a sound footing. To Bishop Las Casas, ardent supporter though he was, this treatment of human beings as so many items in a business account was a source of great distress in retrospect, and one destined to bring little profit to the Admiral.

In another sphere of government, also, Columbus initiated a policy which had far-reaching effects. All attempts, half-hearted as they were, to establish small-holders on the land who would make the colony self-supporting in food-stuffs had failed, not because the country was infertile or inhospitable, the contrary was the case, but because the Spaniards had no intention of giving up the prospects of a quick fortune in exchange for a life of hard labour. Individuals were therefore allowed to take up private holdings of land, as the Roldan party had done, and with the land went the native people already living on it. This system soon evolved into the grant, not merely of a specific area, but of a particular Indian chief and his community, who were thereby put at the unfettered disposal of the grantee, whom they sustained by their labour. Thus in the long run the officials and gentry had triumphed at the expense both of the central authority and the native peoples. In place of a bureaucracy administering the tribute system for the benefit of the Crown, and incidentally of Columbus and his family, there grew up a property-holding oligarchy with absolute rights over their labourers, a subtle blend of feudalism and slavery. This system of *repartimiento*, later known as *encomiendas*, was to become for centuries the basis of Spanish rule in the Americas. Those who were not fortunate enough to obtain such grants clearly demonstrated their lack of faith in the island's future when in 1499 three hundred took advantage of the offer of a free passage home.

These innovations did little to improve the immediate condition of the island. The *repartimiento* system tended to limit the number of slaves available for export, while the revenue from the gold tribute, such as it was, tended to dwindle away. Stability was ultimately achieved only with the introduction of cash crops such as sugar and cotton. The terrible decline in the native population, whose traditional way of life had been ruthlessly obliterated, brought about a scarcity of labour, and this in turn led first to slaving raids on the neighbouring islands and finally to the import of slaves from South America and Africa. Thus in seven years a living culture, in balance with its environment and satisfying the needs of its members, had been replaced by a harsh and wasteful alien rule.

Columbus, however, was not to witness the full effects of this policy. Though he was maintaining a certain order in Hispaniola—his son claimed that a Christian could travel through the island unmolested—the authorities at home had lost faith in his abilities and credibility. It appeared to many that he had not reached the Indies; his promises of great wealth in precious metals and spices were unfulfilled; the demands on the royal treasury were insatiable at a time of financial strain; complaints by returning officials about his administration were loud and venomous; and Queen Isabella was disturbed by the growing traffic in slaves, and angered by his disregard of their instructions to treat the native peoples humanely. To crown everything, the Admiral was obviously in poor condition physically and mentally, increasingly given to putting the blame for the state of Hispaniola on those around him, and conducting himself in the profound conviction that his mission was divinely inspired and assisted by miraculous interventions. His utterances grew more and more self-centred and fantastical, even appearing at times to threaten the Sovereigns with divine punishment: 'God our lord who knows well my intention and the truth of everything will save me as

He has until now, because until this day there is no person of malice toward me whom He has not castigated.'

No government worthy of the name, faced with this disastrous trend to anarchy, could refrain from action, despite the Capitulations, and at this juncture the first step could only be the supersession of the Admiral in favour of a more reliable officer. For this task, requiring firmness and tact, the Sovereigns chose Francisco de Bobadilla, a trusted courtier with a good record in their service. He was accordingly sent out with instructions to hold an enquiry into the state of Hispaniola, to relieve the Admiral of his post, and to assume office himself.

Bobadilla acted decisively but precipitately, in a manner calculated to shatter Columbus's self-confidence. When he arrived in Santo Domingo, the first thing to catch his eye was the bodies of two Spaniards hanging from the gallows, and he soon learnt that five had recently been hanged and another five were awaiting execution. He looked no further for evidence of the Admiral's iniquities. The following day he assumed full powers without communicating with Columbus and won over the support of the settlers by making up arrears of pay and suspending the levy on gold. The ineffectual Diego, in charge at Santo Domingo while his brothers were hunting rebels, was promptly arrested, while—rendering all understanding with Columbus impossible—Bobadilla declared that the three brothers were to be sent back to Spain in chains. Columbus at first could not believe that his Sovereigns would countenance such humiliating treatment, but this hope was dashed when it was made clear that the envoy's credentials were unimpeachable. Resolving to temporize until he could get word home to Spain, he attempted to negotiate with his successor. Events moved too fast for him, however; he was arrested and placed in chains on board a ship for Spain. The same treatment was suffered by Bartholomew, who on his brother's advice had also submitted to Bobadilla's authority. Within weeks the three prisoners were on their way across the Atlantic.

This action has earned Bobadilla universal condemnation. Certainly his conduct was hasty and unnecessarily offensive—the culmination of the long feud between the Aragonese and Castilian nobility and the Genoese bourgeois, brought to a head by the provocative display on the gallows. The arrest of Bartholomew and Diego without preliminary investigation was also an arbitrary proceeding, since theoretically they were simply obeying the Admiral's orders. From the manner in which the Sovereigns received the brothers it is none the less clear that they regarded Bobadilla as being at fault only for the manner in which he had carried out their instructions. However, the thought of the Discoverer of the Indies returning to Europe in chains was too sentimental an incident for the romantic historians of the nineteenth century to neglect, hence the abuse heaped upon Bobadilla; for Columbus the unforgivable insult was his supersession without warning, and for this the ultimate responsibility rested on King Ferdinand. It was he, with his moves to repudiate the Capitulations, who ensured that Columbus's last years were lonely and unhappy, though to do the King justice he saw to it that his personal position, together with his possessions confiscated by Bobadilla, were restored to him, and there was never any intention that the trial anticipated by the latter would be initiated.

Columbus's own views on his fall from favour are set out in the wordy and confused *Letter* which he addressed to his friend, the governess of Prince Juan. He reiterated that he himself had asked for a royal enquiry, but had waited in vain, until this bombshell had burst upon him. His deeds had been accomplished with the help of Our Lord and the Queen against great odds and in the face of petty, ignorant and malicious opposition—and for what reward? 'My reputation is such that though I were to build churches and hospitals, they would always be "lairs for brigands".' Then, recollecting that these offences had been committed with the royal authority, he indulged in abject self-criticism. He had fallen into error through ignorance and force of circumstances; but, given time and the support of his Sovereigns, all would yet be well and gold would flow into the royal treasury. Above all, he pleaded to be judged as a knight (*caballero*) in the high tradition, pursuing a great ideal in the service of God and King through years of danger and loneliness, not as a dull governor of a petty province or as a man of letters befuddled by much study.

There was an ironical twist to this tragedy which he savoured maliciously and from which he drew appropriate conclusions. When he was lying off Santo Domingo at the outset of his last exploration, the coast was ravaged by a great storm which virtually destroyed a sizeable fleet assembled for the return to Spain. Columbus and his ships weathered it, but among the many who lost their lives was the governor, Francisco de Bobadilla.

Chapter IX

THE ADMIRAL'S LAST THROW

IT was generally considered in Spain that Bobadilla had exceeded his instructions in humiliating the Admiral. Accordingly, on his arrival, he was released from confinement on the order of Queen Isabella and received honourable treatment at the Court. Instructions were also given that whatever had been improperly taken away from him was to be restored, but the negotiations were complicated, and the Admiral failed in the end to obtain what he considered to be complete satisfaction. Mocked and derided by those with bitter memories, he saw all hope of returning as Viceroy gradually fade, until he had the final mortification of seeing Nicholas de Ovando appointed in his place and about to sail with thirty vessels, the largest fleet which up till then had left for the West. Nevertheless, if the spoils of office were not for him, he still clung obstinately to his fixed idea, importuning the Sovereigns for permission to make one more voyage before he was too old and infirm. During four years of pleading, exhortation, complaint and argument, the royal authority was withheld, until changes in the international situation alerted the Crown to the thought that the Admiral could perform one more useful service.

It had become apparent that Portugal was about to reap the rewards for which she had striven so persistently and so courageously. In 1496, a fleet under Vasco da Gama circumnavigated the Cape of Good Hope and, crossing the Indian Ocean with the aid of an Arab pilot, had reached the south Indian port of Calicut, loaded a valuable cargo of the highly prized pepper and other spices, and returned safely to Lisbon. There was no delay in pushing the advantage home. In 1500, Cabral took another fleet to the East, touching *en route* the north-east promontory of South America, to be followed by da Gama once again, and then by Albuquerque, the great Viceroy who firmly established Portuguese control with a base at Cochin. There was, therefore, no doubt that the true Indies would be reached by sailing south and east, and that the threat which had hung over

Venice and other Italian merchant states had materialized. As for Spain, unless some drastic and decisive operation were mounted, she had no choice but to recognize that in the race for the wealth of the Indies she had been defeated by her rival. A possible solution was to accede to the importunities of the Admiral and allow him to stake all on one more venture to reach the coveted goal. Columbus, eagerly grasping this last chance to vindicate his contentions, required no second bidding.

The instructions he received envisaged the exciting possibility that the Portuguese and Spanish fleets might meet in East Indian waters, and the Admiral was accordingly provided with a passport, addressed not to that shadowy potentate, the Great Khan, but to Vasco da Gama himself: 'We send you [Columbus] herewith our letter which you have requested for his Captain [da Gama], in which we inform him of your voyage to the west, as we have been informed of his voyage to the east. If you should meet at sea, you should treat each other as friends, as is proper between Captains and subjects of Kings bound together by such kinship, love and affection.' Columbus was also given permission to recruit two men who could speak Arabic, another sign that he was still hoping to contact traders in the Indian seas, though in fact no such men could be found to accompany him. As to the controversial matters concerning his finances which he had raised, he must cease worrying about them, leave his son in charge of negotiations and, most emphatically, embark on his voyage at once.

The more specific instructions accompanying this letter, establishing the procedure to be followed, show the influence of Portugal's triumph. He was to draw up a detailed and accurate account of all the gold, silver, pearls, spices and other products which he might obtain, to be certified by the royal notary assigned to the expedition, and all members of the crews were to make similar declarations. These products were to be handed over to Francisco de Porras, who was sailing as captain of the *Santiago de Palos*, in the presence of a notary, and stringent precautions must be taken against smuggling. Evidently the Sovereigns were not prepared to leave Columbus as free a hand as he had once had, and, very significantly, they stipulated that there must be no recriminations or disputes on the return—no more charges and counter-charges, appeals and demands from the Admiral or his discontented companions.

The character of the ships' companies testifies at once to the magnitude of the effort which the Admiral was contemplating and the importance attached to it. He gathered round him many of those who had served earlier with him, among them Pedro de Terrenos, captain of the *Gallega*, the only man other than the Admiral definitely known to have sailed on all four voyages, who had begun as his servant; Juan Quintero, who had certainly been on two, and possibly all three, earlier expeditions, and Pero Fernandes Coronel, who sailed as a 'gentleman' but had been a captain on two previous voyages. Then on the *Capitana* he had a strong team of navigators, Diego Tristan as captain, Ambrosio Sanches as master and Juan Sanches, his brother, as chief pilot of the fleet. He was also supported and comforted by two members of his own family, his right-hand man and brother Bartholomew, and his young son Ferdinand, aged thirteen, who was later to record many vivid recollections of those dangerous and frustrating, yet thrilling, years. Equally significant was the presence of several fellow-countrymen, the most prominent of whom was a remarkable Genoese patrician, Bartolomeo Fieschi. This man went as captain of the *Viscayo*, survived the voyage, had an exciting career in the service of the Genoese Republic, which conferred on him the title of 'Father of the Commune', and was a witness to the Admiral's will. Rumours circulating at this time, to the effect that Columbus had been endeavouring to 'sell' his discoveries to his native city, had no doubt arisen from the fact that Genoese bankers were once more assisting with the finances, and that Fieschi had been given this important post. Finally there was one representative of the Church only, Friar Alexander, a sufficient comment on the decline of the missionary spirit.

The royal instructions gave no detailed indication of the objective. The voyage would be long, and Columbus would take a direct course for 'the islands and mainland which are in the Indies which belong to us' (those west of the line of demarcation). However, what was in everyone's mind was the arrival of the Portuguese in India proper, and this must be countered at all cost. That Columbus should contemplate a voyage of circumnavigation, after all his untoward experiences in the Caribbean, appears to us, looking back nearly five centuries later, and knowing the true distance which separated him from the East Indian Archipelago, to verge on the preposterous; but to the Admiral, with his exaggerated notion of his progress westwards in longitude, it was, with divine assistance, to be the climax of his life's work.

More specifically, at intervals during the course of the voyage he declared his belief in the existence of a 'strait' in the west through which he might enter the Sea of India. This belief does not imply that what he hoped to find was a sixteenth-century equivalent of the Panama Canal, that is, a passage through a great continental mass. The concept that the western limit of the Atlantic Ocean was a continuous coastline extending from near the Arctic Pole across the Equator towards the Antarctic Pole had not yet been clearly formulated. Nothing was yet known of the North American continent south of Newfoundland, for no one had explored the whole coast of northern Cuba or sighted the peninsula of Florida. It is sometimes asserted that the celebrated Portuguese pilot, Duarte Pacheco Pereira, in his manuscript manual of hydrography and geography entitled *Esmeraldo de situ orbis*, implied that this coastline was continuous, but there is no contemporary evidence of any kind which corroborates or lends support to his ambiguous statement. The passage reads: 'Therefore most fortunate Prince [King Manuel of Portugal] we have known and seen how in the third year of your reign in the year of Our Lord 1498, in which your Highness ordered us to discover the western region, a very large land-mass with many large islands adjacent, extending 70 degrees north of the Equator, and located beyond the greatness of the Ocean, has been discovered and navigated. This distant land is densely populated and extends $28\frac{1}{2}$ degrees on the other side of the Equator towards the Antarctic Pole. Such is its greatness and length that on either side its end has not been seen or known, so that it is certain that it goes round the whole globe.'

Certain points emphasize the difficulty of accepting this statement as it stands. Fourteen hundred and ninety-eight is the year of Vasco da Gama's voyage to southern India and, on the face of it, Portugal would be exceedingly unlikely to have mounted simultaneously a second expedition of the size suggested by Pacheco Pereira. Secondly, Gonçalo Coelho and Fernão de Noronha sailed in 1501 and 1502 southwards along the South American coast to approximately the point mentioned by Pacheco Pereira ($28\frac{1}{2}$ degrees south). This is probably one of the voyages he had in mind; the other was undoubtedly the Corte Real voyages of 1500 and 1502 along the coasts of far north-eastern America. That the huge distance between these two fields of exploration were joined by a continuous coastline was at that time purely a conjecture, but a conjecture that had been made before Pacheco Pereira wrote his version. This is seen in a report from Pietro Pasqualigo, a Venetian official in Lisbon, to the Seignory dated 1501, in which he commented: 'The people of the caravels believe that the above land [Labrador] is the mainland and that it joins the other land that in the previous year was discovered to the north by another caravel of His Majesty. But they were not able to reach it because the sea was frozen over with vast quantities of snow like mountains on the land. They also think that it is joined to the Antilles which were discovered by the Sovereigns of Spain and with the land of Papagia [Brazil] lately discovered by the ship of this King [Manuel] when on its way to Calicut. This belief is caused, in the first place, because having coasted along the said land for a distance of 600 miles and more, they did not come to any termination, also because the report of the discovery of many very large rivers which fall into the sea . . .' In another letter he reports that this land is very populous. This is the basis of Pacheco Pereira's report, which had nothing to do with a voyage in 1498.

The mention of this year, however, prompts another thought: it was widely believed at the time that the Corte Real and Cabot discoveries were made on the north-east coast of Asia, and it is therefore possible that the coastline referred to is the Asian, not the American. If the Ruysch map is consulted, it will be seen that the north-eastern point of Asia is in 70 degrees north, and that Ceylon to the extreme south is in approximately $28\frac{1}{2}$ degrees south, near enough the positions quoted by Pereira. It may well be, therefore, that two passages are here run into one, and that Pacheco Pereira is referring in one of them to the Portuguese approach to eastern Asia. Since the text of his manual is imperfect at this point, such an interpretation cannot be ruled out. As the earliest date for the composition is 1505, after Columbus had returned from his last exploit, we may say that, although the idea was in the air, there is no reason for assuming that Columbus shared it. The contrary is more likely: from his experiences to date, much of the area through which this postulated coastline ran was an archipelago, and its continuity was not established until fifteen years later.

On his fourth voyage, therefore, Columbus was not looking for a 'proto-Panama Canal' but for a way through to the cluster of islands which contemporary cartographers scattered over the southern ocean, and which the Portuguese were thought to be approaching. At one time he believed he was near Java Major, and near it he could also see on the map Neucara, the home of the dog-headed men. Nevertheless he did not altogether abandon hope that he might also be near his original objective, for among the names in his mind when off the Central American isthmus were Ciamba and Mangi, both of which could also be found on the map.

The first of these objectives was clearly to be sought for in the south-west, where the powerful rush of fresh water possibly from Paradise itself, which had so intrigued him on the third voyage, might provide the final solution of his problems. Since he had been on the coast of Paria, others had explored to the west—incidentally reaping a rich reward in the pearls which had then eluded him—and the first step was clearly to push along this coast westwards. This therefore was his original plan for his last and what he regarded as his greatest expedition.

Landfall, as on his second exploration, was made on the island of Martinique, where the crews went ashore for refreshment. As early as this, he was complaining of their discontent and lack of spirit and of the poor condition of the ships. Despite the explicit orders to the contrary, he decided to sail to Santo Domingo in Hispaniola in the hope of replacing one of them. There, as he might have foreseen, he was forbidden to land, a rebuff which produced one of those outbursts of rage and self-pity now becoming habitual to him. 'What man has been born, not excepting Job himself, who would not have died of despair that in such a storm, for my own safety, and that of my little son and brother and comrades, I should be forbidden to land on that shore which by God's will I had sweated blood to gain for Spain?' He was still cruising in the neighbourhood when the region was swept by the fierce and destructive tornado which caused the loss of the large fleet, loaded with gold for Spain, and the death of Bobadilla himself. Columbus of course saw in the destruction of his enemy the hand of divine justice. Equally true to form, he attributed his own survival to his skill in finding a safe haven, while Bartholomew was commended for saving himself by standing out to sea. The upshot of all this commotion was the abandonment of the proposed southerly course, in favour of one via the north coast of Jamaica. The little fleet was then carried by a great current in the direction of Cuba, to that 'Garden of the Queen' where he had spent memorable days in 1494. As far as regards discovery, therefore, he was almost back to his position of seven years earlier.

At last, course was set for the south-west and the island of Guanacca off the north coast of Honduras was sighted on September 12, 1502. No coherent or complete account of this crossing has survived, for Columbus's *Lettera rarissima* as printed is filled with almost hysterical outbursts, and the number of days and distances are absurdly exaggerated. Of one of the storms which harassed them he declared rhetorically: 'The ship's seams were opened, the sails torn, the anchors, boats and equipment were lost, the crew for the most part sick and all were disheartened, some thinking only of vows and pilgrimages, and confiding in each other doubts as to whether they were confessed, expecting death from hour to hour. Though experiencing many other hazards, none were so long and so tumultuous. The most experienced seamen amongst us lost heart.' He was also anxious about his brother who was in an even more unseaworthy ship. He himself was sick, many times at the point of death, he said, and was obliged to direct the ship from a little cabin set up on the poop. Both Ferdinand Columbus and Porras are silent about this storm, so that it is possible that Columbus was really describing the great tornado off Santo Domingo.

While they were among these islands, an incident occurred which, unappreciated by the participants at the time, stands out as another critical turning-point in Columbus's career. On proceeding to examine one of the islands more closely, Bartholomew Columbus discovered a party of thirty or more Indians in an unusually long canoe, hollowed out of a single tree-trunk and eight feet in breadth. In the centre was a canopy of palm leaves, resembling that of a Venetian gondola, and below it, securely protected from the rain and other hazards, were the women and children surrounded by a great quantity of varied merchandise. The crew being too dispirited to flee or fight off the Spanish boats, the great canoe was conducted to the flagship, where to the delight of the Admiral the wide range of its cargo was revealed; declaring that, without any labour or danger to themselves, God had revealed to them the products of the country at one view, he ordered that all that was rare or costly be transferred to his ship. Among the goods, Ferdinand relates, were shirts and coats in divers colours, cloths with which they covered their private parts, and cloaks after the style of the Moors of Granada and similar to those worn by the native crew, hatchets for woodcutting, copper bells and crucibles for smelting. But what particularly engaged Ferdinand's interest were some long wooden laths with grooves on two sides into which pieces of sharp, finely polished stone were bound—weapons, he declared, which would cut through a naked man like steel. Plainly this was a boat engaged in trading the produce of a more sophisticated culture than that of the Arawak islanders.

For years Columbus had been anticipating the moment when he would sight the richly-laden merchant ships plying between Zaiton

and the islands of the East. At this moment, off a coast almost on the
exact parallel of latitude which he had forecast, he had encountered,
not a great Chinese junk, certainly, but signs of a commercial system
on a not inconsiderable scale. Indeed there was also evidence,
in the quantities of small beans which the merchant carried, of a
system of currency. He made, however, no enquiries into the trade
route he had intercepted, nor into the seat of the civilization to which
it led. Thus the way to the Maya cultural area of Yucatan and perhaps even to the Aztec civilization—to the wealth of gold for which
he had longed—escaped him; the chief merchant was taken aboard
as a guide, and the fleet sailed on in search of the non-existent strait
and the elusive treasures of the East. When Ferdinand came to
write up the voyage years later, he was conscious of this lost opportunity, but excused his father on the grounds that he was not to be
diverted from his life-long quest by a side-issue which could be
followed up at any time. Columbus, in fact, obsessed by a fixed idea
which for many observers had been exploded by the hard facts of
geography, had not at that point in his career the strength or supple-
ness of mind to adjust his plans to a sudden opportunity. It was left
to Hernando Cortés, a score of years later, to seize for Spain the
wealth of the Aztec empire.

After this incident among the islands, they followed the coastline
eastwards, landing at one point to take formal possession. They
then reached a cape where they were relieved to find that the coast
began to trend southwards, in token of which they named it Cabo
Gracias à Dios (Thanks be to God). Ferdinand gives a confused com-
mentary on his father's decision then to sail south and east along the
coast in search of 'the strait of the mainland, to open navigation into
the South Sea, which was required in order to discover the Land of
Spices'. Part of the difficulty in following Ferdinand lies in the fact
that he was writing years later when others had explored the area,
and that he uses the later nomenclature. He also confused matters by
arguing that the term 'strait' could be applied to either water or land,
that it could be a channel or an isthmus. There is no reason, however, to suppose that Columbus himself made any such distinction.
The whole argument in the biography is designed to show, in the
light of after-events, that as the Panama isthmus controlled the rich
traffic between the South Sea and the Caribbean, it must be the
'strait' Columbus was seeking and of which he was the true discoverer. In point of fact, the ships were off the present entrance to
the Panama Canal on Christmas Day, 1502. Had the Admiral not

been so obsessed with the thought of a water channel and had understood the Indians, he might have been the first westerner to hear of
the Pacific and to anticipate Balboa.

Nine months were spent sailing up and down the coast of Veragua,
as he learnt the district was called. His furthest point was short of the
Gulf of Darien, for the trend of the coast eastwards was carrying him
away from his objective. Over one-third of this time was spent at
Santa Maria de Belén, where he set up his base for, as he hoped, the
exploitation of the 'gold-mines' of Veragua. Their stay, however,
came with an ace of disaster, partly due to navigational hazards but
mainly because of Indian hostility. The explorers soon recognized
that they were in contact with a new culture area, whose inhabitants
were certainly unlike the gentle Arawaks. The plain truth is that
these pugnacious and courageous people drove out the first wave of
invaders of their country, just as the Britons had driven off Julius
Caesar and his legions at his first attempt. Affairs started unpropi-
tiously when part of a boat's crew was lost in an estuary. Worse
trouble arose from the behaviour of the men, many of whom were of
low reputation and resentful of orders from a foreigner whose conduct was suspect and whose actions in Hispaniola had been repudiated by his Sovereigns. Their discontent, as usual, was further
stimulated by the rigours of a stay in the tropics. Columbus, on his
side, behaved in a manner which showed frustration, vacillation and
loss of confidence in himself. Handicapped also by illness, he fell
into his old habit of blaming his men. The trouble grew as they
raided the Indians for gold and fresh food, and outbreaks of
violence followed. He was able to control them for a time until
conditions deteriorated further, and they took to firing on the
Indians. Another violent tropical storm complete with water-spout
added to their discomfiture. After eight months at sea, all supplies
were running short, the bread was infested with maggots, the ships
had suffered further damage, and the demoralized crews were not
cheered by the sight of sharks following in their wake.

Fairer weather returned when they crossed the bar at the mouth
of the Rio Belén. Supplies of maize, water and wood were obtained,
and morale improved at the sight of gold in small quantities. Columbus in line with his instructions then decided that he had found a site
for the fort he was to set up on any discovery. His plan was to put
his brother Bartholomew in charge of a small garrison while he
returned to Spain with the news, leaving one ship at Belén. What
his brother thought of the idea is not recorded—he had joined the

expedition unwillingly in the first place—but once embarked he acquitted himself resolutely, and accepted the responsibility. The men were less happy, with the tales of the first disastrous failure at La Navidad in their minds, but there was always the chance of a fortune from the 'mines'. Contact had already been made with an Indian village some miles upstream, the chief of which was known to the Spaniards as El Quiban. Plans were accordingly prepared to take a party under the chief's guidance to alluvial gold deposits some distance into the interior. But, before these were completed, another tornado struck with fury, and the ships came near to destruction before they could be moored in safety. Once a measure of security had been restored, Bartholomew set out with a large party to ascend a neighbouring river. After four days' travel up it and through the tropical forest, they reached these 'Mines of Veragua'. They were not in fact mines, but deposits of alluvial gold in the river-bed. The boy Ferdinand recorded: 'In the space of two hours after their arrival each of them had collected gold from around the roots of trees, which are very thick in that country and high as Heaven. The sample of that gold was much esteemed because none of the party carried any tools for digging, nor had they collected gold before. Since the purpose of their journey was merely to get information about the mines, they returned very merry the same day to sleep at Veragua, and the day after to the ships. To tell the truth, these were not the mines of Veragua, which were afterwards ascertained to be much nearer, but the mines of Urira, an enemy people. Since there was war between them and Veragua, the Quiban gave orders that the Christians be guided thither, hoping to get them into trouble, and so leave his country alone.'

This experience, however, had encouraged Bartholomew, for a week later he took another party of sixty men to the Rio Urira, about fifteen miles to the west of Belén. Some distance upstream they were met by a cacique who conducted them to a village, where they received gifts of food and some 'gold mirrors', that is, plaques of gold leaf which the Indians hung round their necks. They were hospitably lodged for the night in a large hut with ample supplies of food, and later visited by the cacique of Urira and his men, bringing more 'mirrours' for barter, and also reports of many caciques in the interior who had quantities of gold and were 'armed like us'. The following day Bartholomew, sending most of his party back, took thirty men and visited two villages where they were received with similar courtesies. In their neighbourhood, 'the land for over six leagues was cultivated with maize, which looked like fields of wheat'. Having gone a considerable distance without finding a suitable site for his settlement he returned to Belén after an absence of nine days. Elated by the gold he had found and by reports of more in the interior, he set about with vigour the construction of a fort on the shore in the shape of a dozen palm-leafed huts with a central store for cannon and munitions. For greater safety wine, food, and fishing equipment were placed in the *Gallega*, moored close by. Columbus for his part prepared to leave, but found that, the flood water having fallen, his ships were shoal-bound in the estuary. All that he could do was to pray for a tropical downpour.

At this critical moment, native politics took a decisive hand. Having failed to embroil the newcomers in strife with his enemies of Urira, the local cacique was increasingly resentful of their presence in his territory and his men were more restless, so much so that the Indian interpreter reported they were planning to fire the huts and slay the Spaniards. Unhappily at this juncture the Admiral committed a grave error of judgement. The intrepid Diego Mendez, who had been appointed to the command of the fort, came forward with a plan to seize the cacique and his counsellors and carry them off to Spain. To this Columbus, neglecting the lessons to be drawn from his experiences in Hispaniola, agreed, with the idea of subjecting the native village to the service of the garrison. Bartholomew had once again to carry out a tough assignment. Behaving with great resolution he personally seized the cacique and sent him with fifty other prisoners and the loot back to the ships under the charge of the reliable Juan Sanches the pilot. In a moment of absent-mindedness, Sanches allowed his prisoners to escape. According to de Porras, the Spaniards also burned down the Indian village. The next day Bartholomew, recognizing the futility of chasing after Indians over the densely forested equatorial hillsides, returned to the ships; Columbus promptly divided the booty, such as it was, among the party and bestowed a gold coronet on his brother in token of his achievements. Now that the river was again in flood, he ordered the ships in which he proposed to sail to Hispaniola to be towed out over the bar. Bidding farewell to his brother, he sent him ashore in the *Capitana*'s barge which, under Diego Tristan's charge, was to refill the water barrels. The Indians, seeing the majority of their enemies about to depart, suddenly threw themselves upon the half-finished settlement. As the boat party scrambled up the beach, they were ambushed by one band and in the mêlée several Spaniards were

wounded. Bartholomew spiritedly rallied his men, though himself
suffering from a spear wound. Simultaneously other bands of Indians
had fired the huts. Despite the uproar, Diego Tristan continued
unperturbed up the river in search of fresh water, until, a league upstream, he and his companions were set upon by a fleet of canoes.
Tristan, living up to the concept of a true knight, continued stoically
to exhort his men to fight on, though wounded several times. But
the Indians were not to be denied, and eventually all the boat's
crew were slain with the exception of one Juan de Noja, who
escaped by swimming underwater. On the shore, the Spaniards,
demoralized by the sudden change of circumstances, and by the
sight of their comrades' dead bodies floating downstream, failed to
reach the ships standing offshore, while the Admiral was unable to
help them. Bartholomew and Mendes then rallied the survivors: a
stockade was hastily built on the beach and with the help of the guns
was held against native attacks for four days.

During these tumultuous days, the Admiral lay at anchor three
miles offshore, helplessly, awaiting a break in the weather. However
he had his own troubles. Several Indian captives, sons and relatives
of the chiefs, succeeded in breaking out of the hold and swimming
ashore. The remainder, frustrated in their attempts, hanged themselves in despair, Ferdinand commenting callously that 'their loss
was no great harm to the ships'.

In this period of hesitation and disillusionment, another knightly
Spaniard came to the rescue when Pedro de Ledesma volunteered
to swim ashore and make contact with the garrison. Beating the
offshore breakers, he reached the stockade, where he was told
roundly that they expected the Admiral to bring them all off. With
this message he swam back to the *Capitana* and the Admiral reluc-
tantly complied with the demand. In after-years Mendes, who,
though no mere boaster, was proud of his deeds and could tell a
good story, liked to relate how he had been the last to leave the
beach and how the Admiral on the deck of the *Capitana* had kissed
him on both cheeks and made him captain of the flagship. So, we
are told, 'rejoicing that we were all together again, we made sail
eastwards up the coast'.

This was the climax of the voyage. The months that followed,
exciting as they were and marked by deeds of bravery as well as
treachery, contributed nothing to exploration. Although he came
within reach of Cape Santa Cruz in southern Cuba, the Admiral
insisted on making for Jamaica. There they were marooned for

several months while the ever-ready Diego Mendes in one canoe, and Fieschi in another, gallantly made the passage back to Hispaniola and secured their ultimate relief after a series of dangerous mutinies instigated mainly by Francisco de Porras. These were quelled by resolute action on Bartholomew's part. So great was the demoralization that de Ledesma, who had acquitted himself courageously at Belén, was among the mutineers. The leader, Porras, was finally placed in chains but when the survivors reached Hispaniola the authorities refused to proceed against him and he was released. The Admiral in fact obtained no support in Santo Domingo and did not delay long before setting out with his brother and son for Spain.

Much may be learnt from the incidents of this last voyage. By the time he had reached Jamaica, Columbus was physically, and perhaps also mentally, unfit for command. It is true that most of his companions were also deteriorating in the unaccustomed environment, though men of the calibre of his brother Bartholomew, de Ledesma, Diego Tristan, Diego Mendes, and Fieschi, in their different ways and animated by the vision of a knightly ideal, had preserved their personal integrity. It was men of their stature who, for better or worse, finally established Spanish rule in America. Sick man though Columbus was at times—by his own account he was often in a high fever—he presented a pitiable figure in these emergencies. From the first landfall in the lesser Antilles until his departure from Santo Domingo he was never in command of events. He had learnt little from, or forgotten much of, his earlier experiences in Hispaniola. Haunted as he must have been with the fate of La Navidad, he could still contemplate leaving another party on a hostile shore while he sailed off with three ships for Hispaniola—not an action to sustain faith in his leadership. The plan to carry off the cacique to Spain destroyed in advance any prospect of survival the shore party might have had. From the second visit to Belén onwards the *de facto* leader was Bartholomew, who was not one to shilly-shally at a crisis, a contrast to his brother of which Ferdinand Columbus, when he came to write his father's biography, was acutely conscious. The relevant section of his narrative was on the face of it an apologia for his father's failure; storms occur at critical moments just a little too conveniently, and he even sees the sending of the watering party ashore at the last moment as an act of divine providence, though what benefit it brought about he does not state; perhaps because it probably saved the lives of the majority of the garrison, though at the expense of several of their comrades.

Columbus's own account, contained in the so-called *Lettera rarissima* which is generally accepted as authentic, harped on this theme. He was still recording hearsay reports that 'there is gold without limit', and made the astonishing statement that 'wherever I had been I found that all that I had heard was true . . . [In Ciguare] the people are clothed and there are horses in the land. They are accustomed to warfare, wear rich clothing, and have fine houses. They tell me too that the sea encompasses Ciguare and that it is a ten days' journey to the Ganges river.' This may have been a faint, garbled rumour of the Aztec and Maya cultures, but was more likely a tale which had reached Honduras concerning the strangers who had invaded Hispaniola. He recited all the old tags from classical and biblical authors and maintained his contention about the length of a degree which for all but himself was thoroughly discredited. The contrast between his aims and his achievements on that 'grim and arduous yet most noble and profitable voyage' was always before him. Many times he had been at the point of death—he does not say whether through disease or tempest. 'At one moment my old wound opened up, and for nine days I gave myself up as lost, without hope of life.'

At the height of the Veragua crisis, during a storm, he orates: 'I was outside [the harbour] very much alone. There was no hope of escape. In this state I climbed painfully to the highest part of the ship and cried out for help with a fearful voice, weeping, to Your Highnesses' war captains in every direction, but none replied. At length, groaning with exhaustion, I fell asleep and heard a compassionate voice saying: "O fool, and slow to believe and serve thy God, the God of every man . . . From thy birth He has ever held thee in special charge. When He saw thee at man's estate, He did marvellously cause thy name to resound over the earth. The Indies, so rich a portion of the world, He gave thee for thine own, and thou hast divided them as it pleased thee. Of those barriers of the open sea, which were closed with such mighty chains, He has given thee the keys . . . The privileges and promises which God bestows He does not revoke, nor doth He say, after having received service, that that was not His intention, and that it is to be understood otherwise. Nor does He mete out suffering to make a show of His might. Whatever He promises He fulfils with interest; that is His way . . . He has now revealed to me a portion of the rewards for so many toils and dangers thou hast borne in the service of others." '

The 'compassionate voice' was certainly expressing dangerous thoughts. It is difficult to understand how Columbus fancied this scarcely veiled attack on the Crown would restore his fortunes. But the tone of the *Lettera* becomes increasingly incoherent. In Cariai sorcerers had sent two young girls, 'no better than whores', to seduce him. No one would ever find Veragua again but himself, no matter how hard sailors and other good-for-nothings might try. Even his pilots were completely out in their reckonings; four hundred leagues in fact ('we were in the vicinity of Mangi, four hundred leagues further west'). This was the old story, but Columbus was unable to abandon it, despite the fact that others were busily extending his discoveries. And then self-pity completely overcomes him: 'Alone, desolate, infirm, daily expecting death, surrounded by a million savages full of cruelty and our enemies, and thus deprived of the Holy Sacraments of Holy Church, how neglected if here I part from the body. Weep for me whoever has charity, truth and justice.' In contrast with the insinuations of the compassionate voice, however, the letter ends on a more diplomatic note. He begs his Sovereigns to pardon him, to restore his losses, and to allow him to make a pilgrimage to Rome. Reading the letter dispassionately, one is almost inclined to exclaim 'an enemy hath done this thing', but that was the state to which the Admiral had been reduced.

In Spain his reception was decidedly lukewarm; Queen Isabella was dead and the 'cold and unfriendly' attitude of King Ferdinand showed only too plainly that as far as he was concerned the Admiral's sun had set. Within seven months of his return, the discoverer of America died at Valladolid, at the age of fifty-five.

The character of Columbus has aroused almost as much debate as have his ideas and achievements. This is in part due to the nature of the evidence available to the biographer. For his life before 1492, except for the Genoese notorial documents, there is little of importance which did not originate at a later date from Columbus himself or members of his family. His critics, on the other hand, found much material in the legal suit which the family brought against the Crown to protect the Privileges. Fortunately, there are documents in the Spanish archives which provide a framework for the period from the granting of the Capitulations in 1492 until the end of his Viceroyalty in 1500. Then, there is a good deal to be learnt from his supporters and opponents at Court. Men like Bishop Fonseca, who controlled the affairs of the Indies, and other high officers of state were engaged in constructing a rigid governmental system, and had little patience with a semi-independent power which disturbed its symmetry. To

King Ferdinand he was simply one weapon to be used when necessary in a series of extensive and complex political manœuvres: up to a point he was ready to back the Admiral but, when it was apparent that his usefulness was failing, he was prepared to put him aside while maintaining a minimum decency of behaviour. To these men the increasing complaints, claims, disputes, and hallucinations were simply an irritating nuisance. It was this attitude rather than his foreign origin which provoked hostility to him in the upper ranks of the hierarchy, but lower in the scale his foreign birth fanned the enmity of the fiercely individualistic Spaniards and the disillusioned adventurers. The recurrent gossip that he might sell out to a rival power added venom to their attacks. Against this opposition he had the support of the Queen and a section of the Church, noticeably the friars imbued with the missionary spirit, and of his countrymen who were prepared to back the enterprise financially.

In all the controversies which have arisen, what Columbus actually achieved is almost forgotten in the turmoil. Stating it in as general terms as possible, he had attained the position of Viceroy of the first considerable Spanish possession overseas and the first permanent European settlement in the New World, and had held it for seven years from 1493 to 1500. He achieved this through inspiring and successfully conducting the first crossing of the Atlantic which is indisputably authenticated (apart from the Viking episode in the north). The effect of this on world affairs was incalculable: in one field alone he triggered off a wave of exploration which within the remarkably short period of thirty years revealed the contours of a second hemisphere. Whether or not he was preceded by a skipper who caught a fleeting glimpse of some mainland or island in the far west is, beside the immensity of this achievement, a matter of little weight. Undoubtedly he built upon the advances of others, the practical seamanship of the Portuguese and Spaniards, the missionary yearnings of the Queen and the friars, and the merchant system of the Italians. But such conjunctions are common in all great historical movements, and there is little point in arguing that, if Columbus had not succeeded in 1492, some other leader would have done so within a decade at most. The plain fact is that Columbus, a Genoese in the service of Spain, reached tropical America in 1492—and from that landfall a certain course of events flowed.

It is perhaps only natural that later generations, impressed by the magnitude of his exploits, should have pictured him as a man of genius, devoted to high ideals, and of a blameless character, an attitude which has led to many misconceptions. He was certainly not a scholar in any strict sense of the word, nor were his intellectual powers conspicuous in relation to the giants of the Renaissance. He drew support for his grand design from the out-dated medieval cosmography, rejecting the more accurate observations of contemporary navigators. Even the plan for a voyage to the west had been formulated in principle at least fifty years earlier. He had acquired some knowledge of astronomy but put it to little practical use—he scarcely ever made an accurate observation for latitude and his calculations for longitude were laughable. He protested too much about his powers as a navigator and seamanship for all his claims to be accepted at face value. Undoubtedly he had picked up a certain amount of experience on his voyages, but he was essentially a commander of a maritime expedition, and in his day that office did not demand a thorough knowledge of seamanship, any more, or less, than it necessarily required a profound knowledge of the art of war. The commander's rôle was to command, and in carrying out that duty he might call upon the experts available, including the pilots.

It was through the lack of the ultimate sanction of power that Columbus finally came to grief, though the difficulty of his position must be recognized. In Hispaniola he could maintain control only if he was backed by appropriate military force, bound to him by strong ties of personal loyalty. This he never possessed after the first exciting days, when the individualistic Spaniards revolted against the control of a foreigner and the home government lost faith in him. His decline was greatly accelerated by the dejection into which the failure to find great quantities of gold in Cibao threw him. From that moment, his complaints against fortune grew shriller as his claims grew wilder and more confused; at moments of crisis he was hesitant, uttered veiled threats, blamed others—and relied more and more upon his brother Bartholomew to maintain control.

To what then is his success to be attributed? In the first place he had the acumen to perceive, while on the 'new frontier', that a great field of opportunity lay beyond, as the Portuguese had found to their profit. Once he had grasped that fact he pursued it with astonishing persistence, supported by great powers of persuasion, and a keen sense of business. (The image of the Discoverer in chains has so seized the general imagination that it is often overlooked that he died a wealthy man.) In time the conviction grew upon him that his mission was divinely directed and he himself was an instrument of God's will. So, as his fortunes declined, he began to exhibit the reverse side of this character, particularly in the development of a persecution mania, and the constant complaints of ill-health. All these characteristics have laid him open to attack by critics, often moved by nationalistic feelings, though in many ways as much harm has been done to his reputation by enthusiastic defenders.

But judged only against his own high aspirations could he be regarded as a failure. Early in his career he had understood the implications of the sphericity of the globe and had applied these with great persistence to the furtherance of his plans for aggrandizement. With considerable astuteness he had perceived 'the way things were going' in the contemporary world and had turned them to his own advantage. What is really astonishing, and instructive in his character, is that against all the odds and in the savage rough and tumble of fifteenth-century Spanish politics he succeeded up to a point in holding his own and bringing to a conclusion an enterprise founded largely on ideas of an age that was past. He could not have accomplished this without great self-confidence, obstinacy, and the conviction that he was an agent of the divine will. If he was not a great seaman, a first-class scientific mind, or a born leader of men, he was something much more remarkable, a man apparently lacking all the necessary requirements for success in his time—birth, rank, wealth, formal education—who yet conceived and carried out an enterprise which led Europe into a new and challenging world. He remains an extraordinary man who accomplished extraordinary things.

Chapter X

THE NEW WORLD OF AMERIGO VESPUCCI

IN THE course of his four voyages between 1492 and 1504, Columbus had discovered and explored Hispaniola, Jamaica, the eastern half of Cuba, Trinidad and the adjacent coast of South America, and the eastern coast of Central America from Honduras to Panama. These four areas are widely scattered around the Caribbean; nevertheless he made no sustained attempt to ascertain their relationship to each other. Indeed he appears to have deliberately refrained from doing so. When on the northern and southern coasts of Cuba he turned back without proving beyond all doubt his contention that it was not insular but continental land; after discovering Trinidad and exploring the Gulf of Parias, he left hurriedly for Hispaniola, and on the last voyage, though ostensibly looking for a passage to the west, he did not ascertain whether the coast of Veragua was continuous with that of Parias. On each occasion he considered that there were sufficient local difficulties to make him call off the voyage. Looking at his procedure as a whole, however, there is a pattern in the succession of these voyages: his first important discovery, Hispaniola, was in the east; he then tried the north, Cuba; this is followed by a probe to the south, Trinidad, and finally he goes west to explore Veragua for a possible strait. Though he never explicitly admitted it, the results as they unrolled led to the deduction that these new lands were not 'the Indies'. The plan for the fourth voyage was almost a tacit admission of this and an attempt to break out to the west towards the Islands of Spices. He never definitely reached the conclusion that he was in a 'new world' in the sense that he had found a hitherto unknown land-mass of continental proportions quite separate from Asia. He thought rather that he was in a 'new heaven and a new world' in which the natural laws of the old world did not hold invariably. Whenever he had sailed three hundred leagues west of the Canary Islands, this sense of other-worldliness would overcome him. The compass needles behaved so oddly; a great river of fresh water would appear without any apparent explanation; the ports of Cathay were never found on their proper parallels at the estimated distance: surely the surface of the hemisphere must be pear-shaped or like a woman's nipple. But whatever all this added up to, it was not Cathay—he must still seek a 'strait' to the west.

It could only be a matter of time, however, before others filled up these gaps in the coastline, with or without his sanction, and so revealed the true picture. As early as 1495, the Spanish Crown had begun to ease restrictions on voyages made independently of Columbus, and by the close of the century a new wave of exploration had set in. The Sovereigns were stimulated to renewed search for a westward route to the Indies by the success which was attending Portugal's efforts and by a disinclination to leave this task to the Admiral, whose powers were only too obviously failing. This increased activity revealed the indisputable existence of a New World at no great distance from the Old, and it is one of the ironies of history that Amerigo Vespucci, the man who publicized this news, should have his name attached to the continent which, whatever he believed it to be, was Columbus's discovery.

Vespucci's background and interests were similar to those of Columbus, and indeed of Cabot. All three were Italians who spent part of their career in Spain. Each was associated in some degree with an Italian merchant state—Columbus with Genoa, Cabot with Venice, and Vespucci with Florence—and each had engaged in mercantile affairs. Not one of them was a trained practical seaman but each had acquired an extensive though sometimes superficial knowledge of cosmography and a smattering of general astronomy. It is noteworthy also that all were skilled, or became skilled, in constructing charts. These resemblances, however, do not place them all on one level. It was one thing to conceive and persist in a plan to reach the Indies by the western route, but quite another to consort with overseas explorers *after* the Discovery and strive to carve out a career in the new phase of European expansion. After Columbus's triumphant return in 1493, his news had a particular interest for those with some knowledge of affairs and of 'the secrets of the world', and possessing a spirit of enquiry. These might hope, along with Spanish grandees and the ubiquitous Italian bankers, to win wealth, and even fame, overseas. In the following century controversy inevitably arose as to their respective contributions to the march of knowledge. The Spanish Crown denigrated Columbus, and gave some support to possible rivals such as the Pinzons and Vespucci; the supporters of

Columbus, prominent among whom was Bishop Las Casas, retaliated by attacking Vespucci and magnifying the achievements of the Admiral; while the Portuguese historians endeavoured to build up their own navigators at his expense, some going so far as to laud the unlikely claims of the German Martin Behaim. So the controversy developed, producing confusion and uncertainty for the historian. To add to all this, Martin Waldseemüller, the German geographer, seduced by Vespucci's rhetoric, firmly fixed the name 'America' on the world map.

Yet the path by which Amerigo Vespucci acquired his reputation is not difficult to follow. Born in Florence in 1454 of a family of standing, he received—what Columbus lacked—a humane education from an uncle, as is reflected in the classical quotations and allusions scattered through his writings. As a young man he attended his uncle as secretary on a mission to the Court of France, and shortly afterwards joined a branch of the great Medici banking family. Early in the *annus mirabilis* of 1492 he was working for them in Seville, as assistant to Gianoto Berardi who had had some connection with Columbus at an earlier date. It is also possible that he witnessed the Admiral's return to Seville *en route* for Barcelona and the royal Court in the following year. In the ensuing years he was in an exceptional position to keep abreast of events in the Indies, for his superior, Berardi, was engaged in fitting out a series of relief ships for Hispaniola, work which brought the two men into contact with Fonseca, the director of Indian affairs, who disliked Columbus intensely, and other important officials. Though Vespucci succeeded to Berardi's post on the latter's death, his affairs, according to his own account, were not in a prosperous state, so that he gladly accepted an invitation from Fonseca to take part in one of the 'free' voyages to the Indies. The account of this venture, attributed to Vespucci himself, places the voyage in the year 1497, but does not mention the name of the captain or any other participant; nor does it contain sufficient data to enable the route to be fixed with precision. The most generous interpretation takes him right round the shores of the Caribbean from Costa Rica to Florida and thence to Bermuda. This is difficult to reconcile with the contemporary limit of exploration (Columbus for instance was not in the Costa Rica area until five years later) and a voyage of this extent is not supported by the La Cosa chart. Either there is an error in the date, or the account was written up later by a panegyrist.

There is, however, no doubt about Vespucci's 'second' voyage,

1499 to 1500, for it is supported by the independent statements of his companions. These formed a remarkable group, which suggests that Spain attached much importance to this voyage, and those in charge were in many ways the pick of the Spanish experts. The leader was the indefatigable and daring Hojeda, a considerable thorn in Columbus's side—he was indeed later accused of having stolen the Admiral's chart of the third voyage for this venture, but it seems that Fonseca regarded such material as Crown property and made it generally available. With him was Bartolomeo Roldan, the expert pilot of the first voyage, and Juan de la Cosa the map-maker, who had been on the first two Columban voyages. On this high-powered staff Vespucci's position was seemingly that of cosmographer and commercial adviser, perhaps with the duty of drawing up a report on the peoples and natural resources of any lands discovered.

After a crossing of forty-four days from the Cape Verde Islands, land was sighted in 5° south latitude on what is now the coast of Brazil near Cape San Roque. It was a well-watered land of huge rivers and very verdant, with great trees. The expedition made numerous attempts to work up the rivers, but 'owing to the great floods which the rivers carried down, in spite of all our efforts we could find no spot which was not flooded with water'. At the outset they sailed south-eastwards along the coast for some forty leagues, against a strong ocean current. Since progress was slow, they agreed to put about and examine the coast northwards, eventually reaching Trinidad, the Gulf of Parias, and the Coast of Pearls to the west. At various points, they made efforts to establish contact with the natives, at first without great success; but in the Parias region the people were more friendly. From them they learned of the methods of pearl-fishing and the great quantities to be found further on, and the customary tales of the depredations of the 'Cannibles'. As the voyage was nearing its end, some less conventional incidents occurred. On one island they found 'the most bestial and most ugly people that were ever seen, and also the most lovable and kind'. Vespucci then goes on to describe the practice of coca chewing in some detail: 'They were very ugly of demeanour and countenance, and all had their cheeks stuffed out inside with a green grass which they continually chewed like cattle, so that they could scarcely speak: and each had around his neck two dried gourds, one of which was filled with that grass which they had in their mouths, and the other with a white flour which seemed like powdered chalk, and from time to time they would dip into the flour gourd a splinter which they would keep

PORTUGUESE CARRACKS

The painting by Cornelis Anthoniszoon, c. 1521.

THE ENGLISH REACH VIRGINIA, 1585

Engraving by T. de Bry from a drawing by John White, a member of the expedition. 'Roanoke' was at the northern end of Pamlico Sound, and Trinity Harbour near the modern Wanchese.

moistening in the mouth; then they would insert it into their mouths, powdering the grass therein. Astonished at such a thing, we could not guess this secret, nor for what purpose they did so.'

On a neighbouring island, after landing for fresh water, they were walking along the beach when they saw 'human footprints of huge size in the sand and judged that if the other limbs corresponded to that measure, they must be very large men'. Reasoning that, as the island was small, it could not carry a large population, Vespucci and eight companions set off to investigate. One league inland, in a small group of huts, they came on five women of astonishing stature, who received them hospitably. The party then planned to carry off three of the younger women as curiosities. They were disconcerted however by the arrival of some thirty men, even taller than the women and well-built, with enormous bows and arrows and great knobbed clubs. The explorers then decided the wisest plan was to slip away secretly. They failed to elude the giants, who followed them at a distance to the ships, chattering continually. As the visitors were re-embarking, the crowd rushed forward shooting off their arrows. Greatly relieved to be aboard, the explorers fired off two mortars to frighten them; this had the desired effect and the giants fled inland. The Island of Giants, identified as Curaçao, duly appeared on La Cosa's chart.

Shortly after this incident the expedition encountered a people who received them with great kindness, and from whom they obtained by barter a large quantity of pearls. According to his own account Vespucci came into possession of one oyster which contained 130 pearls, and he adds that this was taken from him by the Queen but that he hid others for himself. After a stay of six weeks, during which the ships were repaired, they sailed off to Hispaniola. (It is worth noting that Vespucci uses the name Antilia for this island.) Their reception, understandably enough, was not cordial. In Vespucci's words: 'There we suffered many perils and hardships with those selfsame Christians who were in this island with Columbus, out of envy, I think. I refrain from recounting them, to avoid prolixity.' When they arrived in Cadiz after a six weeks' crossing, they were enthusiastically received.

Reports of the wealth of the new land, particularly in pearls, were drawing other skippers to the South American coasts. Shortly after the Hojeda-Vespucci expedition, Vicente Yañez Pinzon left Cadiz with four ships and struck the coast somewhere in the neighbourhood of Hojeda's landfall, about 540 leagues south-west of the Cape

Verde Islands. On the second night, seeing a number of lights flickering along the coast, the commander sent an armed party ashore. They encountered a huge array of people from whom a group of warriors, of great stature and fierce appearance, and armed with bows and spears, advanced menacingly upon the Spaniards. After complete failure to parley with them the landing party withdrew, proposing to return in the morning. But next day no trace could be found of them, and the Spaniards concluded that they were wanderers like the gypsies or Tartars, having no fixed dwellings but living in brushwood shelters.

Some distance along the coast they reached the estuary of a large river but found it too shallow to navigate. Four boats were then sent ashore to negotiate with a large crowd of natives which had assembled. After some efforts had been made to traffic with them, the Indians suddenly surged forward killing eight of the Spaniards and seizing one of their boats. The other three boats made off to the fleet, and course was set for the north. After forty leagues they encountered the 'Sea of fresh water', a *bocha* which rushed into the ocean with great force.* There were many islands here; but, though the people were humane and peaceable, they were not able to establish contact although they departed with thirty-six slaves. Sailing on past *terra peyra* (Columbus's Parias), they reached the 'Bocca di Dragone' and examined a large number of islands. After collecting a great deal of *verzi* (logwood) and *cassia fistula*, and finding many ruined huts, attributable to 'cannibal' raids, they sailed for Hispaniola. They later claimed to have continued four hundred leagues to the west but, after losing two ships and other misadventures, they finally sailed for Spain. Pinzon estimated he had examined over six hundred leagues of coast, which, since no termination to it was discovered, must be the coast of a continent.

The report of the wealth of pearls to be found on the Venezuelan coast attracted other voyagers to that region, among them Peralonso Niño, a member of the family which had owned the *Niña* and a pilot on the first voyage, and Diego Lepe who extended knowledge of the coast at its south-eastern extremity. All these captains were instructed not to enter the Portuguese zone, but with their inability to determine exactly where the line of demarcation lay, there was naturally some confusion on this point. These demarcation disputes inevitably brought the Portuguese into western waters, as complementary to their voyages via the Cape of Good Hope. For instance,

* Probably the discharge of the Amazon, or alternatively the Orinoco.

when Cabral sailed for India in the spring of 1500, he made a wide sweep from the Cape Verde Islands into the western Atlantic and sighted part of the mainland, well to the south of the area of Spanish activity, on April 22. In the words of one of his companions: 'At Vespers we sighted land, first a great mountain, very high and rounded, with other lower ranges to the south, and land covered with great forests. To this mountain the Captain gave the name Monte Pascoal, and to the land the name "Terra de Vera Cruz" [Land of the True Cross].' The fleet then sailed some distance northwards and found a good harbour protected by an extensive reef. The harbour is now known as Bahia Cabriala, and the reef as Coroa Vermelha. On the 22nd, a party went ashore, a friar celebrated the first Mass on South American soil, and a great cross of wood was set up to signify possession of the land. A vessel was sent back to Portugal with news of the discovery, and on May 2 the fleet sailed on the long run to the Cape. This discovery was represented by some cartographers as an island decorated with drawings of the parrots which the explorers reported to be in great numbers.

These discoveries again brought the problem of the line of demarcation to the fore, and Vespucci became involved in the consequent activities. If his account is accepted, the King of Portugal planned to follow up Cabral's discovery and at the same time to sort out the problem of the line. It all began rather unexpectedly with Vespucci transferring his services from Spain to Portugal, an action of which he makes a great mystery. First there was a message imploring him to go to Lisbon for consultation with the King, but Vespucci declined on the grounds of ill-health. Whereupon an Italian resident in Lisbon, one Giuliano di Bartolomeo del Giocondo, arrived to persuade him to accept the invitation. After some further resistance, Vespucci yielded with extreme reluctance, implying that he was being forced to go, and left Spain hurriedly. 'My going,' he wrote, 'was taken amiss by all who knew me, because I left Castile where honour had been shown me and the King held me in good repute.'

In Lisbon he was persuaded to sail with a squadron of three ships which were fitting out to go on an expedition under the command of Gonzalo Coelho. After a voyage during which they experienced 'the worst weather that ever man encountered' they sighted land at 700 leagues south-west of Guinea, significantly near that of the expedition of 1499 to 1500. Course was then set for the south, since the Portuguese had no interest in sailing north-west into the Spanish zone. Precisely how far they proceeded is difficult to establish. The Argentine historian, Dr. R. Levillier, has argued that their turning-point was well down the Patagonian coast, supporting his argument by an analysis of the complicated cartographical evidence. In the immediate context of the voyage, the case he makes is strong, but the precise limit of the voyage is not of overriding importance. What interested Vespucci's contemporaries, and secured him his place in history, were his striking descriptions of peoples and scenes encountered in the earlier part of the voyage and his claim to have revealed a new world. From the literary point of view, if not from the geographical, this was certainly true. Others, including Columbus, had hinted before him that this was indeed a new world, but it was Vespucci's achievement to present it so vividly to his readers that the phrase became for them a concrete reality. His lively account of the first close contact with the Indians gives a good example of his ability as a story-teller. Two importunate sailors were given leave to reconnoitre inland. Their companions waited six days for their return. On the seventh day large crowds began to gather on the beach, women in the forefront. A young sailor went out to parley with them while his companions withdrew to the boats. The women made a circle around the youth, who was then clubbed from behind and dragged away. At once the men discharged their arrows at the Portuguese, who, taken off guard, made no effective reply, though later they fired off four lombards. The women cut up the body, and roasted and ate it in sight of the strangers. The Portuguese wished to rush ashore and avenge their comrades, having learnt that the first two had been similarly treated, but their cautious commander forbade this action; so, dispirited and shamed, they sailed away. This incident made a great stir among contemporaries, and maps of the time carry carefully drawn vignettes illustrating the tragedy.

Nothing quite so dramatic occurred later, but there is one incident, unusual and not fully explained, which excites curiosity. When they reached 32 degrees south latitude, Vespucci reported, 'it was decided that we should follow that course which seemed fitting to me, and the whole direction of the fleet was committed to me'. Under his command the fleet continued on its southerly course to, as he claimed, the latitude of 52 degrees south. At this point another storm struck and the ships were driven to within sight of a barren, rocky and uninhabited island; but as the stormy weather continued, Vespucci gave the order to return to Portugal. As to the identity of the land sighted in the far south, some have rather boldly asserted that it was one of the Falkland Islands or South Georgia; more probably it was a portion of the mainland.

The story of the change in command has been rather ingeniously explained on the grounds that the expedition, having at that point passed into the Spanish sphere, it was thought fitting that Vespucci as one recently in the Spanish service should take command. This line of argument is also used to explain Vespucci's temporary transfer to Portuguese service, this being the result of an understanding between Spain and Portugal to prevent quarrels over the limits of their respective spheres. Certainly this transfer did nothing to affect Vespucci rising later to a high position in the Spanish service, and it is also clear that the two kingdoms were anxious to avoid a clash in the Americas.

From a study of the southerly route followed by this fleet, and statements made elsewhere by Vespucci, it is possible to deduce that its object was to reach the true Indies by sailing round the south of the new continent, in other words it had the same aim as Columbus was pursuing in his search for a 'strait' through the Central American isthmus. Vespucci had failed at this attempt, but he did not on this account abandon the plan, for the fourth voyage attributed to him is considered by some to have been another effort in this direction. That there was a Portuguese voyage in 1503 to 1504 is certain, but our knowledge of it is scant and confused. Its aim, however, was not to seek the Far Eastern islands but to establish a colony of 'new Christians' (converted Jews) in Brazil. The fleet of six vessels, under the command of Fernão Noronha, met with near disaster. Four were wrecked on the newly-discovered island named after the commander, and only two returned with cargoes of dye-wood, parrots and other tropical novelties, having built and garrisoned a fort on the coast near Cape Frio. No further attempts were made by the Portuguese for some years to colonize Brazil, mainly because all the resources of the principal financier of Portuguese expansion, the Florentine banker Bartolomeo Marchioni, were directed to the new trading-stations in the Indian Ocean. When, seven years later, German and Flemish bankers obtained a foothold in overseas trade, Marchioni sought another outlet for his capital and the colonization of Brazil was seriously undertaken.

That Vespucci took any part in this expedition is doubtful, although he appears to have been canvassing support for an expedition by the southern route to the Spice Islands at this time. The only link with him is contained in an anonymous compilation, and there is no direct evidence for it in Portuguese, Spanish, or Italian archives. Whatever the truth of the matter, Vespucci was in rather low water after 1504, as a letter from Columbus to his son Diego illustrates. While Vespucci was returning to the Spanish Court, he visited the Admiral in Seville and had a long discussion with him, which the latter reported in a letter to 'his very dear' Diego dated February 5, 1505. His visitor, who was journeying on matters connected with navigation, the Admiral wrote, had not been treated by fortune as he had deserved. He had expressed a desire to help Columbus to the best of his ability, but it was not clear what he could do in this respect. However, Columbus had told Vespucci all he could about his own affairs and the payments which had been made to him. If we had a verbatim report of this conversation on the subject of adequate rewards for explorers, we should know a great deal more than we do about their characters!

Vespucci's visit to the Court was evidently successful, for two months later he received by order of Ferdinand twelve thousand *maravedis* towards his expenses, and later in the same month he was granted a letter of naturalization 'for his fidelity and the good service he had rendered, and in expectation of the same in future'. This future service was nothing less than the preparation for a voyage 'to discover the Spice Islands'. The royal instructions reveal that Vespucci was to work with Vicente Yañez Pinzon, and also that the King was anxious that the ships should sail before the onset of winter. The preparations, with which Juan de la Cosa was later associated, dragged on for two years and were eventually abandoned when Portugal objected to Spanish intrusion in this quarter. This set-back had no ill results for Vespucci, who went from strength to strength, ending his career as Pilot-Major of Spain. The Royal *Titulo* of 1508 appointing him to this new office recited the need for training pilots in the use of the quadrant and the astrolabe, and laid down that in future all wishing to go on voyages *au long cours* must obtain a certificate of competence from the Pilot-Major, who was also charged with the task, in co-operation with experienced navigators, of compiling and maintaining for general use a master chart, the *Padrón Real*, of all the possessions of Spain in the Indies. No charts were to be used unless they had been approved by him, and all returning pilots were to report any new surveys they had carried out. So there was set up in the Casa de la Contratación de las Indias at Seville one of the first Hydrographic Departments in the world. Vespucci held the office of Pilot-Major with the respect and confidence of the Crown and his contemporaries for four years, and was succeeded on his death in 1512 by Juan de Solis.

It is unfortunate, but probably inevitable, that Vespucci should have been built up as the rival, or at least the equal, of Columbus. This is not to deny his qualifications in cosmography and cartography, which could scarcely have obtained greater recognition in Spain. On the other hand it is no derogation of his achievements to hold that two of his 'four voyages' (the first and the fourth) were probably apocryphal, for no version of either of these is derived directly from him. Nor can any discredit be attached to him for the great popularity of the *Novus Mundus* which led to his name being attached to the new continent. To hazard a suggestion as to what occurred: there are grounds for concluding that, building on the success of the 'second' and 'third' voyages and on Vespucci's reputation as a cosmographer, an enthusiastic popularizer set out to enhance his reputation. Columbus had made four voyages, therefore Vespucci must be credited with four, and accordingly one was added before and one after the established voyages; Columbus suffered shipwreck and left a garrison behind, therefore Vespucci must be made to do the same. (It is noticeable that this incident is added to the doubtful fourth voyage.) The conclusion is that the Vespucci image was worked up by a too enthusiastic, or too successful, public relations officer. But, as has been said, this exaggeration does not affect his true stature as an explorer. The polemics which it occasioned in later years resulted from the involvement of the history of the discoveries in international politics.

Chapter XI

VOYAGERS IN THE NORTH-WEST ATLANTIC

AMONG THE company which Geoffrey Chaucer assembled at the Tabard, Southwark, for the pilgrimage to Canterbury, were several characters whose adventures illustrate the widening outlook of contemporary English society. That any one individual could actually have taken 'part in all the adventures attributed to him is unlikely; nevertheless their stories must have appeared credible to the cultivated circle for which they were written. The Knight, we are told, had fought in one of the numerous campaigns against the Moors in the Iberian peninsula:

> 'And he was in Granada when they sank
> The town of Algeciras, also in
> North Africa, right through Benamarin
>
> . . .
>
> And joisted for our faith at Tramissene
> Thrice in the lists.'

The Skipper from Dartmouth, though he had not ventured far inside the Straits of Gibraltar, knew the coasts of western Europe thoroughly and was adept in his profession:

> 'As for his skill in reckoning his tides
> Currents and many another risk besides,
> Moons, harbours, pilots, he had such despatch
> That none from Hull to Carthage was his match . . .
> And he knew all the havens as they were
> From Gothland to the Cape of Finisterre
> And every creek in Britanny and Spain:
> The barke he owned was called The *Maudelayne*.'

It is worth noting that the references to the Skipper's navigational experience show that it extended only to coastal work: his concern was with moon and tides, harbours and currents which he found described in his pilot books. There is no mention of the astrolabe as an instrument for finding latitude from the heavenly bodies, and rather strangely there is not in this passage a mention of the mariner's compass. These were primarily for 'blue water' navigation. But even when this developed, the pilots for a long time to come relied mainly on dead reckoning to establish their positions. This served so long as one knew approximately the latitude of one's home port and that of one's destination, but to find a small island in the midst of a stormy ocean was another matter.

The tales these pilgrims told were largely drawn from classical and chivalrous authors, and some historians at least would be ready to exchange them for, say, the Knight's adventures at the siege of Algeciras or the Skipper's own story of his experiences in foreign waters. But occasionally fresher details break in. Among those of high degree whose griefs were quoted by the Monk was King Peter of Spain (*circa* 1350) for whom the Black Prince had fought at the battle of Najera, and Chaucer's readers were expected to know something of 'this Tatar Cambuskan' (Kublai Khan).

These wider interests originated in the country's international politics, and more particularly from relations with the nascent kingdom of Portugal. English bowmen contributed to the victory of Aljubarrota in 1385, when Portugal established her independence from Castile. In the following year the Treaty of Windsor decreed that between the two countries 'there shall be inviolate and endure for ever . . . a solid, perpetual and real league, unity, confederacy and union'. To cement this alliance, King John married Philippa, daughter of John of Gaunt, and one child of this union was Dom Henry 'the Navigator'. Throughout the following century the connection flourished: another son, Dom Pedro, received the Order of the Garter.

These relations were founded upon, and in turn fostered, the growing trade between the two countries, and also strengthened England's maritime links with the Mediterranean, which had begun at least as early as the fourteenth century with the annual voyages of the Venetian and Genoese fleets to Southampton and London *en route* for Flanders. By the mid-fifteenth century English politicans and merchants were asking why these Flemings and other strangers should gain exorbitant profits at the expense of their English customers, and were studying the advantages which England might derive from her position commanding the Channel, a vital artery of trade between the South and Flanders, 'the staple of Europe'. These thoughts find vivid expression in the anonymous poem, 'The Libel

of English policie', written in the first half of the fifteenth century.
The poet's thesis is summed up in the lines:

> 'Cherish merchandise, keep the Admiraltie,
> That we be masters of the narrowe see.'

This 'littel book' throws valuable light on the course of overseas
trade and the new areas into which English ships were venturing.
It tells of the Genoese who:

> '. . . comen in sundry wises
> Into this land with divers marchandizes
> In great Caracks, arrayed withouten lacke
> With cloth of gold, silke, and pepper blacke . . .'

There are two other interesting passages. Of Portugal he writes:

> 'The Marchandry also of Portugal
> By divers hands turne into sale.
> Portugalers with us have truth in hand,
> Whose Marchandry cometh much into England.
> They ben our friends, with their commodities;
> And wee English passen into their countries.'

And there are his comments on Iceland, which imply that traffic
with that northern island was by then a commonplace.

> 'Of Island to write is little nede,
> Save of stockfish: yet forsooth in deed
> Out of Bristowe, and costes many one,
> Men have practised by nedle and by stone
> Thider wards within a little while,
> Within twelve years, and without perill,
> Gon and come, as men were wont of old,
> Of Scarborough unto the costes cold.'

The reference to the rudimentary mariner's compass—the needle
and lodestone—is worth attention.

By the middle of the fifteenth century the English fishermen in
Icelandic waters were meeting with severe competition from the
men of the Hanseatic cities who had almost monopolized Norwegian
commerce. This state of affairs was leading them to look for new
fishing grounds, a factor which had some influence on voyages
into the Atlantic, where Bristol men were launching out on a new
venture. In 1480 William Worcestre records under the date of July
15, that 'the ship . . . of John Day junior of 80 tons burden, began

a voyage at the port of Bristol from King Road to the Island of Brasylle on the west part of Ireland, ploughing the seas . . . Thloyde is the ship's master, the most knowledgeable seaman of the whole of England.' After nine weeks Lloyd failed to find the island and was driven back by storm to a port in Ireland where he refitted. The following year two ships, the *Trinity* and *George*, sailed from the same port 'not with the intention of trading but of examining and finding a certain island called the Isle of Brasil'. Lloyd's ship returned safely, but what befell the other two is not known. Since nothing more is heard of the Isle of Brasil for fifteen years the presumption is that the island was not found at this time.

What lay behind these voyages? It has been argued that the island of Brasil had already been discovered and that these were attempts to find it again. It has also been pointed out that as the *Trinity* and *George* had shipped large quantities of salt it was expected that they would find new fishing grounds in the vicinity of the Isle. Thus, if these grounds were the Great Banks, Brasil might very well be part of the North American continent. On the other hand, the reference to the island as being in the western parts of Ireland does not suggest that it was at first thought to lie far out in the Atlantic. Whatever the significance of this evidence, it at least shows that, around 1480, the island of Brasil was much in the minds of Bristol men. In attempting to ascertain why this was so, one is led back to the Portuguese voyagers into the Atlantic. De Teive in 1452 claimed to have come close to land in the north-west, and around 1475 there was another burst of activity among Portuguese seekers of Atlantic islands. It is not known what were the results of this, or even if the ships actually sailed. Equally, there is no evidence of any discovery by the Bristol men at a slightly later date. On the evidence available it is reasonable to suggest that the impetus behind these western voyages came from the Portuguese, and was transmitted to Bristol through skippers and traders. This information might well have been about the existence of promising new fishing grounds, concerning which the sailors of both countries were content to keep silent while exploiting them.

Between 1481 and 1497 there is no direct evidence of further voyages from Bristol. Some years ago, however, a document was found in Spanish archives which suggests, but without giving details, that this activity continued. This was a letter written by John Day* to a

---

* The letter was first published by L. A. Vigneras in *Hispanic American History Review* 36 (1956), 503; see also Quinn, D. B.: *Geographical Journal* 117 (1961), 277.

Spanish notable addressed as Admiral-Major. After describing Cabot's first voyage, the writer continues: 'The cape of the said land [as found by Cabot] was found and discovered in times past by the men from Bristol who found Brasil, as your Lordship well knows. It was called the island of Brasil and it is assumed and believed to be the mainland that the men from Bristol found.' John Day was a man of good family and education who was engaged in business in Spain and in Bristol, although he was later unsuccessful and in trouble with the authorities. He was thus in a position to know what at least was commonly held in Bristol in 1497. The value of his evidence is diminished by uncertainty as to the exact meaning of the phrase 'in times past' (en otros tiempos), which could be either 'many years ago' or equally 'some years ago'. On the first interpretation, in association with the 1480 to 1481 voyages, it has been argued that the discovery was pre-1480. But a less conjectural case can be made out for the years 1490 to 1495. This is supported by the statement made by Ayala, the Spanish agent in London, to King Ferdinand in the following year: 'For the last seven years the people of Bristol have equipped two, three and four caravels to go in search of the island of Brasil and the Seven Cities, according to the reckoning of this Genoese [Cabot]. The king made up his mind to send him thither, because last year sure proof was brought him they had found land.'

Taken literally, this implies a search starting about 1490, and concluding successfully with Cabot's first voyage. The reference to 'sure proof' suggests that the earlier attempts had probably brought back rather vague rumours of land. Putting all these stories together, it might be concluded that the earlier voyages were to fishing grounds and that it was not for some time that a definitely located and reported landfall was made. There are suggestions, however, that these efforts added up to something more than mere fishing voyages. Ayala's mention of the 'Seven Cities' is important as a pointer to some Portuguese association with them, for throughout the century this had been one of their objectives. Apart from the general relations between the two countries, there are other grounds for this suggestion. In 1486 two Portuguese, Fernandes and Gonçalves, made a trading voyage from Madeira to Bristol where they evidently became well established for, five years later, a João Fernandes was exporting goods thence to Lisbon. Again in 1488 a João Fernandes of Terceira obtained a licence from the King of Portugal to seek out and discover at his own expense some islands lying in the Portuguese sphere of influence. Evidently something went wrong with his plans

—he may have been unable to raise the necessary funds—for two years later, João Fernandes, this time joined by João Gonçalves and three citizens of Bristol, obtained letters patent from Henry VII authorizing them at their own expense 'to find, recover, discover and search out whatsoever islands, countries, regions or provinces of heathens or infidels, in whatever part of the world they may lie'. It is likely that the Fernandes and Gonçalves referred to in these three texts were the same two individuals in each case. A less reliable piece of evidence is a legal document from which it can be deduced that Fernandes was on an exploring voyage from 1492 to 1495. These last dates are not firmly established, but there is at least a case to be made out for a voyage from Bristol with Portuguese co-operation within the period to which Ayala refers.

The obscurity which surrounds the activities of Bristol seamen in the northern Atlantic in the late fifteenth century is finally dispelled in the last decade when John Cabot (the English rendering of Zuan Caboto) enters the scene. Within a mere three years this man had inaugurated English overseas expansion and was the first European indubitably to sight the mainland of America, north or south, before he perished in the waters of the Atlantic. The records of his career, though only too scanty for our complete satisfaction, are sufficient to explain his achievements and, what is of more importance, enable them to be fitted intelligibly into the contemporary pattern. While it would be uncritical to place him without reservation on an equality with Columbus, who cannot be deprived of the fame of having first put to the test the ideas and speculations of geographers through many centuries, Cabot stands not far below him as a man of sufficient ability and determination to grasp the significance and potentialities of his fellow-countryman's achievements and to seize an opportunity to apply his conclusions in an appropriate quarter. Even his major error, the belief that his discovery was a part of the Asian mainland, was no worse than that of Columbus.

Many of Cabot's contemporaries regarded him as a native of Genoa, and this seems to be correct; the important fact is that he became a naturalized citizen of Venice in March 1476, the year, incidentally, in which Columbus arrived in Lisbon; the qualification for Venetian citizenship was then fifteen years' residence. By 1484 he was a married man with three children, his second son, Sebastian, being destined to be another notable and enigmatic figure in the history of exploration. As a citizen of Venice, it is not surprising to find that at some stage of his career he engaged in the spice trade: he later told an acquaintance in England that he had been several times to Mecca, 'whither spices are borne by caravans from distant countries'. In reply to his questions as to their origin, the traders were unable to give him definite information except that they came a very great distance and passed several times from one group of merchants to another. 'He therefore reasons,' his friend reported, 'that these things come from places far away from them, and so on from one to another; also assuming that the world is round, it follows as a matter of course that the last of all must take them in the north towards the west.'

Although this conversation was taken down in 1497, after Columbus had reached what he claimed to be the Indies, and may therefore be an afterthought on Cabot's part, he at least knew that the spices reached the eastern Mediterranean through a number of intermediaries. Though he does not specify them, contemporaries such as Martin Behaim, for instance, knew that they went by sea from the south-eastern islands to southern India; Arab traders carried them to Ormuz or to ports in southern Arabia and from there they were transported by caravan to Cairo and similar cities of the Levant where they were purchased by Venetian and other merchants. It was the dues levied at each stage of these lengthy transactions, plus the monopoly exercised by the Ottoman Turks at the Levantine termini, that made the spices so costly to Europeans.

The only puzzling statement in Cabot's remarks is why he had concluded that the distant source was 'in the north towards the west', and not 'in the south towards the west'. 'West' here means the quarter reached by travelling eastwards through ninety degrees, as Cabot could demonstrate on his globe. It is 'north' that is a little strange. This idea may have arisen from a misunderstanding of Marco Polo's account, which Cabot had probably read. After discussing Cipangu, Polo refers to the 7,448 islands in the surrounding Sea of Chin, where spices, including black and white pepper, were grown. Since Cipangu was generally placed to the east, and not south-east, of the Asian mainland, Cabot may have concluded that the Spice Islands were also in that quarter. Alternatively, his information may have been obtained from traders who had travelled across Asia and who would regard the spices they brought as originating north of the island. Whatever the reason, this concept helped to convince Cabot that he had discovered part of Asia.

We next hear of him in Spain in 1490 as a professional man of some competence charged with preparing a scheme for the construction of a harbour at Valencia, for which he had designed and painted plans.* This was official work and brought Cabot into brief contact with King Ferdinand in the exciting years of 1490 to 1492. The harbour contract was ultimately abandoned, and Cabot is said to have attempted to gain support in Seville and Lisbon for an expedition westwards. This is possible but rather unlikely, as the chance of obtaining preference among the throng endeavouring to cash in on Columbus's success would be small. It is more probable that, stimulated by what was going on around him, he saw an opportunity to make use of his knowledge of the spice trade and of cosmography. The important factor, however, was his decision to take his ideas to England and, basing them on news of the Bristol voyages, to try to interest King Henry in a more northerly approach.

Accordingly he journeyed to London with his wife and family to open negotiations. The close attention which Their Catholic Majesties gave to matters of discovery, and also the excellence of their intelligence system, are shown by the fact that Cabot's arrival was at once reported to them and they sent back without delay instructions on the way in which the affair was to be handled. They wrote: 'In regard to what you say of the arrival there of one like Columbus for the purpose of inducing the King of England to enter upon another undertaking like that of the Indies, without prejudice to Spain or Portugal, if the King aids him as he has us, the Indies will be well rid of the man ... It is also clear that no arrangement can be concluded in this matter in that country [England] without harm to us or to the King of Portugal.' The Ambassador, de Puebla, was to make this plain to King Henry and not to let him be persuaded by the King of France into becoming involved in opposition to Spain and Portugal.

Henry, however, was playing his hand in his own way and was not deterred by these manœuvres. Some weeks before de Puebla's representations, and in reply to a petition from John Cabot and his sons, he had granted letters patent authorizing their proposed voyage. The relative ease with which these were obtained suggests that Henry was well abreast of developments in this field and had determined the course he should pursue internationally; perhaps he had learnt something from Bartholomew Columbus's visit a few years before. The clauses of the letters patent cover most of the points made in the Capitulations granted by Their Catholic Majesties to Columbus. It

* The identification of this engineer with the explorer is not completely established, but appears probable.

would probably be going too far to assume that the English agreement was modelled on them, but it is significant that the first English document of this type should have been drawn up in so workmanlike a fashion. Ignoring Papal Bulls and the Treaty of Tordesillas, the King authorizes Cabot, his sons and their heirs to 'sail to all parts, regions and coasts of the eastern, western and northern seas . . . at their own proper costs and charges, to find, discover and investigate whatsoever islands, countries, regions or provinces of heathens and infidels which before this time were unknown to all Christians', and to set up royal banners and ensigns in 'any town, city, castle, island or mainland whatsoever, newly founded by them'. The only regions, therefore, which were barred to them were the southern seas, no doubt in consideration of the alliance with Portugal, and the discoveries of the Spanish in the West Indies, for any parts of Asia which they might reach, certainly of eastern Asia, could be regarded as 'unknown to all Christians'. They were to hold these possessions as vassals of the Crown in return for one-tenth of the net profits of the voyage. Furthermore, no one was to trade in any of the discoveries without a licence from the Cabots.

John Day, in the letter already quoted, refers to an abortive voyage later that year, but there is no record of this elsewhere. The successful expedition set sail in one small vessel, the *Mathew*, in May 1497. No journal or report by any member of the crew has survived, and what we know of it, apart from Day's account, is derived from two Italians resident in London, Lorenzo Pasqualigo, who corresponded with his brother in Venice, and Raimondo de Soncino, an agent of the Duke of Milan. That the news should have had such interest for Italians testifies to their anxiety about the future of the spice trade. There are also some entries in the Exchequer accounts of payments to those who took part, and brief entries in contemporary chronicles. From all these a general account of the voyage can be constructed. After a voyage of thirty-three days from Bristol, Cabot sighted land, 'which is the country of the Great Khan', at a distance of 700 leagues, and examined 300 leagues of the coast. At one point he went ashore to take possession and to replenish his water supply. No great effort was made to penetrate inland or to make contact with the inhabitants, though he brought back some of their implements. One account added that he had also discovered the 'Island of the Seven Cities', 400 leagues from England, and another that he had seen great quantities of stockfish. John Day was able to give more precise details of the new land, for he had seen Cabot's chart; the cape nearest to Ireland was 450 leagues west of Dursey Head, the southernmost part of the 'Island of the Seven Cities' lay west of Bordeaux river, and most of the coast was explored on the return. The land was wooded, with tall trees of the kind masts are made of, and was very rich in grass. These details, most commentators agree, fix Cabot's discoveries on the south-east coasts of Nova Scotia and Newfoundland, that is, between Cape Sable and Cape Race.* If the reference to Bordeaux river was based on an observation for latitude, or even on accurate dead reckoning, then the southern part of the Isle of the Seven Cities was very close to the position of Halifax, Nova Scotia. Cabot had therefore made the first authenticated land-fall on the American mainland.

Cabot received a warm welcome on his return. Within four days he was received in London by the King who was highly delighted with his success, having, as de Soncino supposed, 'gained a part of Asia without a stroke of the sword'. Cabot was granted an annual pension of twenty pounds to be drawn from the Bristol customs, and was promised ten armed ships to follow up his discovery. Pasqualigo added one of the few human touches in the record. Cabot 'is called the Great Admiral and vast honour is paid to him. He goes dressed in silk and these English run after him like mad, and indeed he can enlist as many of them as he pleases, and a number of our rogues as well.'

With the aid of his globe, Cabot demonstrated his contention that his discovery lay on the north-east projection of Asia as drawn by contemporary map-makers; if the parallel of Bordeaux is traced on the world map (Ruysch's, for example) it intercepts the 'Asian' coastline at the point named 'C. de Portugesi'. From a point in this vicinity he proposed to sail westwards and southwards until he reached Cipangu, in fact around the shores of the 'Sinus Plisacus'. He would then be in the equinoctial regions where he believed all the spices and jewels in the world originated. That this was his general intention is clear from the documents already cited, although it is not stated in the new letters patent which he received in February 1498. These permitted him to take six ships, again at his own expense, to convey and lead them 'to the londe and Iles of late founde by the seid John'.

* From Day's report it appears that the new coasts were charted on the return, in other words after the landfall at Cape Sable, Cabot sailed eastwards, leaving the land at Cape Race. Day's figure for the distance west of Dursey Head is approximately correct.

All this talk about Asia and its spices naturally disturbed the Spanish agent at King Henry's Court. Pedro de Ayala made strong representations that Cabot's cape fell within the Spanish sphere, to the west of the Tordesillas demarcation line, and that the islands were those which Columbus had found. As for Cabot's world map, he poured scorn upon it: 'so far as I can see [it is] exceedingly false, in order to make believe that those are not part of the said islands,' he wrote to his Sovereigns. But Henry was not prepared to listen to such arguments, and allowed Cabot to proceed.

After this preparation and the high hopes entertained by its promoters, the voyage proved a tragic anti-climax. Cabot left Bristol with five ships in 1498. Of the ship in which he himself sailed nothing more was heard, and it must be presumed to have been lost with all hands. Some at least of the other vessels returned, though in what circumstances is unknown. If they reached American waters, their course can only be conjectured. Dr. J. A. Williamson has argued that one or more may have sailed southwards, even to the extent of penetrating into the Caribbean but for this there is no independent contemporary evidence. The epitaph of the expedition is written in the Great Chronicle of London: 'of whom in this mayor's time returned no tidings'.

Nevertheless the Bristol merchants continued to invest their capital in the enterprise, and in circumstances which point to competition with Portugal, but with the aid of Portuguese venturers. Within a year of the Cabot disaster, João Fernandes had obtained a licence from King Manuel to look for 'some islands lying in our sphere of influence'. What then happened is obscure; the outcome however was that another resident in Terceira, a Portuguese noble, Gaspar Corte Real, sailed for the northern Atlantic with three caravels, while Fernandes took himself off to Bristol to promote a similar scheme. Portugal, having tapped the spice trade, was unwilling to see a rival pass beyond the demarcation line and reach the Spice Islands by another route. The obvious rejoinder was to reconnoitre it herself or at least to take possession of strategically placed islands or mainland and so control access.

Corte Real's voyages were similar in pattern to those of Cabot's; a successful reconnaissance on which he reached the east coast of Greenland, circumnavigated Cape Farewell and sailed some distance up the west coast, and a disastrous follow up, in the course of which, having gained the west side of David Strait and sailed southwards, he and his crew disappeared without trace off the coast of Newfoundland. Two subsequent search expeditions led by his brother Miguel were fruitless, Miguel himself perishing on the second.

Meanwhile a parallel effort had been mounted in Bristol, where Fernandes with two companions had found partners in Richard Warde, Thomas Asshehurst, and John Thomas, 'merchants of your town of Bristol'. The first letters patent which they obtained from Henry recall those granted to Cabot, but they gave the merchant venturers a very much wider field of action. The wording ran: 'all ports regions and territories of the eastern, western, southern, arctic and northern seas'. They were no longer enjoined to keep out of the Portuguese zone, or apparently to worry whether any discoveries might be known to Christians. The remaining clauses, drawn in greater detail, define the future position of the enterprise more closely. The trade monopoly was to extend to ten years, but for the first four years imports into Bristol were exempt from all custom duties. Interlopers were once more forbidden, and half the profits of any such illegal voyages were to be divided between the Crown and the associates. Fernandes and his friends were to receive equal treatment, provided they did homage to the King and observed the laws of England.

Nine months later a new patent was granted which greatly limited their field of action, for the adventurers are forbidden to enter or occupy any of 'the lands, countries, regions or provinces of heathens or infidels first discovered by the subjects of our very dear brother and cousin the King of Portugal, or by the subjects of any other princes soever, our friends and confederates, and in possession of which these same princes now find themselves'. The business of the Company then hung fire for almost two years, perhaps because of difficulties in raising the necessary capital, or through the intervention of the Portuguese. When a new patent was granted in December 1502 its field of operations set out in the reference to the four seas was considerably qualified.

What the Company adventuring to the New Found Land accomplished under these letters patent is uncertain. There are records which point to preparations for voyages and to some activity in the new lands, but these peter out by the year 1510, and certainly no colony or settlement as foreshadowed in the letters patent materialized. As with the Spanish discoveries in the West Indies, after the first excitements had evaporated a period of disillusionment with overseas expansion set in. In the case of Portugal and England, the resources still employed were concentrated on developing the new fishing grounds. Contact was thus maintained with the discoveries, which left the way open for the resumption of exploration when a new expansionist movement set in.

During the first decades of the century the maritime countries of the western seaboard were steadily exploiting the Grand Bank and other fishing grounds of the north-west Atlantic and developing important markets for their catches in western Europe, in face of strong competition from the Hanseatic League in control of Icelandic waters. These voyages were not concerned with advancing geographical knowledge, but when the region was once again drawn into the arena of international politics, as offering the possibility of an alternative route to the East, explorers had a firm base from which to advance and were able to make rapid progress. It was at this point that France, under Francis I, seeking to embarrass her Spanish rival, took a first step in overseas expansion. By the year 1504, fishermen from Brittany and Normandy had joined the Portuguese, Basque and English fleets on the Grand Banks and had set up shore stations on the southern coasts of Newfoundland, where during the summer their catches were dried or salted. Dried cod, the principal product, was known by its Portuguese name, *bacalhau*, from which the land derived its name, Tierra de Bacalaos. Prominent in these affairs was the Portuguese merchant João Alvares Fagundes of Vianna, who by 1520 had established stations on Miquelon island and at Placentia on the mainland.

The next advance came when France took up the quest for a strait through to the West. The persistence of this concept for years after Columbus had pursued it in vain at first sight seems remarkable, but on examination it is easily reconcilable with the geographical knowledge of the period. It maintained its position as long as the belief that the new lands were part of Asia had any currency. If ships were to reach eastern Asia, they clearly had to negotiate an area of the world occupied to a large extent by continental land, whether united or separate from Asia, although many were coming to believe that its eastern coastline was continuous from north to south, even though this would constitute the longest continuous meridional coast on the sphere. The cosmographers could see quite clearly from their globes that the arc of a great circle running through points off the east coast of North America and the Moluccas was considerably shorter than the long and dangerous route through the Strait of Magellan. Somewhere, surely, between the stretches of known coast from Newfoundland to these Straits, there must be a navigable passage to the great

South Sea sighted by Balboa. When, therefore, Francis I of France, in his quarrel with the Emperor Charles V, looked for a means of challenging his rival's position, it was logical that he should turn to the search for a short cut to the Spice Islands via an area outside Spanish control.

For this enterprise he found the necessary support among a powerful body of merchants in Dieppe and Lyons. At the head of this group was Jean Ango, an enterprising and cultivated citizen of Dieppe who was already financing overseas voyages. Ango was in touch with the silk merchants of Lyons who were professionally interested in Eastern trade, and had connections with Florence, the city where the whole idea of a westward voyage had originated nearly a century earlier. The merchants of Florence, like their confrères in Lyons and Dieppe, were looking anxiously for new commercial outlets, as the growing tide of treasure flowing into Spain was leading to monetary inflation, a serious threat to the economies of other nations. All these trends influenced the attitude of Jean Ango and exiled artists and cosmographers from Florence flocked to Dieppe. It is not surprising, therefore, that when the French expedition sailed from Rouen in 1524 it did so under the command of a Florentine, Giovanni de Verazzano.

Most of our knowledge of his voyage is drawn from a chart made by his brother some years later. From this it appears that he examined with some care the coast between the Spanish zone in Florida and Nova Scotia in search of a western passage. His landfalls are not known in detail, but 'the very wide, deep river which he named Deep River' and up which he sailed in the belief that he had found the strait was probably either the Penobscot river or the Bay of Fundy. In Verazzano's view they came very near to finding the elusive strait, for they discovered a thin neck of land separating the Atlantic from the 'Sea of Verazzano'. This feature was described as an isthmus about two hundred miles long and one mile in width (another account gives the width as six miles). They reported that 'from the ships they could see the eastern sea to the north-west and that this was undoubtedly the Ocean which washed the shores of farther India, China and Cathay'. It seems likely that this feature was the long series of banks and shoals which border Pamlico Sound on the east, the most easterly point of which is Cape Hatteras. Verazzano continued the voyage north-westwards but failed to find a channel into the 'eastern sea'. To the land of his discovery he affixed the name 'Terre Franciscane' in honour of the King.

This initiative by the French did not escape the attention of the Emperor Charles, sensitive to any encroachment on what he still maintained was the Spanish zone by virtue of the Papal Bulls. He was also apprehensive lest a rival should find the strait, for the experience of Magellan's expedition had shown too forcibly that the route around the southern extremity of the Americas was even more tedious than the Portuguese route by the Cape. He accordingly despatched Estevão Gomes, another Portuguese pilot in the service of Spain who had been with Magellan as far as the Straits, to north-eastern America. The royal hydrographer, Alonso de Santa Cruz, makes it plain that Gomes was seeking 'to discover Cathay or the eastern city of India, as well as that so-much-sought-for strait or passage leading to the sea commonly called the South Sea'. He makes it equally clear that Gomes was not attempting a passage to the north between Greenland and Labrador. Santa Cruz gives as a reason for this that Gomes 'was convinced it was unnecessary to attempt it because of the cold in those parts, which would always be a bar'. The details of his course have yet to be established definitively, but he probably coasted northern New England.

With Verazzano and Gomes the search for a strait in the north ceased for a decade, to be revived and carried much further by Jacques Cartier, sailing from St. Malo. When he set forth, fishing vessels had begun to frequent the Gulf of St. Lawrence, but their skippers, not being interested in discovery, had little knowledge of one island or coast or another. Cartier's achievement, in four voyages between 1534 and 1542, was to find in the west the entrance to the St. Lawrence and to ascend the river as far as the site of Montreal. There he heard of a country in the interior called Saguenay, reportedly rich in gold, and also of a great river flowing to the south (the Mississippi). At this point, therefore, the story of the discovery of the coast of North America ends and that of the exploration of the interior begins. The continuing search for the passage, now located north of the Arctic Circle, is part of the British contribution to Polar exploration.

Chapter XII

EARLY DAYS IN HISPANIOLA

COLUMBUS CEASED to have any responsibility for the governance of Hispaniola in the year 1500 when Francisco de Bobadilla arrived on his fateful mission, and by that time it was quite apparent that he had accomplished nothing as an administrator. In the eight years since he had first anchored off San Salvador the Admiral was actually in Hispaniola for little more than half this time, and during his absences his brothers lacked full authority in facing the unruly Spaniards; for even his own powers were ill-defined, at least in the eyes of the royal officials who considered that their ultimate loyalty was to the Crown. As to the military, they had been organized, despatched and paid by the Crown, and their commanders were disinclined to pay great attention to one who was essentially a civilian, standing outside their rigid hierarchy. Given this situation and the difficulties of establishing order among inexperienced men in a strange environment, it is scarcely surprising that his rule was a failure, setting in motion trends which had a devastating effect on the future of the island.

Before he sailed on his first voyage he had contemplated the establishment of factories trading on the Portuguese model, but the destruction of La Navidad emphasized the necessity of subduing the whole island. Accordingly a number of small forts were garrisoned by Spaniards who were, officially, to collect the gold in return for a fixed percentage. It was also intended that at least a proportion of the men would settle as small-holders raising the food-stuffs which would render the settlement self-supporting. In the nature of things, this project failed—gold-seekers do not make good market-gardeners—and the settlement remained dependent largely upon the arrival of supply ships, which the Crown was increasingly reluctant to furnish.

The next stage was the plan by which the local chiefs were made responsible for collecting a fixed tribute in gold from their people.

For reasons already made plain, this too was a failure, though Bartholomew modified it by offering to take cotton or cassava in lieu of gold. When Bobadilla arrived, Spanish control rested upon one embryo town, Santo Domingo, and a number of forts, strategically placed, a few of which later became settlements. In eastern Hispaniola, Concepción controlled the central Vega, while Esperanza guarded the crossing of the river Yaque between the dying Isabella and the rising Santo Domingo. In the course of opening up new placer deposits in the south, Bartholomew had also founded the small centre of Bonao (now called Monseñor Noel). Outside these posts, the disbanded Spaniards were scattered through the eastern half of the islands, living upon the Indians. In a moment of unguarded frankness, the Admiral described their existence in glowing terms—each attended by several Indians with dogs for hunting, and 'wonderfully handsome women'.

Bobadilla's name and fame are darkened by his high-handed action, beyond the terms of his mandate, in placing the Columbus brothers under arrest, but his record as an administrator in Hispaniola was by no means unworthy. His function was to hold the island for the Crown until the new régime, which Bishop Fonseca was organizing to replace the personal rule of the Admiral, could be initiated. With the revocation of the Capitulations of 1492, Fonseca was to all intents and purposes 'Secretary of State for the Colonies' in Ferdinand's council. The colonial administration was tightened up and centred from 1503 in the Casa de la Contratación at Seville, the equivalent of a government department. Under his scheme Hispaniola became a separate entity, while the new territories on Tierra Firma were gradually brought under distinct administrations, with the object of making each self-supporting, thus ending the continuous drain on Spain's resources of men and finance. With this purpose in view, discovery and trade were thrown open to all who could obtain licences from the Crown—a source of much indignation to the Admiral.

Bobadilla's task in Hispaniola, therefore, was to establish order and to reorganize the traffic in gold under strict control. To the further annoyance of the Admiral, watching the wealth he coveted slipping through his fingers, the Governor immediately issued licences to individuals for the collection of gold in return for a royalty which, as an additional incentive, was remitted for a fixed period. He also saw to it that the collection of these dues was more fairly and systematically carried out. As a consequence gold began to flow into the treasury—it has been estimated that 275 kilograms were collected in 1501—and the following year for the first time a substantial quantity was consigned to the royal exchequer in Spain.

In these circumstances the three hundred or so Spaniards remaining in the island welcomed the new security and ceased troubling the authorities. After two years of tranquillity Fonseca recalled Bobadilla and sent out as Governor with full powers a man almost the direct antithesis of Columbus in character. Frey Nicolas de Ovando, Commander of the military order of Alcantara, was, like Bobadilla, a tried servant of the Crown, of whom Las Casas had a high opinion though he was unable to forgive him for his treatment of the Indians: 'This knight was a very prudent man, fitted to govern great numbers of people; a man of authority and a friend of justice, very honest in his deeds and words, and a great enemy of cupidity and avarice, yet not lacking humility.' With him on the fleet of thirty-one vessels, great and small, came no less than 2,500 men, including nobles, knights and persons of standing—an influx comparable to the crowd which had come out with Columbus in 1493. Also on board were twelve Franciscans, for Ovando had been strictly enjoined to treat the Indians like other vassals of Castile, to ensure them against molestation, and to provide for their conversion to the Christian faith, as Queen Isabella of blessed memory had always wished. These remained for the time merely pious aspirations for the new Governor was determined to exert his authority over the whole island, and particularly over the western part which, thanks to Bartholomew Columbus and, ironically enough, to the rebel Roldan, had preserved much of its aboriginal social system, and was enjoying comparative tranquillity.

Ovando, in his first decisive action, assembled a considerable armed force and marched menacingly into the country. He was everywhere received hospitably and particularly by the remarkable woman Anacoana, widow of the great chief Caonabo, who had summoned an array of lesser caciques to meet him. Without warning, the Spaniards fell upon the unsuspecting assembly, burnt down Anacoana's palace with all the principal chiefs inside, massacred the others, and later hanged the Queen. Ovando defended this insensate action on the grounds that he suspected a revolt was brewing. We may also surmise that the earlier good relations with the Columbus party had some influence on Ovando, making him determined to assert his authority over the whole island. Another ironical twist to the tragedy is that the slaughter was witnessed by Diego Mendes who had just reached Hispaniola with a plea for assistance from the Admiral, then marooned on Jamaica. He recorded that in all eighty-five caciques had been slain or hanged. After the blood-bath Ovando lost no time in destroying every vestige of native authority in the island.

In the meantime things were not going well with the new arrivals —the second wave of adventurers and fortune-seekers. As had happened to those pressed into the building of Isabella in 1493, the foul conditions on the way out, the crowded, badly organized encampments ashore, and the mouldering rations produced an epidemic of dysentery and other tropical diseases. It was estimated that from one cause or another forty per cent of the newcomers were lost within a short time of their arrival. This decline in numbers, however, was not altogether unwelcome to the authorities; at its stage of development the colony could not support a large population of Europeans, and with the crushing of native resistance a strong military force was no longer necessary. They preferred to encourage the emergence of individual entrepreneurs possessing some technical ability and preferably with capital to invest. Such men, as Fonseca had foreseen, were attracted to the Caribbean when he threw it open to independent voyagers. As the phase of exploration waned, trading in pearls, slaves, logwood (for dyes) and, for a period, gold provided the means for further development. Spanish merchants came to reside in Hispaniola and to invest their profits in local enterprises.

This development was tied in with Ovando's general policy. Under his administration, the *encomienda* system was completed. Settlers became the virtual owners of a defined number of Indians whom they could put to work in the gold-mines for their own profit or alternatively hire out to another entrepreneur. Gangs of labourers were thus marched from one end of the island to the other, with little hope of ever returning to their homes. Initially the period of this service was limited, but in the course of time all such restrictions were removed. Alternatively the holder of an *encomienda* could employ his people on the raising of crops such as sugar, which was introduced in 1505. Out of this sprang the system of plantation agriculture, which was to be the foundation of the economy of much of the Americas for centuries, just as the forced-labour gangs prefigured the methods employed in the mines of Peru. The other, and very profitable, occupation was the raising of livestock. Many large ranches were operated throughout the island, over which roamed the descendants of the cattle, horses, pigs and sheep introduced from Europe, and hides and tallow contributed substantially to the flourishing export trade.

The typical form of settlement came to be the Villa, the dwelling house of the *encomiendor* surrounded by the huts of the Indian community, set among the plantations or, in the case of the ranches, surrounded by the gardens which, tended by the Indians, provided the settler with his necessities. At the centre of the economy, the City of Santo Domingo, after being removed across the river to its present site, was growing rapidly with all the attributes of a contemporary European community.

In these conditions, many of the settlers enjoyed more comforts and a higher standard of living than they could hope for at home. In addition to this class, there grew up a body of administrative and judicial officials who served the Crown faithfully. It was with these men that originated the multitude of judicial reports, replies to enquiries from Spain, petitions and returns from which so detailed a knowledge of Spanish rule can be obtained. Industrious, thorough-going, animated by a sense of duty to the Crown, and dedicated to maintaining the system in accord with their training and outlook, these men were largely responsible for the fact that the vast and heterogeneous empire of Spain held together for three centuries and left an indelible imprint on the Americas. Naturally, this system had its obverse side. The very bulk of their paperwork made it difficult for the rulers at home to exercise effective control of events overseas. Half-buried in the flood of papers, the Emperor Charles V is said to have exclaimed in exasperation: 'We know everything about the Indies, except what is really going on there!'

When Ovando retired in 1509, Santo Domingo had become, with its administrative organization and the capital funds created by its citizens, a firm bridgehead for the next wave of expansion. After some years of raiding and failure to get a foothold on the mainland the Spaniards subdued Cuba with such exceptional ruthlessness that Las Casas, who accompanied them, gave up his slaves and began his life-long devotion to the cause of the Indians. In 1513 Ponce de Leon made the first reconnaissance of Florida, and two years later Hernandez was rebuffed after a landing in Yucatan. After the reduction of Cuba, Hernando Cortés recruited a small band of dissatisfied *conquistadores* and set off on his spectacular conquest of the Aztec empire of Mexico.

As no strait leading to the Mar del Sur, or Pacific Ocean, was to be found in this area, the search for a passage shifted to the southern extremity of South America. Success came to Spain when a fleet under the command of Ferdinand Magellan, a Portuguese captain who, after serving in the Moluccas, had transferred to Spanish service, sailed through the Strait which now bears his name, and after a tedious and gruelling voyage across the Pacific reached the Philippines, where he was killed in a local war between two native chiefs. On his death, the flagship *Victoria* reached the Moluccas, took on board a valuable cargo of pepper and other spices and struggled back to Cadiz in 1522. Thus within thirty years of the landing on San Salvador, a Spanish ship had reached the Spice Islands and circumnavigated the globe. A passage in the far north was more elusive and was not discovered until the nineteenth century.

Chapter XIII

EXPANDING HORIZONS

A N ATTEMPT to estimate the results, short- or long-term, of the Age of Discovery raises a fundamental problem in the writing of history. If there were results, there must also have been causes—yet a modern school of historians argues that history is not a record of causality. Some indeed go further, to argue that the result has determined the cause as much as the cause has the result. If this premise were accepted, an essay on the effects of the discovery of the Americas would be a chronology of all that has happened in the world after October 1492. The writer must therefore select, but on what principle? Many would maintain that the result of any selection would not be 'history', but a subjective creation in the mind of a professional, 'with no validity except for himself, and perhaps for fellow historians playing the same game by the same rule'. Professor J. H. Plumb, in the essay from which this quotation is taken, provides a practical solution, starting from the position that 'men believe, accept that the past existed; any other attitude for men in action is impossible'. Every man is aware of his own past, of the decisions he has taken, and equally those taken by others, which have led to his present situation, and has witnessed his fellows acting in a similar belief. Admitting the difficulties that attend the establishment of historical facts, one can apply a parallel trend of thought to the past. This is not to contend that all that has taken place in the Americas has flowed from the single fact of the discoveries; many trends came together to mould the communities that function today—sixteenth-century religious strife, the Age of Enlightenment, the Industrial Revolution, to mention a few only. The discoverers at a particular date in time revealed a vast territory, with its own geographical characteristics, in which these currents intermingled and interacted. Such a point of view has the merit, as Professor Plumb stresses, of producing an historical statement with a present social value, contributing to a deeper understanding of the problems now facing the Americas and the tensions which they create.

In this and the following chapter there is a brief outline first of the general effect on the intellectual outlook of the Age, and then on the immediate political trends in Spain and the rival nations. Finally, as this is not a history of the Americas, the more significant strands in the evolution of the two great cultural areas of North and South America which, in combination with numerous others, can be held to derive from the circumstances of the Discoveries have been sketched.

It is often taken for granted that the Discoveries had a drastic and revolutionary impact upon the European attitude to the world. Contemporaries were certainly in no doubt as to the significance of the achievement: to the Spanish historian Oviedo, for instance, it was the greatest event in history since Hercules broke through the Straits of Gibraltar; and his contemporaries regarded it as the eighth wonder of the world! This association with the deeds of a classical hero is noteworthy, for it demonstrates the extent to which the Spaniards saw themselves as continuing the work of their predecessors, rather than as initiating a complete break with the past. Hence incidentally, the necessity to show that Columbus's success was not accidental.

The Age of Discovery, therefore, was not so much a break with the past and a new departure, but rather a quickening of pace, a stimulus to nascent ideas. The New World provided, as it were, a gigantic laboratory in which the speculations of Renaissance man could be tested, modified and developed. The very size and variety of the new lands, compared with the old world in which men lived, created a mood of excitement which encouraged the bolder spirits to further ventures, and stirred the imagination of the scholars. This movement was slow in getting under way for there was for some decades little printed material available covering this expansion, beyond popular pamphlets such as the first *Letter* and the *Mundus Novus* of Vespucci. As interest spread, collections of voyages were compiled to meet the demand, the first of these, the *Paesi novamente retrovati* (Newly-discovered countries) being published at Vicenza in 1507. Besides summaries of Columbus's four voyages it included a portion of the *Mundus Novus*, Yañez Pinzon's voyage of 1501, and a brief account of the Portuguese in India. In course of time such collections grew larger and more detailed, but the public had to wait until the appearance of Giovanni Battista Ramusio's *Navigazione e Viaggi* in 1550 for a systematic body of explorers' narratives. What finally stimulated the publication of this geographical literature was the entry of other countries, France, England and Holland in particular, into the colonial struggle, and the consequent demand, for political and economic reasons, not only for the narratives of their own explorers but for any available literature on the overseas world. It was to serve these purposes that Richard Hakluyt the younger compiled his splendid *Principall Navigations . . . of the English Nation* in the year 1589. Cartographers were also busy producing their images of the contemporary world from the first surviving engraved map of the world by Giovanni Matteo Contarini in 1507, through the various augmented editions of Ptolemy's *Geography* and the products of Italian cartographers, to the great atlases of Ortelius, Mercator and their Dutch successors.

This collection, arrangement and correlation of the multitude of facts proceeded steadily until there emerged an entirely new conception of the world of man and nature towards the end of the seventeenth century.

How were the multitude of facts eventually revealed to be reconciled with each other, and into what world order were they fitted? Throughout antiquity, the general attitude to the habitable earth was summed up in the 'idea of a designed earth', that is, the earth as a purposely made creation 'designed for man alone'. This concept was taken over almost bodily by medieval Churchmen and theologians who found little difficulty in substituting for the natural laws, by which the Greek philosophers had justified this belief, the Hebrew and Christian concept of 'God the Creator'. This world view was set out clearly and in detail by Saint Augustine, and has been succinctly summarized by Professor Glacken in his historical study of early geographical ideas. 'Man, for example, lives on a divinely created earth harmoniously devised for his needs; his physical qualities such as skin and hair, his physical and mental stimulation are determined by climate, and he fulfils his God-given mission of finishing the creation, bringing order into nature, which God, in giving him mind, the eye and the hand, had intended that he do.'* The achievements of the Renaissance have encouraged the view that this period demolished immediately such theocentric concepts, and that this rejection was stimulated by the discovery of the New World with its unknown races and natural marvels.

The Renaissance had made some breaches in this acceptance of established authority, notably in the eminently practical art of politics, as *The Prince* of Nicolo Machiavelli, in its rejection of any authority overriding that of the statesman grappling with the exigencies of day-to-day affairs, demonstrates. The *conquistadores* in the New World, if they ever felt the need to justify their conduct,

* *Traces on the Rhodian Shore*, 1967.

might well have found such justification in the pages of *The Prince*. Sixteenth-century Europeans, therefore, while struck with wonder at the wealth and marvels of the New World, had no feeling that their homelands were inferior to those newly discovered, since all were the fruit of the same divine benevolence. On the contrary, they prided themselves upon the fact that they and their fellows had more fully and efficiently carried out the divine purpose by exploiting their resources and developing the arts more effectively. So it was that Europe was able to confer on less fortunate peoples those riches 'whereof the poor wretches never knew the want'. It was not until the civilization of China was revealed that this assumed superiority of western Europe was subjected to critical examination. This change in outlook, however, was by no means instantaneous. As Professor Glacken shows, the old concepts continued to prevail for three centuries. 'What greater proof of the wisdom, the power and the creativity, of God, then,' he writes, 'could one ask for than these unexpected tidings from the New Lands? The lushness of the vegetation, the great expanses of the wet tropics, the sight of people living in a manner which demanded immediate answers to questions regarding human origins and the migration not only of man but of domestic animals (the latter a far more difficult problem than the former) were but a few of the observations that evoked wonder.'

In the result, certain cosmographical ideas were strikingly vindicated, while others had eventually to be modified or abandoned. First and foremost, the discoverers proved conclusively that on the surface of the globe there were vast seas and lands 'unknown to Ptolemy'. The area of the Americas alone was approximately four times that of the Old World directly known to them, and to this landmass Magellan added the immensity of the Pacific Ocean. No longer could the *oikoumene* be regarded as a compact unit around the Mediterranean—that term had lost its literal meaning—dominated by a culture largely inherited from Greece and Rome, and drawing spiritual nourishment from the Fathers of the early Christian Church. Secondly, the hypothesis of Ptolemy and other Greek scientists that the earth was a sphere was strikingly justified when the remnants of Magellan's expedition struggled back to Cadiz, having gained a day on their circumnavigation and having carried out the greatest experimental verification of a scientific hypothesis to that date. Their world had been shown to be, not a great island washed on all shores by a seemingly limitless ocean, but a sphere of known dimensions. In the latter respect one medieval estimate, given the

THE NEW WORLD

From Sebastian Munster's edition of Ptolemy's Geography, Basel, 1540

This shows the new discoveries with traces of Columbus's ideas still apparent, e.g. the island of 'Zipangri' in the Pacific, the Asian coastline, Cathay, and the city of Quinsay. In North America there is the narrow isthmus with the Ocean beyond which Verrazano claimed to have sighted; Temistican indicates Cortes's conquest. In South America Magellan's strait is shown; the western coastline results from the conquest of Peru and Chile, but there are no modern names; interestingly, Cattigara, the classical name for a port in the Malay Peninsula, is inserted. The 'Ins. infortunatae' in the South Pacific are the Ladrones of Magellan, or possibly the Philippines. The map therefore depicts the expansion of the known world in the forty years following the first discovery.

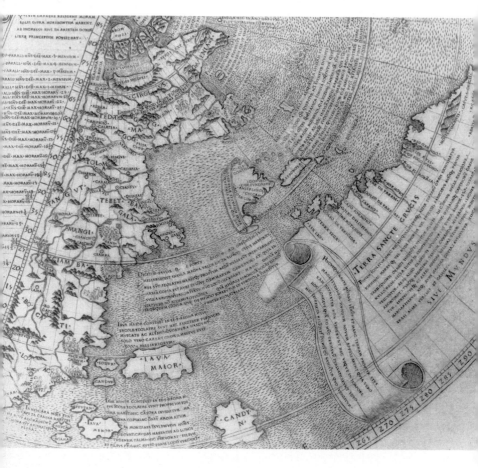

THE NEW WORLD FROM JOHANN RUYSCH'S WORLD MAP
INCLUDED IN THE ROME EDITION OF PTOLEMY'S
GEOGRAPHY, 1507

The islands of the Caribbean and part of the northern coast of South America are based on the first three voyages of Columbus (to 1496). The extension to the south shows knowledge of Cabral's sighting of Brazil (1500). The inscription to the east of 'Spagnola' recounts the story of Antilia and the Seven Cities. The long legend to the west refers to Marco Polo, the port of Zaiton, and the island of 'Sipago' (Cipangu), but doubts whether this is to be identified with the Spanish discoveries. 'Terra nova', the conspicuous promontory in the north, represents the Portuguese and English discoveries attached to the mainland of Asia. The east-west coastline is possibly the shore of 'the sea discovered by the English' of the La Cosa chart.

general uncertainties of the units of measurement involved, was remarkably accurate; this was Fra Mauro's figure of approximately 25,000 miles for the circumference of the earth. The school of thought, summarized in Sacrobosco's work, which believed in the existence of other continents, one antipodal to the Old World, was also vindicated, but the associated idea that there were seas unnavigable and lands uninhabitable had to go by the board. Similarly the theory that the surface of the globe was predominantly land, not water, had to be abandoned, for the oceans proved to cover seventy per cent of the total area.

Another geographical theory which underwent modification in the light of experience was that of 'climates'. This had been the foundation of much of medieval thinking, and at first had seemed to be justified. The corresponding zones of latitude in the New World appeared to be, at least superficially, like those of the home lands in climate, peoples and resources. This was at the root of Columbus's belief that large quantities of gold would be found in tropical America, and also accounted for his frequent comparisons of conditions in the 'Indies' with those in Europe—the sea was as calm as the river of Seville, the climate was as agreeable as that of Andalusia in May. Looked at very broadly, there was a considerable element of truth in this concept, at least as far as climate, in the sense of 'average weather conditions', was concerned, for the great world belts of climate are approximately arranged in zones of latitude. It was further confirmed for the Spaniards when they penetrated to the high dry plains of Mexico and found conditions resembling those of the Spanish *meseta*. In the course of time, however, they were made aware of the considerable differences. The Admiral had at first thought that the Caribbean was remarkably free from storms, but he was soon to become acquainted with the destructive power of the tropical tornadoes, which almost brought his fourth expedition to a disastrous close. Other observers were impressed by what appeared to them to be strange anomalies, snow-capped mountains, for example, near the Equator, or regions of great heat a considerable distance to the north. It thus became apparent that climate was not so closely related to absolute location on the earth's surface. This conclusion was reached at a quite early stage by Peter Martyr, an acute student of geography as well as an able historian. Writing of the contrast between the continents revealed in the narratives of the explorers he concluded: 'Wherefore it is apparent, the course of this so great difference to be rather the disposition of the earth than the constitutions of the Heavens. For we know of snow in the mountains of the Equinoctial or burnt zone, and the same to endure there continually. We know likewise that the inhabitants of the regions far distant from that line toward the north are molested with great heat.' He then goes on to explain that the disposition of the earth included aspect, lie of the land, and the nature of the soils and rocks. Many of the early travellers were astonished by the girth of the trees of the tropical lowlands, and attributed this to the great heat; Peter Martyr argued that it was the result of the abundance of water as much as to the high temperature. Each region had its own characteristics and so its individual products, not directly connected with the constitutions of the heavens. To this extent, men were breaking away from the idea that conditions on the surface of the earth were controlled by the movements of the heavenly bodies, but it still lingered on in the deterministic argument that man was controlled by his environment. The seventeenth-century geographer, Nathaniel Carpenter, following the French political theorist Jean Bodin, expatiated on the 'influence of the temper of the air and soil' upon the affairs of mankind; indeed it was not until late in the last century that such ideas came to be seriously challenged.

Through such experience and reasoning, geography as 'writing about the earth' began to emerge as a discipline in its own right, though progress in this direction was long hindered by the practical value, to a nation of traders, of what might be called the 'capes and bays' or 'products and trade' type of textbooks.

In the field of the humanities, the discoveries brought to the fore, and in an acute form, one problem which had exercised political philosophers from the time of Aristotle, namely the relations between civilized men, that is, Greeks and Romans, and the less advanced and unenlightened races of mankind. For the first time there lay outside the bounds of Europe a vast territory whose population had been reduced to abject submission to its European conquerors' will. This was a new situation, for the Crusading states of the Levant had come to an ignominious and bloody end, while the Portuguese had accomplished nothing on this scale in Africa, indeed they had avoided doing so. How should these people be regarded? Columbus at first had looked benevolently upon them but had soon adopted a more ruthless attitude, and the problem became more acute with the terrible acceleration in the decline of their numbers. The ensuing controversy has raged for centuries. However subject to qualification the statistical evidence may be, it speaks out only too clearly.

One source of dispute was the size of the population of the Caribbean islands at the time of the Spaniards' arrival. Las Casas, for the purpose of his polemics, was no doubt exaggerating when he bandied about the figure of two million souls. Other less committed observers, including royal officers, agreed fairly consistently that the original population of Hispaniola was approximately one million two hundred thousand, a figure also quoted by Peter Martyr. The island was undoubtedly well-populated, for the Arawaks had perfected a way of life closely integrated into the natural environment, although narrowly balanced and dependent upon the continuance of peaceful conditions. Even if for safety this figure is divided by two, the collapse was still rapid and disastrous. Thirteen years later a total of 60,000 persons was returned though this may refer to those of working age only. If we double this figure—and this is probably too great an allowance—we have a decline from 600,000 to 120,000; in other words, three-quarters of the population had disappeared by 1509. From that year the fall can be more precisely followed, for the second Admiral, Diego, a year later gave a figure of 40,000; four years later it had fallen to 23,000 and by 1518 to 11,000. A smallpox epidemic then sealed the fate of the survivors.

The challenge to humanity was not entirely new but in the Americas it had much wider ramifications. For centuries the Iberian kingdoms had been engaged in driving back the Moslem tide of invasion which had swept to the Pyrenees: the Moors were simply mortal enemies and infidels to be exterminated wherever and whenever possible. Having obliterated their last stronghold in the Peninsula and deported large numbers, Castile and Aragon had then turned their attention to the Jewish community in their midst, which was given the alternatives of abjuring its faith or going into exile. The *conquistadores* were in no mood to treat the peoples of the New World any less arbitrarily. They were themselves perfectly frank about their motives; they had gone out to deprive the Indians of their gold, and were ready to employ any means to this end.

The position of the Crown was more complex, since its title in part rested on its declared intention of treating benevolently any peoples subjected to its rule. In seeking the subjection and conversion of the Indians, the Spaniards had considerable theological support: it was accepted that it was a Christian duty to carry the faith to all peoples and to offer them the opportunity of salvation. The Crown emphasized this obligation in its negotiations with Columbus, enjoining him to treat the natives with consideration. Before the depopulation reached frightening proportions, however, the Sovereigns, beyond admonishing their officers from time to time, reminding them that the Indians were their subjects and should be treated accordingly and in principle at least opposing their enslavement, tended to leave the moral aspects to the Church. When extermination rather than slavery was seen to be only too likely, a bitter controversy flared up in which the men on the spot, alarmed by the imminent disappearance of the essential labour force, were ranged against more merciful and enlightened churchmen.

The settlers represented the Indians as lazy, treacherous and improvident, given to cannibalism and a host of other vices—in short, unworthy to be regarded as human beings. In this contention the more sophisticated could quote Aristotle to the effect that there were certain classes of men incapable of exercising the natural rights enjoyed by the more rational and integrated, and that these might properly be enslaved. On the other hand, zealous friars, aghast at the brutality, sprang to the Indians' defence. Mass conversion without proper preparation or instruction was a mockery, and the treatment the Indians received a denial of natural and divine law. These gentle, unwarlike and contented peoples, uncorrupted by the world, must not only be converted but protected and cherished. From this attitude was to develop the concept of the noble savage which, elaborated by Voltaire and Rousseau, exerted considerable influence on political theory in eighteenth-century Europe.

This view was first forcibly expressed by a Dominican friar, otherwise little-known, Antonio de Montesinos, whose stand should be recorded in even the briefest reference to the history of human rights. In Santo Domingo, at Christmas in 1511, he preached a fiery sermon on the text: 'I am a voice crying in the wilderness.' As recorded by Las Casas, Montesinos pulled no punches: 'In order to make your sins against the Indians known to you,' his denunciation proceeded, 'I have come into this pulpit, I who am a voice of Christ crying in the wilderness of this island, and it therefore behoves you to listen not with careless attention but with all your heart and senses, so that you may hear it, for this is going to be the strangest voice that ever you heard, the harshest and hardest and most dangerous that ever you expected to hear . . . This voice says that you are in mortal sin, that you live and die in it, for the cruelty and tyranny you use in dealing with these innocent people. Tell me, by what right or justice do you keep these Indians in such a cruel and horrible servitude? On what authority have you waged a detestable war against these people who dwelt quietly and peaceably on their own land? . . . With the excessive work you demand of them they fall ill and die, or rather you kill with your desire to extract and acquire gold every day. And what care do you take that they should be instructed in religion? Are these not men? Have they not rational souls? . . .'

Despite the wrath aroused in the settlers by this denunciation, Montesinos returned to the attack a week later, elaborating the theme 'Suffer me a little and I will show thee that I have yet to speak on God's behalf'. When reports of the friar's sermons reached Spain, the Dominicans were warned that if they persisted in this attitude, in defiance of Canon Law, they would be withdrawn from the Indies. Accordingly, Montesinos was reprimanded by his superiors and recalled to Spain in 1515. The controversy however did not die down completely, thanks to the powerful support of the Indians' cause by Las Casas, 'the Apostle of the Indies', as he was known to his supporters. Despite fierce opposition he made some headway at least in securing theoretical recognition of their rights. The Laws of Burgos, in 1513, stipulated that the Indians were not to be attacked unless they were aggressive or cannibalistic. Before new territories were annexed, a proclamation must be read, setting forth the Spanish claim to sovereignty, based on the Papal Bulls, and requiring the natives to be of good behaviour. As L. Hanke has commented, 'This discourse, unintelligible to the Indians even if it had been possible to interpret it into their various tongues, soon became a mockery to those entrusted with it.' Whenever a Spaniard produced the document the Indians promptly took to their heels.

Las Casas was not discouraged; for more than half a century, in the Indies and in Spain, by personal effort, through representations to the Crown, by tracts, books and sermons, he fought the cause of the oppressed. Despite failure to translate his teaching into practice—his projected colony in Venezuela came to nothing, as was almost inevitable in the current situation—it seemed at times that he might gain the day. By the Bull, *Sublimus Deus*, the Church came out clearly against slavery, recognizing the Indians as 'truly men capable of understanding the faith'. His advocacy finally won over the Emperor Charles himself and his Council after much disputation, and a fresh approach was embodied in the 'New Laws of the Indies'. The system of *encomienda* was to be abolished and no such grants were to be made in the future; all those held by governors, Crown officials, bishops and monasteries were to lapse immediately, and other grants were to revert to the Crown on the death of the holder.

The Indians were to be treated as direct vassals of the Crown. This sweeping solution was easy enough to proclaim but to execute it was beyond the power of the Crown in face of the consternation and violent opposition the decrees provoked overseas. In Mexico the *conquistadores* refused angrily to surrender the rewards of their services, having already opposed successfully Cortés's desire to improve the status of the Indians. To pacify them the Crown was obliged to grant a dispensing power to the local authorities. In Peru, the reaction was even more violent, leading to some years of civil war, much loss of life and very nearly to a declaration of independence. Ultimately the Crown reasserted its authority through the resolute action of a new Viceroy.

This impact of two worlds, of which the treatment of the Indians was one aspect only, was slow to change the intellectual outlook of Europe, but by the end of the seventeenth century the defenders of the old order were yielding ground, and new ideas of humanity, human culture and the 'revolution of new environments' were being harvested. One facet of this scientific renaissance was exhibited in the work of Sir Isaac Newton and the practitioners of the new physical sciences. (It is significant that Newton edited an edition of Varenius's *Geographia generalis* a standard text of the day.) In the humanities, the movement culminated in the Age of Voltaire and the philosophers of the Enlightenment, who drew their material not only from the New World but to a greater extent from travellers' reports of the civilizations of Egypt, Persia and, above all, China. This development is summarized by Paul Hazard in his survey of seventeenth-century thought:* 'It is perfectly correct to say that all the fundamental concepts, such as Property, Freedom, Justice and so on, were brought under discussion again as a result of the conditions in which they were seen to operate in far-off countries, in the first place because, instead of all differences being referred to one universal archetype, the emphasis was now on the particular, the irreducible, the individual; in the second because notions hitherto taken for granted could now be checked in the light of facts ascertained by actual experience, facts readily available to all inquiring minds . . . Perspectives changed. Concepts which had occupied the lofty sphere of the transcendental were brought down to the level of things governed by circumstance.' At this point, modern scientific thought begins to take shape.

* Hazard, Paul: *The European Mind, 1680–1715.* London, 1964, pp. 26–7.

Chapter XIV

THE TWO AMERICAS, SOUTH AND NORTH

SUCH WAS the intellectual atmosphere in which the work of the discoverers was continued. In the world of everyday affairs and practical politics, men conducted themselves at first in accordance with well-established precedents over a field of action that had been vastly enlarged, offering material rewards apparently unlimited. These opportunities they set about exploiting vigorously although quick returns were not immediately forthcoming. It was not until after 1545 that the gold and silver of Mexico and the silver from the Potosi mines of Peru contributed significantly to building up Spain's position as a great power. Nevertheless, as in the realm of thought, forces were gradually coming to a head which ultimately transformed the world scene, bringing men face to face with new and complex problems.

For Spain the immediate task was to assert unchallengeable sovereignty over her new acquisitions. The arguments that the Admiral was not the true discoverer, that he had been preceded by unknown pilots, or knew of the route to the Indies from other sources, were raised during the political manœuvrings of the early decades. To establish Spain's rights on as broad a basis as possible, the historian Oviedo elaborated a claim that the Indies were the Hesperides of the ancient geographers and had been discovered by early, semi-legendary, Kings of Spain. The significant point about this claim is not its flimsy character but that the Emperor Charles V ignored it, for possession through discovery by the Admiral as the Crown's agent was a more substantial basis than speculations about the deeds of his shadowy predecessors. Similar reasoning no doubt contributed also to the abandonment of the long-drawn-out legal contest over the Admiral's rights and privileges. Basing rights on the Crown's title of possession through discovery and annexation, with Papal support, also made it possible later to ignore the claims advanced by other nations, for instance those which Dr. Dee and other Tudor antiquarians founded on the alleged discoveries of King

Arthur. So far as the Treaty of Tordesillas was concerned, it soon became clear that the meridian would never be demarcated throughout its length; each country therefore simply notified the other of the position of new discoveries in accordance with the spirit of the treaty. Thus from the beginning the principle of discovery and proclamation of sovereignty was accepted in international relations, though this was later qualified by the requirement of effective occupation over a reasonable period.

In line with this policy of exclusion Spain, and to a lesser extent Portugal, endeavoured with considerable success to keep the commerce of the New World in their own hands, on the theory that colonies existed solely for the benefit of the home country, and that to permit other nations to trade directly with them weakened her own economy. This attitude was later adopted by the mercantilist powers of Europe, its best-known manifestation being the English Navigation Acts. The vociferous indignation which the Spanish monopoly excited, particularly among Protestant politicians and historians, therefore, was little more than an expression of self-righteousness, as when the distinguished historian, the late Sir Richard Lodge, wrote of 'the monstrous pretension of the two pioneers of discovery to monopolize all its fruits to themselves'. It was not until the Dutch and the English began, as world carriers, to develop a widely-flung commercial trading system and the principle of the freedom of the seas was introduced into international law that, finally, the nineteenth century looked with approval upon free-trade doctrines. However for three centuries the Spaniards were able to maintain their monopoly, modified by the *assiento* or licence for limited annual transactions. The biggest breach in the system was due to large-scale smuggling and the diversion of silver to the Philippines, where it entered into commercial exchanges with China, instead of crossing the Atlantic to Spain. Smuggling was particularly strong in Brazil where Portugal strove to maintain the same exclusive policy which she initiated in West Africa; but she was not sufficiently in control to curb the illegal activities of the exuberant colonists, although able to drive out the Dutch from their settlement on the north-east coast which had been designed to break through the 'silver curtain'.

During her wars with Spain in the eighteenth century England contemplated from time to time encouraging the Spanish settlements on the Pacific coast to throw off the connection with Spain and assume independent status, but this plan was never seriously pursued—harrying the coasts was scarcely calculated to encourage such a move. One small effort was, however, made to establish a foothold in Central America but the Scottish colony at Darien had a brief and inglorious existence. Any further territorial expansion by European nations was finally checked at independence when the United States formulated the Monroe doctrine. The general effect of this policy was to continue the isolation of the continent from world affairs and to divert the attentions of European countries away from the south to North America, where, beyond the Mexican border, Spain was never strongly established in control.

The Spanish monopoly in the New World was naturally not accepted by the other nations which challenged her hegemony in the sixteenth century—France, England, and later the Dutch. Their efforts to establish footholds in the Caribbean met with success only after a period of harassment of the Spanish settlements and treasure fleets, and participation in the slave trade. It was not until the mid-seventeenth century that the English first made considerable progress, when Cromwell obtained Jamaica from Spain. On the South American mainland the Spaniards and Portuguese succeeded in repelling these assaults by their rivals except on the north-eastern coasts. But the Spaniards were not so successful in the northern continent, although they were able to hold most of the Gulf coast and the Florida peninsula for three centuries, for the English colonized the littoral between the Appalachian mountains and the sea where they found conditions more congenial to their way of life; and still further north the French founded a colony of settlement in the lower St. Lawrence basin and worked down the Mississippi river to link up with fellow-colonists in the delta.

So, for over three centuries, Latin America was almost completely isolated from the outside world, under the control of Spain, and the two cultures, Hispanic and indigenous, were left to work out their destiny alone. Before examining the results of this contact, it is relevant at this point to consider the effects of this overseas empire on Spain herself. After 1550 it was definitely showing a return for the labours and trials of the *conquistadores* for, in addition to the silver and gold from the mainland, the plantations on the islands in the Caribbean were contributing substantially to the export trade. Their success was entirely due to the slave labour imported from West Africa. This traffic accelerated throughout the century and perhaps as many as twelve million negroes were transported across the Atlantic, one of the greatest forced transfers of population in history.

The sugar, rum and chocolate they produced were the price for which the maritime nations strove bitterly until the close of the century; if 'the Indies were the apple of the King of Spain's eye', it was an apple coveted by numerous powerful rivals, who turned these seas into the real cockpit of European conflict. However, whether this splendid empire proved a long-term blessing to Spain herself is debatable. Cortés might write to his Emperor in 1524, when thanking him for much-needed help: 'Your Caesarian Majesty ... need do no more in order to be monarch of the world', and for a period it seemed as though the American treasure would assist Charles V towards placing this prize within his grasp, but in the long run its effects were economically disastrous. Much of this wealth was directed to meeting pressing current liabilities, to raising, equipping and maintaining the famous Spanish infantry which dominated European battlefields, to subsidizing client states, or to paying for imports, mainly brought in by Portuguese ships. Little of the profit was invested, either in the colonies or in Spain, to breed new wealth. The most apparent result was to cause a steep rise in prices not only in Spain but throughout Europe. The nobles and the great landowners enjoyed a luxurious and aloof way of life, but for the smaller men, particularly the peasantry, their lot became harder and wellnigh unendurable. Their reaction was obvious—flight, where possible, from the land. The reply of the landowners was equally predictable, to turn vast tracts into cattle ranches which required little labour, and to take what profit was to be had from the animal products, which, incidentally, were open to the competition of hides and tallow from the overseas territories. Thus the Spanish economy lost the foundation of a settled and prosperous agriculture. As a contemporary proverb had it, 'A Spaniard could exist for a week on a German's dinner'. A weak, poor rural population and the absence of a prosperous middle class were additional factors in the failure of Spain to develop popular institutions. However, Spain could take legitimate pride in the thought that she had carried her culture and religion overseas and in watching it spread across a continent. Even today the Spanish language is a major force in world communications, commerce and literature.

For the outside world these widening horizons initiated a revolution in international affairs by obliging statesmen to think globally; about the precise location, on the other side of the world, of the Spice Islands, about the best route to them (was the theoretically shorter way by the Arctic practical?), about the best sites for overseas settlements or the best markets for their goods. The paramount importance of command of the sea was recognized at an early date and western Europe embarked upon its maritime phase, with a shift of the centre of power away from the Mediterranean to the English Channel and its approaches and to West Indian waters. The characteristic world map ceased to be the circular *mappa mundi* centred on Jerusalem; the new configuration was that of the Mercator chart divided by the Greenwich meridian with the Americas and Asia conveniently placed to west and east.

In this revolution those who first profited greatly were the merchants and bankers of the Empire in the Low Countries and the Rhineland. There the rising commercial and industrial classes, already established before the arrival of the wealth from the Indies, applied their gains to extending their activities not only in Spain but throughout western Europe and to stimulating further growth. During the fifteenth century Flemings and Germans had flocked to Portugal as merchants and colonists of the Atlantic islands. This trend then spread to Spain, with increasing strength when the Hapsburg alliances brought the countries closer together. Charles V's advisers were largely of this origin—he himself had little proficiency in Spanish—and German bankers, among whom the Fuggers of Augsburg were prominent, replaced Italian firms of the old dispensation as financiers of foreign trade and of the costly campaigns in northern Europe. A similar shift had taken place in Portugal. When the centre of the traffic in pepper and other oriental products was removed to Antwerp, Portugal became little more than a carrier of seaborne products with a declining share in the profits. As a result, Antwerp and Augsburg came to be the banking centres of Europe.

This opening-up of sources of supply outside Europe was the beginning of the worldwide system of commercial exchange, which reached a zenith in the nineteenth century, to give place in turn to the present nexus of interrelated national economies. Again, this was not the case of the discoveries having initiated an entirely new trend—Venice and other Italian cities had drawn their profits from the spice trade with southern Asia—but an acceleration and enlargement of the trend to such a degree as to bring about a difference in kind. The import of overseas products ceased to be the mark of an extractive or 'robber' economy, but set in motion an export of manufactured goods and development capital in return. Spain and Portugal were not to be the lasting beneficiaries of this revolution; these who ultimately flourished upon it were the countries of the north-west, initially Flanders and the Rhineland, followed later by Holland, France and England. Out of the profits of this prospering commerce accumulated the capital which fertilized and nourished their incipient industries until, led by Britain, they became the 'workshops of the world'. This international exchange developed, not under the rigid and hampering control of a central government, but through new institutions and climates of opinion, chartered and joint-stock companies, and the liberal free-trade and worldwide market pinpointed by Adam Smith as the true source of the 'Wealth of nations'.

Until around the year 1800, Latin America was thus scarcely affected by what was going on across the Atlantic, and its political and social structure largely retained the form it had been given in the early days of the conquest. At its base was the Indian population, untouched by the invaders in areas such as Mexico and Peru, where it was numerous enough to preserve much of the ancient ways and traditions. As Poole comments: 'The Indian was not Europeanized; rather he took over certain Old World techniques that allowed him to root himself more firmly in the soil. The essential fact and pattern of his life remained the subsistence cultivation of maize.'* This applied only in closely-settled regions; the fate of Indians conscripted into the Mexican gold- or Peruvian silver-mines was tragic. For the others, the introductions were few and minor, iron for simple tools, small axes for clearing bush, domestic fowl and donkeys. The major techniques were applied by the new masters, whose triumph itself rested upon the horse and the steel sword, 'a cutting instrument much superior to any the Indian possessed'. They also experimented with, rejected, or finally developed on a large scale other introductions, among them wheat, sugar cane, olives, vines and other plants, and, in addition to the horse, cattle, sheep and goats. Another aspect of the European advent was the opening-up of regions hitherto unexploited by man, the most conspicuous being the scrub and grasslands of northern Mexico. There the Spaniards, with their horses and cattle, successfully built up a valuable local economy. Unable to run this unaided, they gave to the *mestizo* population an opening which provided one outlet for their abilities. Much of this area was to pass later under American control, and it was here that the cowboy of western legend was born. Thus at the base of Latin-American life there was, over vast areas, an Indian population, little changed

* Poole, D. M.: 'The Spanish Conquest of Mexico', *Geographical Journal* 117 (1951) 27.

in its way of life; intermingled with it was the *mestizo* people, a class created and influenced by the newcomers, and, over all, the Spanish officials, landed families, churchmen, and bourgeoisie (relatively restricted in numbers) who controlled the whole and welded it by a rigid governmental structure into an enduring organization which for three centuries functioned from California to Patagonia.

Over these territories the utilization of the land was based upon the *encomienda*, or division, which developed out of the *repartimiento*. The latter conferred rights over groups of Indians, not over defined areas of land. The new system recognized outright ownership of land in estates frequently of great extent, while the neighbouring Indians were obliged to take service with the landowners. It was in the latter's own interest to make sure that the Indians had at least a minimum standard of existence. Outside the Caribbean area, therefore, although the master-man relationship was in this way preserved, the Spaniards, unlike the Portuguese in Brazil, had no necessity to import slave labour.

Upon this indigenous population pressed the alien and rigid rule of the Spaniards. This imported system, basically Mediterranean, was built around the city and city life; the concrete sign of the occupation was the building of cities and the creation of civic institutions. Santo Domingo, the first modern American city founded in 1500, was soon followed by others; the ruined native capital of Mexico, Tenochtitlan, was rebuilt by Cortés and renamed Mexico City, and Lima was founded in 1535. Thus the split between the city (Hispanic in origin and culture) and the rural areas (Indian and aboriginal) which is a characteristic, and so far imperfectly resolved, problem of Latin-American life, is not a twentieth-century phenomenon.

All political power centred in the Viceroys acting under instructions from Spain through the official hierarchy and in co-operation with the Church. Apart from the city and town councils, whose functions were largely ceremonial, there were no representative institutions. The territorial extent of the first two Viceroyalties reflected the stages in the establishment of Spanish sovereignty; the Caribbean, Mexico and the lands immediately to the south comprised the Viceroyalty of New Spain, while the remainder of South America, minus Brazil, formed the Viceroyalty of Peru, with Lima as the centre. The great distances involved, the growth of local differences, arising partly from geographical conditions and partly from the variety of the indigenous populations, ultimately broke up this artificial unity. Before the end of the eighteenth century, two further

Viceroyalties had been created, New Granada and Rio de la Plata, and some lesser administrative units had been formed, the Captaincies of Guatemala, Venezuela, Cuba and Chile. Thus the structure of the overseas territory resembled that of the Spanish kingdom, the Viceroyalties having their counterparts in the kingdoms of Castile, Aragon, Catalonia and others, all under the supreme authority of the Spanish Crown.

The Church was efficiently organized territorially, with impressive cathedrals and monasteries. The first universities were founded at Mexico and Lima in 1551 by imperial charter. As in contemporary Europe, classics and theology were the main studies, and several universities were noted for their law schools, but all were controlled in the interests of Church and State. The concentration on the humanities and legal studies, to the neglect of more practical and scientific pursui s, in universities of the time continued after the Wars of Independence. By the close of the eighteenth century western Europe, with the spread of the mechanical arts and the progress of the industrial revolution, had a body of trained and skilful technicians and industrialists to conduct her along the road to the modern world. In Latin America such a source of skilled labour scarcely existed—a lack which seriously retarded national progress and left affairs to be run by lawyers and military officers, a bias which persists to a slightly lesser extent today. The local craftsmen were competent to furnish the needs of colonial societies, but any considerable growth in trade and manufacture was hindered by the prohibition of inter-colonial trade—everything must pass through the home ports.

This transference of a complete constitutional and cultural system, with little alteration, from one hemisphere to another is remarkable in itself; but its success and its endurance had one defect—when the break with Spain came the liberators had to face manifold problems with little or no experience in self-government. Allowing for all the defects, however, it is difficult to accept the nineteenth-century statesman Lord Bryce's condemnation of Hispanic rule as 'the most ill-conceived and ill-administered scheme of government that selfishness and stupidity ever combined to devise'.*

Ideas, however, proved more difficult to keep out than interlopers, and were even more inimical to the established order. The works of the eighteenth-century philosophers, political theorists and demagogues, despite the efforts of the governments at suppression, spread

* Bryce, J. A.: *South America* 1912.

rapidly and eventually undermined the old order between the years 1810 and 1826. The early years of independence however were not easy for the new republics: the disorganization of government, the growth of separate local interests, the losses consequent on the wars, hindered marked advance. Despite the break with Spain, the influx of revolutionary ideas, and a widening of political and commercial horizons to include Britain and the United States, the social structure underwent little fundamental change. As far as the lower classes, *mestizo* and Indian, were concerned, the descendants of the *conquistadores* remained firmly in control and in possession of great estates. This dichotomy between the wielders of political power and the ruled still persists to a lesser but still significant extent.

This is manifest particularly in the problem of land ownership. In modern Chile the proportion of large holdings is high, no less than three-fifths of the farmed land being comprised in only three per cent of the total number of holdings; in Argentina, where farming approaches more closely European intensity, the corresponding figures are three-quarters and six per cent. These figures to some extent reflect the character of the agriculture, extensive sheep ranching in Chile and the raising of beef cattle in Argentina (where wheat growing reduces the proportion), but fundamentally they demonstrate the persistence of the social structure inherited from the past.

The composition of the various populations also results from the course of events in the early centuries of Spanish rule. In the Caribbean the Spanish and other European nations imported great numbers of negro slaves to replace the aboriginals, and their descendants form a considerable part of the present population. To a much lesser extent Africans were also imported into the north-east, and in more recent times there has been some movement of negroes from the islands into the Central American isthmus. Elsewhere in the regions opened up by the Spaniards the negro stock is not significant. Figures for this intermingling of races are not easy to disentangle, for the republics are anxious to emphasize their Hispanic heritage. In the north, in Venezuela, Columbia and Ecuador, the 'unmixed European population' averages from fifteen to twenty per cent, *mestizos* sixty-five per cent, with Indians and negroes forming the balance. In Chile by contrast the European element is approximately one-third, and the pure-blooded Indians, mostly Arucanians, five per cent only. Where the Spanish influence was less strong, the Indian strain predominates, almost fifty per cent in Peru and seventy-five per cent in areas of Bolivia. Where migrants from Europe have been numerous, as in Argentina, it is stated that ninety-five per cent of the population is of European stock. Large numbers of Indians, living at barely subsistence level, knowing no Spanish and with no aptitude for the skills required in the modern world, present those republics anxious to develop their economies with complex and daunting problems.

In economic affairs the 'robber' economy of the early period had ensured that little or none of the gains from the exploitation of the great natural resources of the continent had been invested actually in the continent; the gold, silver and diamonds went to enrich the Crown and the grandees, and the restrictions on inter-colonial exchange had hampered the growth of a broadly-based economy. Thus Latin America remained outside the new industrial world for most of the nineteenth century as the supplier of primary raw materials to the rapidly growing industrial populations of western Europe. At various times and to a varying extent, natural rubber from Brazil, tin from Bolivia, saltpetre from Chile, beef and wheat from Argentina have been an important factor in international trade, but nevertheless subordinate to the requirements of the great industrial countries. Today oil is the foundation of the economies of Venezuela, Columbia and Netherlands Surinam. In this way Latin America shares the handicaps which beset all developing countries which are primarily exporters of pastoral and agricultural produce, especially those in the tropics. Unless the terms of world trade are particularly advantageous, these are subject to wide and often sudden fluctuations in price with a general long-term tendency to decline in relation to the prices of heavy industrial and manufactured goods. This is due to the fact that agricultural output tends to expand rapidly to meet the requirements of a particular market, to which other producers are then attracted, leading to a sharp price fall. Again, technical advances in industry result in a change from one raw material to another, leaving the old product with a much reduced market. The fluctuations in the fortunes of Brazilian coffee-growers are a case in point. Thus, outside secondary industries for domestic needs, Latin America is still largely a producer of raw materials, with large sections of its population living at subsistence level. Some countries, however, are nearing the point of 'take-off' into a modern industrialized state, obviously those which have profited from the impetus of large-scale immigration from Europe or of foreign capital investment. Argentina is a notable example of this type; the *pampas* which form the kernel of her economy as producers of wheat and beef were developed largely by immigrants from Spain, Italy and Germany, while the construction of the necessary railroads was financed originally by British capitalists, who also supplied the equipment, and by the export of beef. At the moment, however, Argentina's progress in this direction appears to have been checked by the adoption of a policy of autarchy and by domestic political differences. The oil-producing countries of the north seem to be better placed to break away from the old, more or less stationary economy.

Brazil stands apart from the other countries of Latin America through its own national history and its geographical situation. With Brazilian Portuguese as the national language its culture is not identified with that of the Hispanic countries. It took no part in the wars of independence nor did it immediately reject the authority of the home country, and constitutionally it was for a period first the seat of a government in exile from Portugal and later an Empire under Dom Pedro. There was less break, therefore, with the past, and the life of the country continued without internal or external war. Largely because of this continuity and the Portuguese tradition of national solidarity, the military class, unlike those of other South American states, did not intervene directly in civil affairs, and came to regard itself as the guarantor of the constitution. Although slavery continued until well into the nineteenth century, and the position of the lower social strata was little different from that in the other countries, there were no strongly marked racial divisions. The population of Brazil, as varied in origin as any in the continent—Portuguese, negro, European from many countries, aboriginal, and Asian—is thus closely integrated.

Despite these individual characteristics Brazil shares many of the problems of Latin America as a whole, some indeed in a more acute form. A large proportion of its area is still scarcely known, much less developed, for in contrast to the 'national territory', that is, the coastal belt and the more closely settled south-eastern states from Bahia southwards, stands the vast area of the Amazon basin of equatorial rain forest bordered on the south by parched upland plateaus of thorn and scrub. (Brazil has a greater extent of territory lying about the Equator than any other country in the world.) This vast river and its numerous and lengthy tributaries were probably as well known in the eighteenth century as they are today and many sections have scarcely been traversed since the days of the wild rubber collectors; as a waterway when not in flood it provides access to a great area, which however is largely unexploited and in present conditions unexploitable. The sparse and widely scattered Indian population where it is in contact with the agents of civilization is fading away, but elsewhere in the untraversed areas it maintains a precarious way of life. A further handicap to development is the fact that the main axis of communication, the Amazon, runs eastwards to the Atlantic, while the core of Brazil lies at a considerable distance to the south-east.

The Brazilians aware of the unfavourable situation have in the present century begun the tremendous task of overcoming this isolation, though without large capital investment and immigrants progress must inevitably be slow. One considerable step was the foundation of the new federal capital of Brasilia far to the north-west of Rio de Janeiro. One of its principal functions will be to act as a link between the latter and the upper Amazon basin, and for this purpose a twelve-hundred-mile highway to the river port of Manaus is planned. The main problem will then be to offer sufficient inducements to settlers and to find capital to undertake large-scale development, a problem which concerns the general question of the future of the tropical world and the developing countries. At present the Amazon region is not a significant contributor to world production and trade; one of its principal resources is the extensive forest, but tropical trees do not in general yield commercially valuable timber. Early in this century, wild rubber yielded considerable revenue, but this has declined with the development of synthetic substitutes, and the area of rubber under plantation is not great. Without extensive prospecting it is not possible to forecast what exploitable minerals are present on a commercial scale, and similarly the chances for oil production are not known. One possibility is that medicinal plants might prove economically rewarding. The other problem concerns the source of potential population. In this respect Brazil is perhaps better placed, with its characteristic racial stock, to undertake large-scale settlement in a tropical environment than many other countries. This would require, first of all, the overcoming of the current, and unfortunate, attraction of the great cities for the rural peasantry fleeing the land. As with many cities in the tropics, this has resulted in the growth of 'shanty towns' in their suburbs, where the migrants live in conditions of squalor at a standard little if any above that of their village homes. It is, however, scarcely conceivable that with the pressure on food supplies, minerals and other requirements of modern industry which the world must experience before the end of this century, so large and potentially productive an area will remain in its present state as a virtually uninhabited desert. Brazil, in the unusual position of a country with a vast unexploited 'colonial' territory adjacent to its land frontiers, must surely have a great future in the evolving world order. Is it too fanciful to believe that in the near future Brazil may, in relation to the Amazon basin, stand in the same position as the United States were when the pioneers were breaking through the eastern mountain barrier to exploit the resources of the northern continent's interior?

Whatever the future of these Latin-American republics may be, it is unlikely to resemble that of the North American states. Indeed, the contrasts, geographical, political and social, cannot fail to strike the most superficial observer. South of the Rio Grande the Iberian stamp is unmistakable on the cultural landscapes and in the outlook of their peoples. North of that river there is another cultural unit, also with its own regional variations: over the greater part of the inhabitable area the twentieth-century American way of life pre-dominates, north-west European in origin but modified by later contributions from most countries in the world. Only to a slight degree has the original population survived, but in its place stands a significant section of African origin. To elaborate this theme in detail would require a history of the United States and Canada, with excursions into Mexican history; certain main lines of development, flowing from the circumstances of the discoveries and the early decades, may however be isolated, providing a theme which requires considerations of geography as well as history. Climatically the main region of settlement in North America lies well to the north of the tropics, with a markedly maritime belt east of the Appalachians. Beyond this barrier a great extent of country of low relief stretches westwards, much of it not exceeding five hundred feet in altitude until the High Plains of the west are reached. This is essentially the basin of the Mississippi-Missouri, the greatest hydrological system in the world. The dominant vegetation in the east is deciduous, temperate woodland which gives place westwards to the long-grass and short-grass plains. Once the pioneers had crossed the eastern mountain barrier and descended the Ohio and other tributaries of the Mississippi, there was no serious obstacle to their progress until they were confronted by the high desert and mountains of the west. There is little need to stress the contrast between the conditions which faced them and those which challenged the exploiters of South America—the vast areas of the Amazonian rain forest and swamp-bordered rivers, the parched scrubland of interior Matto

Grosso, or the cold deserts of the Andes. This east to west advance was not seriously hindered by the southward trend of the rivers, and these later served as a bond between north and south.

The great westward advance was not fully under way until two centuries after the foundation of the New England colonies. Up to the time of the Pilgrim fathers, the tropics continued to draw the attention of Europe, fascinated by the rewards which the Spaniards had gained with such apparent ease. When it was also apparent that the Spaniards were firmly in control, England and France looked northwards for areas suitable for expansion, where they calculated upon finding an environment not too different from their own. So it was that North America was colonized by west European rather than Mediterranean men.

The founders of New England were not Renaissance Catholics, frankly actuated by the prospect of great and immediate wealth, which in fact eluded most of them, but men of the Reformation, seeking to create a society after their own fashion, free from the restrictions hampering them at home. From the first they were in America to stay, to settle on the land and to found homogeneous societies, not to chase El Dorado across a continent. By investing the capital produced by the labours of their own hands they created a firm base between the coast and the mountains for future expansion inland. It is perhaps not too severe a judgement to pronounce that the Iberians were 'strippers' while the founding fathers were investors, but this goes little futher than the dictum of the distinguished historian Gilberto Freyre, that in Brazil 'the Portuguese economy became possessed of the furious and parasitic passion of exploiting and transporting in place of producing wealth'.

By farming and fishing, by exploiting the woods and local iron ores in a primtiive way, the New Englanders built up six small states, bound together by the sea and animated by a spirit of sturdy if narrow independence. Unlike the Spaniards, they had left their homes to escape authority and looked forward to eventual political independence of England. In the south, progress took another direction, and a different social system evolved. Virginia and Carolina found their prosperity in plantations of cotton, tobacco and rice, worked by imported negro labour from an early date. This contrast, persisting with dire consequences for the American Union, was reflected in differing relations with England: the southern economy was more closely integrated with the home country, while the northern states resented and finally rejected English attempts through the Navigation Acts to control the direction of their trade. Between the six New England and the three southern colonies the 'Tidewater States' were late in developing, though these have been called 'the most important British landfalls'. Farming stock from England and Hanover, including William Penn and his Quakers, succeeded by cultivating a variety of crops by new techniques in transforming this area into the home of American mixed farming, less traditional than that to the north and freed from the south's dependence on plantation labour. Their farming folk intermingled profitably with seafarers and to them were added later, as the westward drive progressed, the industrial pioneers; all of which combined to make this the political and economic core of the young Republic, and Pennsylvania the 'Keystone State'. But it was through the New England ports that the waves of European immigrants poured into the continent and proceeded by stages to carry the frontier of settlement across the mountains and the Mississippi until it came to rest on the Pacific shores.

When, therefore, the exodus of population from Europe began around the beginning of the eighteenth century and built up into the great movements of the nineteenth, there was across the North Atlantic a vast area capable of providing not only a new home but the prospect of a better life. The stimuli which produced this migration were manifold: a sharp rise in the natural increase of population (which has not been fully explained*); economic distress in western Europe; political strife and insecurity in the Germanic lands under the constant threat of war; and aspirations towards a freer life encouraged by the philosophers of the Age of Enlightenment: all these considerations must be reckoned with, but doubtless the fundamental impulse was the urge to exploit the opportunities which, by report, the new lands in the west offered to bolder and more enterprising spirits.

The New Englanders, narrow as their outlook may appear to the permissive societies of today, were inspired by an ethic which placed a premium on work, moulded a cohesive society out of a mass of individuals, and inculcated an assurance of ultimate success, all qualities which fitted individuals for the rough and strenuous life

* Carlo Cipolla considers that by 1750 the European population figure was 'in a way the "historical" maximum for the agricultural phase of the story of man ... Under the push of internal demographic pressure and with the advantage of technological superiority, the Europeans spread all over the world, peacefully and otherwise.' *World Population*, p. 99.

of the frontier, where they were free from the restraints of life in the east. Translated into terms of the pioneering life, they stood for personal initiative, determination, self-reliance, regard for one's neighbours, rough justice, and a spirit of optimism. In spite of the sectional interests which the new environment created—cattlemen versus ranchers, agriculturalists against industrialists, the small man against the capitalist—the sense of being one nation prevailed. With free homesteads and universal free education, each man had an opportunity to advance himself, irrespective of his national origin.

This spirit held the Union together in the supreme test of the war between the States, after the sectional interests of the south had been subordinated, but leaving the problem of the integration of the emancipated negroes unsolved. With the disappearance of the frontier, when all land had been allotted, the severe restriction of immigration after the First World War, and the profound changes in economic and social organization which followed, the feeling of 'one nation' still holds together a country with a population approaching two hundred million.

*

The Age of Discovery was the first act in the drama of a great human migration, without doubt the greatest in human history, which was played out over four centuries. As it unfolded a great new culture, part Hispanic part Indian, rose in Latin America; vast areas of virgin land were brought into the human economy: geographical location acquired a new significance, transforming international politics. Western Europe rose for a period to world supremacy; millions of Europeans poured across the ocean to occupy the North American continent and to lay the foundations of a new and mighty state which was a challenger for world power. In the opening act there were many characters, some barely emerging from obscurity, others better known but no less enigmatic; they play their parts, great and small, often savagely but never without conviction. None have captured the imagination of succeeding generations more powerfully, and rightly so, than Christopher Columbus, the weaver's son from Genoa.

Appendix

NAVIGATION AND CARTOGRAPHY
OF THE DISCOVERY

COLUMBUS'S FIRST voyage from the Canary Islands to the West Indies was almost certainly the longest open sea passage, of which there is undisputed record, to be made by navigators of a western European nation before 1492. Since he sailed directly out into unknown waters with such success it has usually been assumed that, as he was commander of the squadron, he must have been an expert and outstanding navigator. This thesis has been strenuously advanced by the distinguished American historian and navigator, Admiral S. E. Morison. Basing his arguments on the results of the Harvard Columbus Expedition which he led, he has identified the landfalls, harbours and other coastal features recorded in the accounts of the four voyages, and has expounded and praised the conduct of the squadrons in the difficult and dangerous circumstances in which they were often placed. Without challenging so authoritative a work—indeed it would be impertinent for a mere 'armchair navigator' to do so—I would submit with respect that this judgement may rest upon misconceptions of Columbus's abilities and the circumstances in which he devised and carried out his great enterprise.

He certainly maintained that he had navigated since his youth and was well versed in the affairs of the sea, but this does not necessarily imply that he had sailed in the capacity of a ship's officer. From what we know of the circumstances, his position was that of a merchant or commercial adviser interested in cosmography. On his voyages of discovery, however, his position was different; he sailed as commander, with soldiers, sailors and officials under his orders. From a study of the records, it is apparent that he conformed by and large to a contemporary code of conduct for those, not necessarily seamen, in charge of such a maritime undertaking. This is apparent in the fixing of a rendezvous in the event of separation after 700 leagues; in the method of maintaining contact by the display of lights, the firing of lombards, and the passing of charts from one vessel to another; in the periodic consultations with the pilots on the distance run, with the masters on change of course, and on the continuation of the voyage. No code of this nature has survived from the fifteenth century, but from the following century a code of this type was drawn up for the Admiral of Castile. To put it briefly, Columbus stood to a certain extent in relation to his officers and crews as Alonso Perez de Guzman el Bueno, Duke of Medina Sidonia, the commander of the 'Invincible Armada', did to the naval experts of that fleet.*

The method of navigation practised by the pilots and masters, dead reckoning, was by modern methods simple and in skilled hands effective. It explains how difficult it was for the early navigators to rediscover an island in the midst of an ocean, and the difficulty the cartographers had in relating one discovery to an earlier. Course was controlled by the magnetic compass and noted at each change of wind; the distance run, as the log-line had not been invented, was based on an estimate of the mileage made good along each 'leg', based in turn on the strength of the wind, state of the sea, general weather conditions and a knowledge of the usual performance of the particular ship. There were some courses on which a vessel would be happier than on others. The obvious people to know these characteristics would be the master who had sailed on her before, or the owner if he ever went to sea—an additional reason for believing that the seamen would be more accurate navigators than Columbus.

The chief instrument used was the ship's compass, mounted on a binnacle. This was checked by observing the bearing of the North Star, corrected in accordance with a standard set of rules ('The regiment of the North Star') which allowed for its movement around the Pole. Other instruments were designed to measure time; they included sand-glasses, dials, and nocturnals. The sand-glass, turned every half-hour, indicated the time run along a leg and this, with the bearing, was noted on a board, together with the estimated speed; from these figures the vessel's position, or the 'dead reckoning', was calculated from time to time.

This method was satisfactory for navigating the waters of western Europe, where it was supplemented by the master's knowledge of

---

* 'I know by experience of the little I have been at sea that I am always sea-sick and always catch cold. . . . I have had no experience either of the sea, or of war': the Duke's reaction to his appointment to the command. (Mattingly, G.: *The Defeat of the Spanish Armada*, p. 222.)

tides, currents, nature of the sea bottom, and the appearance of the land from the sea. The problem was more complex when seamen began to venture into the high seas; but by the time of the discoveries the Portuguese were in the process of evolving more precise methods. In their progress along the African coasts there came a point when the North Star could no longer conveniently be observed, and astronomers were then given the task of preparing tables of the sun's declination at noon as a substitute. With the aid of a development of the astrolabe, latitude could then be determined. Owing to the clumsy nature of the instruments and the difficulty of observing on an unstable deck, accurate observations were rarely made at sea, consequently it was necessary to go ashore to set up the instrument, until a lighter and handier instrument, the quadrant, was evolved. At an early stage, the names of relevant ports or of prominent coastal landmarks were engraved on the quadrant with their latitude in degrees. On a southern run, such as the Portuguese were making to Africa, the pilot could take the latitude, and calculate his distance from any point marked on the instrument. This developed into the practice known as 'running down the latitude'; in other words, to make a point on the African coast, one sailed southwards until its latitude was reached and then turned eastwards until a landfall could be made.

From the late fifteenth century the Portuguese astronomers and pilots had developed these methods, and in time their manuals and instructions were translated into numerous other languages. As the pilots and seamen of Portugal and Spain intermingled freely, the Spaniards were aware of these developments at an early stage. The Spanish historian, J. F. Guillin y Tato, has shown that Portuguese nautical expressions and terms can be traced in the *Journal*, evidence that Columbus had picked up some seafaring knowledge from them, and Professor Eva Taylor has sought to explain some of his errors by showing that he may have misunderstood an out-of-date Portuguese navigation manual. Not the least of the services of Portugal to the discoveries was the provision of this information to other nations.

It is interesting to note that in planning his voyages Columbus appears to have had the method of 'running down the latitude' in mind; aiming at a point on the Asian coast in approximately the latitude of the Canaries he first sailed southwards to those islands and then set a course due westwards. Similarly on the third voyage, wishing to make for and explore the regions south of the Caribbean, he sailed to the Azores before turning westwards.

Columbus's views on the length of a degree of latitude, held despite the accurate calculations of the Portuguese, is another consideration which makes it difficult to accept his expertise, especially on account of his claim to have actually measured it in a voyage to Guinea. The error is more likely to have arisen in his cosmographical reading than in the experience of a practical seaman.

I conclude from this summary that Columbus was not a navigator or a seaman in the sense that, as the result of long experience, he had the capacity to sail and navigate a vessel without the services of a pilot or master; this is despite the claims of his biographers who, however, had little practical knowledge of the sea and consequently did not put up a very convincing case on his behalf. Columbus on his first voyage was the commander of an expedition systematically organized, he was assisted by a skilful staff and had acquired some knowledge of astronomy and cosmography. That is the only conclusion which can safely be reached.

The method of navigation employed had some effect on the development of cartography, and thus on the interpretation of early charts. The plane chart made no allowance for the sphericity of the earth, consequently considerable errors could occur in locating new discoveries at the end of a long ocean voyage; for a course plotted by dead reckoning would not be correlated with the parallels of latitude or the meridians of longitude, or, in other words, a course on a constant bearing, when plotted on a plane chart, is not a straight line. This problem was ultimately solved by Mercator's projection, but in the meantime the location of a new coastline could be very inaccurate until latitude could be determined with accuracy and observations made for longitude. Another complication for the cartographer was introduced when the explorers entered the north-west Atlantic, where the magnetic variation greatly increased. Until this had been accurately determined the result was that a coastline might, for example, be charted by the explorer as trending north and south, whereas its true bearing was twenty degrees west of north. These are some of the considerations which should be kept in mind in discussing the cartography of the discoveries.

The biographers of Columbus state that both he and his brother were skilled chart-makers, but no charts have survived which can with certainty be attributed to either of them. Charts, however, must have been carried on all the voyages for the purposes of navigation, but again we have no precise details. Las Casas stated many years later that he had seen the Toscanelli chart among Columbus's papers and that this had been taken on the first voyage. There are also a few references in the *Journal* to a chart or charts, for example to the fact that a group of islands was depicted in mid-Atlantic; and from other references the position of Cipangu and the Asian mainland relative to the course set by Columbus may be deduced. In the following paragraphs an attempt is made to relate Columbus's proceedings to contemporary maps and to estimate the value of the information that can be drawn from them.

Few if any early maps are the work of one man, recording his own observations over a definite period of time; in other words, they are compilations in which the cartographer has used what he considered to be the best contemporary material, or rather the best material available to him. In the Age of Discovery, therefore, a new map of the discoveries incorporates pieces of coastline resulting from the work of several explorers into a conventional framework, perhaps of considerable age. The cartographer will also have had to form his judgement as to the relationship of the separate voyages. This had to be done at a time when few observations for latitude were made, and longitude depended upon dead reckoning. Also to be taken into consideration is the time-lag between the voyages and the data reaching the cartographer. This type of problem makes it difficult to determine what contemporary ideas on the discoveries were at a particular date. The confusion increases with the appearance of engraved maps, for they were one further stage removed from the original sources, and the significance of the dates they bear may be misleading. The absence of a particular feature, for example, does not necessarily imply that the map must date from before its discovery; the cartographer may have been ignorant of it, or did not consider its inclusion relevant to his purpose. For the sake of example, a map dated 1510 may include data from a voyage made three years earlier, while a map dated 1512 may use material at least six years old. The result is that, for the particular area in question, the 1512 map is the earlier. In problems of this nature reliance must first be placed emphatically on the written record to control the cartographical data. Where written records are wanting, the evaluation of the evidence from maps is more difficult and even hazardous. This has led in the history of exploration to various conflicting conclusions being drawn, and in some instances extravagant hypotheses.

In examining the map evidence for the discoveries one is at first surprised by its scarcity. No chart of the new lands has survived from the period of 1492 to 1500, the crucial stage. The first to depict any part of the New World is the great chart of Juan de la Cosa, the pilot who took part in the first two voyages, dated 1500. This delineates the Caribbean islands with considerable accuracy; Cuba is shown as an island, and well to the north the results of John Cabot's voyage of 1498. All this section forms part of a vague continental coastline which extends far to the south but which is not indicated as the mainland of Asia. So far as the voyages of Columbus are concerned, the representation of the Caribbean does not include anything discovered after the third voyage. In the extreme south some Portuguese exploration is included. La Cosa, who was on the first two voyages and later sailed to the Caribbean on his own account, confines himself closely to actual observations, though there are some traces, in the numerous islands scattered about unnamed and in the mainland coast, of reminiscences of earlier maps of eastern Asia. After 1500 the number of surviving maps of the New World increases, so that the extension of knowledge can be traced in some detail. Among these are the Cantino map of 1501 to 1502, on which 'The land of the King of Portugal' (Labrador) appears as a large island. On the Caveiro map of 1504 Cuba is shown as an island, but the eastern half, with its nomenclature, has been duplicated as part of the mainland. This has been taken by some to show that the peninsula of Florida had been explored by this date, but this is to misinterpret the map evidence. The mistake persisted among the cosmographers for a number of years and appears on Waldseemüller's *Carta marina* as late as 1516. The earliest engraved map to show any part of the new lands is the Contarini world map of 1506.

This paucity of cartographic material may seem surprising at first sight, as there were undoubtedly several made during the years before 1500. Columbus and his brother are stated by contemporaries to have been chart-makers, yet the sole example of Christopher's to survive is a small rapid sketch of a portion of the northern coast of Hispaniola. Except for some small maplets the work of Bartholomew has also disappeared, and even the extent of his share in these is a matter of uncertainty. Nevertheless there is much evidence in the Admiral's writings and in Las Casas's history that charts were at least made under his direction in response to repeated demands from his Sovereigns. It is probable that these were retained by Court officials and deposited later in the Casa de la Contratación, where they were eventually discarded when more accurate surveys were forthcoming. It is also clear that charts were circulating unofficially, to judge from the Admiral's anger when the chart made on his third voyage was obtained by Hojeda and put to good profit by him. No doubt efforts were made to keep the results of voyages secret for a time at least, but this policy was not completely successful. Pilots passed from the service of one country to another, probably taking their charts with them, and after the navigation of the Indies had been thrown open, many ships sailed to that region. It has been suggested by Professor Armando Cortesão that some maps were deliberately falsified to induce the Spaniards to believe that the southern extremity of Africa was in a more southerly latitude than Bartholomew Diaz had ascertained, with the object of discouraging competition on the sea route to India. Whether this is a correct interpretation of the false latitudes is debatable; but, although there is much uncertainty over early American latitudes, there is no reason for believing that these were faked deliberately.

If these considerations and qualifications are kept in mind, however, it is possible to gain some enlightenment from a chronological and comparative review of the cartographic record. It has always been a matter of speculation as to what the chart which Columbus used on his first voyage, and on which he consulted Pinzon, was like. An answer to this question would also throw light on his aims, and why he considered almost to the end that he had discovered 'the Indies'. In the following paragraphs, I have endeavoured to answer this question by placing in logical order the representation of the east coast of Asia in relation to the delineations of the Caribbean on four maps.

The pre-Columban concept is drawn from the type of world map associated with the German cartographer, Henricus Martellus, who worked in Florence in co-operation with the engraver Francesco Roselli. Four manuscript copies and two engraved copies have survived, so that it is clear that this model was popular around the year 1489. Further evidence of this is the fact that the Behaim globe of 1492 was based on it or on a common source. The outline from the latter forms the basis of the first maplet on page 208. This shows part of the east coast of Asia with the position of certain place-names which are also referred to by Columbus. The prominent features are the characteristic projection of the coastline and the rectangular outline of the island of Cipangu lying to the east with its main axis extending from north to south. The surrounding ocean is scattered with numerous islands. Most of these features can be identified on the succeeding outlines.

The second maplet is of special importance. It is a chart of the

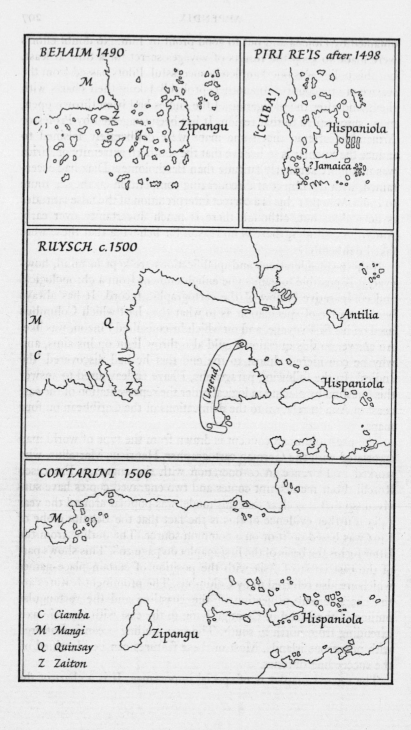

Atlantic Ocean drawn by a Turkish scribe at Gallipoli in 1513, and clearly based in the main on Spanish and Portuguese charts. It has been established by Paul Kahle that for part of it, i.e. the Caribbean, it is a copy of a chart associated definitely with Columbus. The Turkish Admiral for whom it was drawn had obtained the original from a Spanish vessel captured off the Spanish Mediterranean coast in 1501. Probably equally important was his carrying off into slavery of a Spaniard who had made three voyages to the Caribbean and from whom he obtained much important information. There is considerable justification, therefore, in accepting this chart as a fairly accurate copy of a Spanish original, while allowing that the nomenclature, and possibly the long legends, all in Turkish, contain some misunderstanding of the original Spanish. The outline of the Caribbean is extremely interesting: the island named Hispaniola recalls forcibly the Behaim-Martellus island of Zipangu, and the coastline to the west with a projecting cape the continental coastline on the same. The general outlines of the two maps are sufficiently alike to suggest that they are at least based on the same original. The false orientation of Hispaniola derives from the fact that Columbus was anxious to show that the island was Zipangu. It is evident from the nomenclature of the western coastline that another, and extremely rash, attempt had been made to reconcile the charting on the second voyage with the idea that he had reached eastern Asia, for the names that occur here are names bestowed on the south coast of Cuba! Notice the configuration of this coast and particularly the large bay in the south.

The identification of the coastline on the west with the south coast of Cuba rests upon the nomenclature and the configuration. The Turkish *porta grande* is Puerto Grande, and *kaw punta orofai* is Ornofay, a district of southern Cuba; both these names are recorded by Andres Bernaldez in his account of the second voyage. As to the coastline, the bay with islands at the lower end of this stretch is clearly the great bay delineated by Ruysch and La Cosa. Subsequently, when the Turkish chart was being assembled, this coastline was joined up with that of northern South America.

The third outline shows the first efforts to replace preconceived ideas by observations. It is based upon a 'modern' world map by Johannes Ruysch in the 1507 Rome edition of Ptolemy's *Geography*. Hispaniola is more accurately oriented: the eastern end of Cuba is shown on the basis of the results of the first and second voyages, so that the southern coast is properly related to Hispaniola;

and Jamaica is shown with the name 'Tamariqva'. The question as
to whether Cuba is part of the mainland is left unresolved, for the
legend across the island indicates that this is the limit reached by the
ships of Spain on the second voyage. Doubts as to whether the island
was part of the mainland, which is represented to the north and west,
were obviously increasing. In this area also appears an indication of the curious curved shape given to the western portion of the
island on La Cosa's chart. Thus we have a representation of the
results achieved on the first two voyages, between 1492 and 1494,
probably based on charts by Juan de la Cosa. It should be noted that
Cipangu has been removed completely from the map.

The fourth outline, from the world map by G. M. Contarini
engraved in 1506 by Roselli (British Museum, Map Room), shows
the completion of the charting of Cuba, although it was engraved a
year earlier than the Ruysch map. Cuba is now an island, with the
claw-like western end the beginning of which is apparent on Ruysch.
The island of Cipangu is removed to the west, although still closer
to Cuba than to the Asian mainland. This is the last of 'the Indies' as
part of Asia; the islands are henceforth 'The Antilles of the King of
Spain'.

*

It appears permissible to draw several conclusions from this cartographic evolution: first, that Columbus set out on his first voyage
with the hope of reaching the Indies of eastern Asia; secondly, that
the chart which he consulted with Pinzon in the course of the voyage
embodied this hope, in other words, its western border resembled
outline B; and thirdly that the insularity of Cuba was accepted at
some date between 1494 and 1500, probably nearer the latter date,
since the older idea circulated for some years longer.

If it is accepted that the Columbus-Pinzon chart resembled that
incorporated in the Turkish chart, then we may take a further tenta-
tive step and accept Las Casas's statement, made many years later,
that this was the chart sent to Lisbon by Paolo Toscanelli. Support
for this long shot is provided by its resemblance to the reconstruction
of the latter by H. Wagner.

BIBLIOGRAPHY

The literature on Columbus and the Discoveries is immense and any attempt to cover it comprehensively would be useless to the general reader. This bibliography is intended to indicate the original source material on which all research must be based, useful general histories, biographies of the principal explorers, and recent literature on cosmography, navigation, politics and economics which I have consulted in writing the text. This section is not complete, but further guidance can be obtained from the bibliographies which accompany most of the entries. For current work the reader should consult issues of the *Geographical Journal* and *Imago Mundi*.

I. *Source material*

Coleccion de documentos ineditos relativos al Descubrimiento . . . ultramar. Madrid, 1892–4.

Colleção de documentos relativos ao descobrimento e povamento dos Açores. Edited by Manuel Montiero Velho Arruda. Ponta Delgado, 1932.

COLUMBUS, CHRISTOPHER. *Select documents illustrating the four voyages of Columbus.* Translated and edited by Cecil Jane, two volumes. Hakluyt Society, 2nd series, 65, 70. 1930.

— *Christopher Columbus: documents and proofs of his Genoese origin.* Bergamo, 1932. Published by the City of Genoa.

— *The voyages of Christopher Columbus.* Edited by Cecil Jane. Argonaut Press, 1935.

— *The Journal of Christopher Columbus.* Edited by L. A. Vigneras, with Appendix by R. A. Skelton, 'Cartography of Columbus's first voyage'. 1960.

— *Journals and other documents on the life and voyages of Christopher Columbus.* Translated and edited by S. E. Morison. New York, 1963.

COLUMBUS, FERDINAND. *Le Historie della vita e dei fatti di Cristofero Colombo.* Edited by Rinaldo Caddeo, two volumes. Milan, 1930. The best annotated edition of this work, with useful appendices.

— *The life of the Admiral Christopher Columbus by his son Ferdinand.* Translated and edited by B. Keen. New Brunswick, N.J., 1959.

GATHORNE HARDY, G. M. *The Norse Discoverers of America*. Oxford, 1921.

LAS CASAS, BARTOLOME DE. *Historia de Las Indias*. Edited A. Millares Carlo and Lewis Hanke, three volumes. Mexico, 2nd edition, 1965. With an illuminating introduction 'Las Casas, historiador' by L. Hanke.

— *Tratados*. Edited by L. Hanke and M. Gimenez Fernandez, three volumes. Mexico, 1965.

Mostra Colombiana Internazionale 1950-51. Elenco illustrativo. Edited by Paolo Revelli. Genoa, 1950.

NAVARRETE, MARTIN FERNÁNDEZ DE. *Coleccion de los viajes y descubrimientos que hicieron por mar los Españoles . . .*, five volumes. Madrid, 1825-37.

OVIEDO, GONZALO FERNANDEZ DE. *Sumario de la natural historia de las Indias, 1526*. With an introduction by José Miranda. Mexico, 1950.

Raccolta di documenti e studi pubblicata dalla R. Commissione Columbiana. Six parts in fourteen volumes. Rome, 1892-4. The major Italian contribution to Columban studies. Printed and manuscript sources for Columbus and his family; Italian histories of the Discoveries; biographies of Toscanelli, Peter Martyr, etc.

TAYLOR, EVA G. R. 'A letter dated 1577 from Mercator to John Dee'. *Imago Mundi* 13 (1956), 56-68. The source for Nicholas of Lynn.

VESPUCCI, AMERIGO. *El nuevo mundo; Cartas*. Edited by Roberto Levillier. Buenos Aires, 1957. Texts of Letters in Italian, Spanish and English.

VIGNERAS, L. A. 'A letter of John Day, 1497'. *Hispanic American Historical Review* 36 (1956), 503-9.

WILLIAMSON, JAMES A. *The Cabot voyages and Bristol discovery under Henry VII*. Hakluyt Society, 2nd series 120, 1961.

II. *General works on the Discoveries*

ALMAGIA, ROBERTO. *Gli Italiani primi esploratori dell' America*. Rome. 1937. A well-documented work, strong on the cartographical aspects, emphasizing the share of Italian explorers.

BAKER, J. N. L. *History of geographical discovery and exploration*. 2nd ed. 1937. The best general account available in English with good references.

BROCHADO, COSTA. *History of the Portuguese discoveries*. Lisbon, 1960.

CORTESÃO, JAIME. *Os Descobrimentos portugueses*. Lisbon, 1960. A detailed history from the Portuguese angle, the result of much research.

GODHINO, VITORINO MAGALHÃES. *Les grandes découvertes*. Coimbra, 1953.

HERRMANN, PAUL. *Conquest by man*. 1954.

KIRKPATRICK, F. A. *The Spanish conquistadores*. 1934.

LEITHAUSER, JOACHIM. *Worlds beyond the horizon*. 1956.

NUNN, GEORGE E. *The geographical conceptions of Columbus*. American Geographical Society, 1924.

PERES, DAMIANO. *Portuguese discoveries in the Atlantic*. Lisbon, 1960.

SAUER, CARL ORTWIN. *The early Spanish Main*. Berkeley, 1966.

III. Biographies

Columbus

HARRISSE, HENRY. *Christophe Colomb*, two volumes. Paris, 1884.

IRVING, WASHINGTON. *Life and voyages of Christopher Columbus*, four volumes. 1828.

LOLLIS, CESARE DE. *Cristofero Colombo nella legenda e nella storia*. Milan, 1892.

MARKHAM, CLEMENTS ROBERT. *Life of Christopher Columbus*. 1892.

MORISON, SAMUEL ELIOT. *Admiral of the Ocean Sea ; a life of Christopher Columbus*, two volumes. Boston, 1942. Primarily a study of 'where Columbus sailed on his four voyages, and what sort of a seaman he was', and the final word on the courses sailed. Includes a good personal life of the Admiral but does not cover the political or economic aspects in detail.

MUGRIDGE, DONALD H. *Christopher Columbus: a selected list of books and articles by American authors or published in America, 1892–1950*. Library of Congress, Washington, 1950.

THACHER, JOHN BOYD. *Christopher Columbus ; life, work and remains*, two volumes. New York. An uncritical work, but useful for the material it reprints and for the essays on Peter Martyr and Las Casas.

UZIELLI, GUSTAVO. 'La vita e i tempi di Paolo del Pozzo Toscanelli'. In *Raccolta*, Rome, 1894.

VIGNAUD, HENRY. *Histoire critique de la grande enterprise de Christophe Colomb*, two volumes. Paris. The prime critic of the contention that Columbus's object on the first voyage was to reach the 'Indies'; indispensable for any study of Columbus.

WAGNER, HENRY. 'Marco Polo's narrative becomes propaganda to inspire Colón'. *Imago Mundi* 6 (1949), 3–14.

Vespucci

CARACI, GIUSEPPE. 'The Vespucian problems—what point have they reached ?' *Imago Mundi* 18 (1964), 12–23. A critique of Levillier's works.

LEVILLIER, ROBERTO. *Americo Vespucio*. Madrid, 1966. Concentrates on the third voyage, which he holds to have reached 50 degrees south latitude, and subsequent Spanish voyages; detailed analysis of the cartography.

— *America, la bien llamada*, two volumes. Buenos Aires, 1948. Maintains the authenticity of the 'four voyages', basing his argument mainly upon contemporary charts.

MAGNAGHI, ALBERTO. *Amerigho Vespucci*. Rome, 1924. Accepts the 'second' and 'third' voyages only, on the basis of the literary evidence.

Others

HANKE, LEWIS. *Bartolome de las Casas; an interpretation of his life and writings*. The Hague, 1951.

SANCEAU, ELAINE. *The perfect prince; a biography of the King Dom João II*. Lisbon, 1959.

IV. *Cosmography, navigation, cartography*

AILLY, PIERRE D'. *Ymago mundi*. Edited by E. Buron, three volumes. Paris, 1930. Latin text with French translation.

ALMAGIÀ, ROBERTO. 'On the cartographic work of Francesco Roselli'. *Imago Mundi* (1951) 27–34.

CORTESÃO, ARMANDO. *Cartografia y cartografos portuguesas*, two volumes. Lisbon, 1935.

CRONE, GERALD ROE. *Maps and their makers*. 3rd revised edition, 1965.

GLACKEN, CLARENCE J. *Traces on the Rhodian Shore; nature and culture in western thought from ancient times to the end of the eighteenth century*. Berkeley, California, 1967. A valuable study, with a comprehensive bibliography.

KAHLE, PAUL. *Die verschollene Columbus-Karte von 1498 in einer turk-ischen Weltkarte von 1513*. Berlin, 1933.

LANGLOIS, CHARLES V. *La connaissance de la nature et du monde au moyen âge*. Paris, 1911.

MCELROY, J. W. 'The ocean navigation of Columbus on his first voyage.' *American Neptune*, Salem, Mass. 1 (1941), 209–40.

RAVENSTEIN, ERNEST GEORGE. *Martin Behaim and his globe.* 1908. With facsimile.

SANZ, CARLOS. *Primera representación del mundo con los dos hemisferios.* Madrid, 1967.

SKELTON, RALEIGH ASHLEY, and others. *The Vinland Map and the Tatar relation.* New Haven, Conn., 1965. In addition to the study of the Map there is a widely-ranging history of Northern cartography.

TAYLOR, EVA G. R. *The haven-finding art.* 1956. The clearest study of the art of navigation to the time of James Cook.

— 'The navigating manual of Columbus'. *Bollettino civico Istituto Colombiano,* Genoa 1 (1953), 32–45.

WRIGHT, JOHN KIRTLAND. *Geographical lore of the time of the Crusades.* American Geographical Society, 1925. A valuable study of medieval geographical ideas.

V. *Political and economic*

CADDEO, RINALDO. 'Il financiamento del primo viaggio e l'opera dei capitalisti italiani di Spagna', in Caddeo, R. *Le Historie . . .* Appendix F.

CHAUNU, HUGUETTE and PIERRE. *Seville et l'Atlantique 1540–1650.* Paris, 1955–60. (Title from Smith, Robert S., see below.)

CIPOLLA, CARLO. *The economic history of world population.* 1962.

DAVIES, ARTHUR. 'Columbus divides the world'. *Geographical Journal* 133 (1967), 337–44. Takes the view that Isabella finally accepted Columbus's proposals because he undertook to secure possession of the new lands without royal aid.

FREYRE, GILBERTO. *The Portuguese and the Tropics.* Lisbon, 1961.

HAY, DENIS. *Europe, the emergence of an idea.* Edinburgh, 1957.

MADARIAGA, SALVADOR DE. *Spain, a modern history.* New edition, 1961.

MEAD, W. R., and BROWN, E. H. *The United States and Canada; a regional geography.* 1962.

PENDLE, GEORGE. *A history of Latin America.* 1963.

PIKE, RUTH. 'The Genoese in Seville'. *Journal of economic history,* New York 22 (1962), 348–78.

RIEGEL, ROBERT E. 'American frontier theory', in *The nineteenth-century world.* Edited by G. S. Metraux and F. Crouzet. UNESCO, New York, 1963.

SMITH, ROBERT S. 'Seville and the Atlantic; cycles in Spanish colonial trade'. *Journal of economic history,* New York 22 (1962), 348–78.

ACKNOWLEDGMENTS

My debt to scholars who have studied the Age of Discoveries will be apparent in the pages of this book. I hope that the Bibliography will be regarded by them as some acknowledgment of the extent of this indebtedness. I am particularly grateful to Admiral S. E. Morison for permitting me to quote extensively from the documents he has published in *Journals and other documents on the life and voyages of Christopher Columbus*. Acknowledgments are also due to the Council of the Hakluyt Society; to the Clarendon Press for permission to quote from R. Flower's *The Irish Tradition*; to Hollis & Carter Ltd. for the extract from Paul Hazard's *The European Mind*, and to the University of North Carolina Press for the passage from L. E. Ayres' *Theory of Economic Progress*.

The illustrations are reproduced by courtesy of the Trustees of the British Museum, the Galleria degli Uffizi, Florence, and the Royal Geographical Society. I wish also to thank Mr. George Naish of the National Maritime Museum, my colleagues in the Library of the Royal Geographical Society, and Dr. F. A. Toufar, Reference Librarian, Ealing Central Library, for their help so readily given, and especially Mr. G. S. Holland, head of the Drawing Office, for the skill and patience he has given to drawing the maps. It is perhaps scarcely necessary to add that none of them are responsible for any errors which may occur.

G.R.C.

INDEX

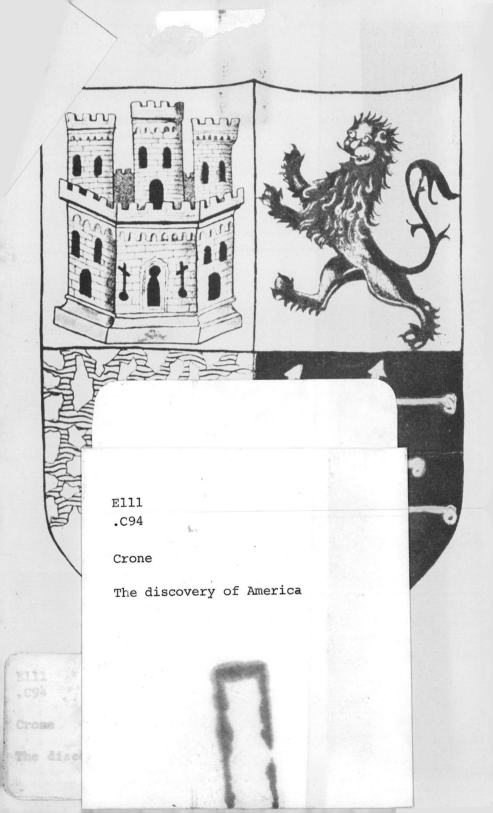